College Is Only the Beginning

A Student Guide to Higher Education
Second Edition

Edited by

John N. Gardner

DIRECTOR, UNIVERSITY 101
UNIVERSITY OF SOUTH CAROLINA, COLUMBIA

and

A. Jerome Jewler

CO-DIRECTOR, UNIVERSITY 101
UNIVERSITY OF SOUTH CAROLINA, COLUMBIA

Wadsworth Publishing Company
Belmont, California
A Division of Wadsworth, Inc.

The Freshman Year Experience$_{SM}$ Series Editor: Henry Staat
Production Editor: Gary Mcdonald / Deborah Cogan
Managing Designer: Carolyn Deacy
Print Buyer: Karen Hunt
Interior and Cover Design: Seventeenth Street Studios
Copy Editor: Pat Tompkins
Compositor: Better Graphics, Inc.
Signing Representative: Neil Oatley

The Freshman Year Experience is a servicemark of the University of South Carolina. A license may be granted upon written request to use the term *The Freshman Year Experience* in association with educational programmatic approaches to enhance the freshman year. This license is not transferable and does not apply to the use of the servicemark in any other programs or on any other literature without the written approval of the University of South Carolina.

Printed in the United States of America   19

4 5 6 7 8 9 10—93 92 91 90 89

Library of Congress Cataloging-in-Publication Data

College is only the beginning: a student guide to higher
    education / edited by John N. Gardner and A. Jerome Jewler.
        p.   cm.—(The Freshman year experience series)
    Includes index.
    ISBN 0-534-09642-5
    1. College student orientation.   I. Gardner, John N.
II. Jewler, A. Jerome.   III. Series.
LB2343.3.C65 1989
378'.198—dc19   88-25986
                                                    CIP

To Belle, Donna, Melissa, Scott, Wynn, Jonathan, and Vicky.

To the students in our lives.

To college faculty, staff, and administrators everywhere who believe that a college education must go beyond the classroom in order to be educational.

And to college freshmen who are fortunate enough to have these kinds of people around to help them discover their own wonderfully distinctive strengths and talents.

Contents

Preface

Most preface statements aren't read. This one is meant to be.

As editors of *College Is Only the Beginning* and directors of the University 101 program at the University of South Carolina, we believe very strongly that the majority of entering students can accomplish much more during their college years if they know how to play the game.

No, this book can't make you brighter than you are, and it surely doesn't give you an easy way to get through the next several years without working. This point is, you are going to have to work very hard to reap the many benefits of higher education. This book's purpose is to get you off and running in proper fashion.

We know how important it is to begin college in that fashion. Since 1972, we've learned that students who enroll in the University 101 freshman seminar at Carolina tend to survive into their sophomore year at a higher rate than students who don't. It isn't because they're smarter than other students. In fact, the University has predicted that a majority of them won't fare as well as the students who choose not to take this course.

What happens to change them? We believe we know the answers, and that's what this book is all about.

First, these students were made to understand the meaning and significance of higher education, and we know that students who understand why they are in college tend to stay in college longer than those who don't.

Second, they discovered that professors would challenge them in the classroom because professors were interested in helping them succeed, not because they wished them to fail.

Third, they found that getting involved in clubs and activities could also motivate them to succeed in the classroom.

Fourth, because they were encouraged to speak up in class and felt comfortable with other students and the professor, their self-esteem and self-awareness were considerably higher than before. In simple terms, they felt good about themselves.

And finally, they learned a variety of survival skills—how to study, how to write, how to manage stress, how to use the library—that helped them achieve higher grades.

This is what we hope *College Is Only the Beginning* will do for you. In a series of essays by experts in various areas of higher education, we've attempted to provide you with the ammunition for your own college success. While we have attempted to sequence the essays in logical order, don't feel you have to begin with the first and read through to the last. You might gain more by checking the topics in the table of contents and plunging in as the mood strikes you. Your instructor may have similar views when he or she assigns the chapters in this volume.

The first edition of this book emerged just as freshman seminars were coming into their own. When we began to plan the second edition, our experience indicated the need to eliminate certain chapters and add others. We think the changes have resulted in a book that is even more suited to the needs of the typical college freshman of the 1980s and 1990s.

For example, new to this edition is an essay on higher education in the Western world, in which John Orr Dwyer traces the development of what we now know as college through the centuries. Also new is an expanded chapter on study skills by Ken Long of the University of Windsor. Because we know that learning to study properly is a key to academic success in college, this new chapter kicks off our unit on academic blossoming.

Mary Stuart Hunter, our colleague in University 101, tells you what to expect from your academic advisor and also warns you to be prepared when you sit down to discuss your academic future.

Another colleague and friend, Carolyn Matalene, divulges how a caring attitude toward writing can reward you with more than just a semester's worth of essays in your English course.

Thorne Compton of the University of South Carolina stresses the importance of developing critical thinking skills and points to the liberal arts as the basic building blocks of education. Richard Morrill, president of the University of Richmond, urges you to develop your own personal values system and tells you how to begin. Bob Friday of Duquesne University discusses the importance of relationships. Our other authors return in revised versions of previous efforts to complete your program for success.

We would like to thank the publisher's reviewers of the manuscript for this edition: Roger Danchise, Bentley College; Arthur U. Iriarte, Central Connecticut State University; John T. Lewis, West Georgia College; and Frances K. Rauschenberg, University of Georgia.

As with our other work, *Step by Step to College Success,* this book is dedicated to freshmen everywhere. We hope that the wisdom offered on these pages will help you find your niche in college and throughout life. If you're wondering how to begin in college you can start by reading these essays, by practicing what they suggest, and by taking advantage of every opportunity your college offers for personal and professional development.

In these pages we suggest that while college can be tough, it doesn't have to be demeaning. When professors and other college professionals care about helping students develop, both parties benefit. So as you continue your college career, we hope you will use the skills you have learned from this book and from your caring instructors. Use them and use them well, and you will discover that college and life will reward you many times over.

John N. Gardner
A. Jerome Jewler
January 1989

College Is Only the Beginning

UNIT ONE

College as a New Beginning

1 Making the Transition

A. Jerome Jewler

CO-DIRECTOR FOR INSTRUCTION AND FACULTY
  DEVELOPMENT, UNIVERSITY 101
PROFESSOR OF JOURNALISM
UNIVERSITY OF SOUTH CAROLINA

My father had died the year before, my mother had opened a small retail business to support the rest of us, and I found myself entering college as a somewhat bewildered, anxious, and skeptical freshman. That was more than thirty years ago, but I can still remember the smell of the dank, musty field house where the university president welcomed us, although I don't remember a thing he said. I can recall the dirty wooden floor creaking under my feet as I shuffled through line after line in the dusty armory, attempting to sign up for the classes I needed at the times I needed them.

That fall I sat through an early morning English class and three or four other courses in which I vaguely knew the instructor and felt he knew me even less. In the middle of the spring semester, after months of wondering why I was spending this hard-earned money, I announced to my family that I was dropping out of college to help Mom in her business. You can't imagine the panic that set in at my house. "You're the first one ever to go to college in the whole family. You just can't give up," they pleaded. But I insisted that they, who had never been there, could not know how pointless college was.

I was majoring in journalism (at least I knew what major I belonged in!), and my family suggested I might try working on the campus newspaper if classes weren't stimulating. It might make a difference, they said. Knowing what I now know about the importance of participating in such activities, I marvel at their sage advice. Back then, I grudgingly wandered into the newspaper office one evening, thinking no one would want this nerd of a freshman who wasn't even going to stay in school.

Talk about miracles, this turned out to be one. Suddenly, life had meaning. Even though my classes didn't become "beautiful" overnight, I suddenly realized I was at college to grow, to gain new experiences that would make my transition to adulthood more rewarding.

So I did finish college, I did go on to graduate school, and although I never went into the newspaper business (what I thought I was preparing for in college), I did gravitate to advertising, where I used my writing skills to persuade consumers to buy cleaning solutions, milk and ice cream, dog food, and a host of other products and services.

Building on that experience, I began teaching advertising in 1972 and soon became involved in the University 101 freshman seminar program.

It's amazing how one thing leads to another. That's something to remember as you make the transition from high school to college.

—III—III—III—

As many educators are beginning to realize, the college experience can be a more perplexing one for high school graduates these days simply because more of them are going to college.

It wasn't always that way. Not many years ago, college was exclusively for the privileged few. Generally, this meant that only wealthy, white males were even considered to be college material. Nor was the emphasis on preparing for a career, as it tends to be today. Colleges were considered places where those who were about to step into positions of responsibility could prepare for the task. College introduced these young lads to the classics, to critical thinking, to principles of scientific inquiry, and to mathematical logic. At college, they also sampled music, theater, and art. With such a preparation for life as this, a man with a college degree was practically marked for success.

As colleges and universities proliferated and large state universities were founded, more opportunities arose for more people to attend institutions of higher learning. This trend has culminated today in a belief that anyone who can be admitted to college on the basis of academic achievement should be encouraged to pursue a degree. Our present open admissions policies are certainly a far cry from the early days of American higher education, and millions of individuals have reaped the benefits of this change in attitude. But at the same time, many students have found the adjustment difficult.

College — Not Advanced High School

College is not and was never intended to be simply an extension of high school. If you tend to doubt that, take a moment to read the following four statements about college and see whether or not you agree with them:

1. Years ago, college was only for a select group. Today, we're urging everyone to go to college. As a result, colleges are worse off than they were before this open admissions policy.

2. Years ago, people expected to get a liberal education in college. Today, students are generally more interested in using college as a pathway to a career. As a result, college graduates are generally worse off than they used to be.

3. We used to allow students to succeed or fail on their own. Nowadays, we help students too much. For example, we have academic advisement programs, personal counseling, career planning, and freshman seminars. As a result, students are not given the chance to determine on their own whether college is the right place for them. And that can be dangerous.

4. Grades, tests, and lectures interfere with the learning process. Get rid of them and real learning will take place.

Do any of these statements sound like the kinds of things you discussed in high school? Probably not. What about the validity of each of them? Here's how most educators might respond to them, although many might adhere to the opposite point of view:

1. Surely, most of us would agree that *society* is much better off because of the open admissions policies many colleges embrace. Although everyone who wants to attend college cannot have his or her pick of schools, a college education is now within the realm of possibility for millions of young people who previously had no chance whatsoever for this valuable experience.

2. One of the most hotly debated issues in higher education today is whether or not academic programs have become too career oriented. Perhaps the best answer here, and the best advice we can offer you, is that the ideal college education provides a healthy balance between developing the intellect through the liberal arts and sciences and preparing you for a career. If you doubt the value of English, philosophy, speech, history, psychology, and the other scholarly disciplines, you need to rethink your priorities.

3. Dangerous indeed! Most forward-thinking educators, especially those who see college as providing a total developmental experience for young people, see such helping services as not only positive but also positively essential.

4. Would that we could be rid of grades, tests, and lectures—and still manage to evaluate student performance. While memorization of material from a lecture may help you pass a test, which may lead to a higher grade, it ain't what education is all about.

Let's look now at some of the obvious differences between high school and college and try to understand why your first year of higher education is a turning point in your life.

☐ High school, for the most part, is mandatory. College is purely optional.

☐ Unless you attend a private high school, you pay no tuition. In college, you pay to attend classes.

☐ Although you normally attend a high school near your home, you may attend college anywhere in the world. Besides location, you have a choice of a private or public university and a two-year or four-year institution.

☐ Unlike high school, in college you generally pay for textbooks and housing.

But this list is hardly complete. For most freshmen, the most disturbing difference hasn't even been mentioned yet: a newfound sense of freedom. This mixed blessing can be exciting and frightening at the same time. With no mom, dad, or older brother or sister to tell you when to study, how late you can stay out, or even where you can go and with whom, you're pretty much on your own. And that can be scary!

Think of the many decisions you'll need to make daily—without the advice of your parents: Should I roll out of bed or skip class? Do my laundry or be a slob? Eat breakfast or sleep longer? Study regularly or cram for the exam? Eat anything I want? Drink responsibly (if I'm of legal age), drink even though I'm under age, or not drink at all? Avoid the drug scene or experiment? Become sexually involved with someone? Take precautions if I do? Make friends with the right people? Join a sorority or fraternity? Exercise or get fat? Sleep or walk around half awake all day? Keep my room neat or live like a pig? Choose my classes each semester or consult an academic advisor? Select a major or just take courses?

It Helps to Know the Rules

With so many decisions to make—often for the first time in your life—no wonder college can seem awesome during the first days of your first term. And wouldn't it be nice to know in advance what you should do when it's time for a big decision!

That's the purpose of this book—to fill you in on what you need to know, to explain the rules for going to college. If you're enrolled in a freshman seminar or orientation course, so much the better. We know a great deal about these courses through our own University 101 program at the University of South Carolina, and we know that freshmen who enroll in such courses usually find their first year of college more rewarding than do many students who don't take them.

Higher education represents a major developmental step in your life, but not all development takes place in the classroom. At the same time that colleges are encouraging more of you to attend, we've made the rules of going to college more complex than they have ever been. Today, you don't necessarily follow a rigid curriculum; you usually have some choice in deciding what courses to take (within the context of a specific academic subject). You'll certainly need to choose an academic major, but your program may also require you to minor in a related field, or establish a cognate in one or more related fields of study.

Factors in Freshman Success

You'll need to understand more than your curriculum to take advantage of the other developmental experiences of college life. For example, we know that students who live on campus, become involved in campus organizations, seek help from career and counseling centers, exercise regularly, eat sensibly, work to improve their writing skills and study habits, learn how to manage stress and speak up for what they want, and follow other guidelines we'll be suggesting in this book tend to find college a more satisfying and rewarding experience than those who don't.

Here's what one major state university discovered when it set about to determine factors that affected freshman success:

□ Because some nonacademic factors may have as much to do with whether you stay or leave as academic factors, you should work as hard at your personal development outside the classroom as you do at your scholastic development inside the classroom.

- Success doesn't depend on whether you're black or white, rich or poor, or whether your parents went to college. But other things do matter. Be certain about wanting to come to college in the first place. Don't come because it's the thing to do, or because all your friends are going. If you come to college with a specific vocational goal in mind, you'll be more likely to come back for your sophomore year. Uncertainty about a specific major, however, is nothing to worry about as a freshman.

- Whether or not you work in your freshman year won't affect your chances of survival, but how much you work does matter. The dropout rate of those who work more than twenty hours a week is five times that of those who work less than twenty hours a week.

- Certain personal problems may affect your chances of returning for your sophomore year. If you have difficulty getting along with people, if you are lonely, if you are ill, you are more likely to drop out. So deal with these problems before they become overwhelming.

- Live on campus. Freshmen living off campus drop out at a rate nearly twice that of on-campus freshmen. Make a real effort to get along with your roommate, and try to stay with that person during your entire freshman year. But, if you have irresolvable differences, request a room change because prolonged incompatibility will increase your chances of dropping out.

- Finally, be concerned if you run into academic difficulty. Students having trouble with their courses are more likely to drop out than others.

The study goes on to discuss factors that may affect *academic* success:

- Succeeding in college is more than simply a matter of studying hard and applying native intelligence.

- If you have a job, don't overdo it. Going to college full time and working more than twenty hours a week is an open invitation to earning lower grades.

- A good relationship with your parents helps. Students who have very close relationships with parents earn significantly higher grades than those who are incompatible with their parents. Don't assume that just because you're away from home your parents don't matter anymore.

- If you get sick or injure yourself, have financial problems, or have difficulty getting along with people, you are likely to earn lower grades.

Remember, these are generalizations from one study, but they should help you recognize the warning signals and thereby be better prepared to alter them.*

College Requirements

Chances are if you're reading this book, you've already been accepted by a college or university. You should understand that admission does not automatically mean that you are admissible to any academic program on the campus. What's more, should you wish to change majors during your college years, you may discover that the program you are seeking may have higher admission, progression, or graduation requirements than the program in which you are presently enrolled.

Be certain you know the differences among admission, progression, and graduation requirements. An admission requirement is simply the standard (usually a grade-point average or predicted grade-point average) by which you are admitted. A progression requirement is a standard you must uphold while enrolled in the program. Should you fall below the standard at any time, you may be put on probation or asked to leave the program until you can achieve the progression standard through other course work. A graduation requirement is the standard you must achieve at the end of your program in order to graduate. Although many programs have identical requirements for all three stages, you should know what these terms mean.

Academic Requirements

In addition to meeting certain standards, you will also need to complete certain course work to be eligible for graduation. Most academic majors have degree requirements requiring that you take a certain number of specified courses, with the balance of your course requirements coming from electives. With the proliferation of academic majors, the course requirements for each major have become rather complex in many cases. What's more, many courses have prerequisites or other courses that must be completed in order to be eligible for the next course in the sequence. By keeping in touch with

---

* Adapted from "The Academic and Personal Development of Penn State Freshmen," a longitudinal study of the class of 1980 by Lee Upcraft, Patricia Peterson, and Betty Moore, Office of Residential Life Programs, Division of Student Affairs, the Pennsylvania State University. Used by permission.

your academic advisor, you can be certain you are enrolled in the courses that will lead to the degree you seek. You'll learn more about academic advisors in Chapter 6 of this book.

Computing Grades and Grade-Point Averages

Your grade-point average or ratio (GPA or GPR) is computed on the number of course hours you attempt during a term. Each grade represents a certain number of points. Here's the system at most colleges:

- A = 4 points
- B = 3 points
- C = 2 points
- D = 1 point
- F = 0 points

By multiplying the number of points for the grade by the number of credits for the course, you can determine the total points you have earned in that course. Add the points taken for all courses you took that term, then divide this total by the number of hours you attempted that term. This is your GPA, or GPR.

Attendance Policies

Class attendance policies vary dramatically, even among professors on the same campus. Although many colleges allow you to miss class occasionally, their catalogs discuss excused and unexcused absences (never mentioning the word *cut*). And while most colleges publish official attendance policies in their catalogs, professors may have their own ideas about how often they will allow you to miss class. Some may expect you to attend all class sessions. Others may never take attendance, but may remind you that much of the material necessary for passing the course will be given as lecture material. In any event, we know that students who attend regularly tend to achieve better grades. So we urge you never to miss the first few classes of the term. This is when your professor will announce the course policies regarding attendance, requirements for passing, and other vital information. If you are ill and must miss a class, notify your professor or advisor. When you know in advance that you will be missing a class, your professor will appreciate knowing in advance, too.

A New Beginning

Although we've introduced a wide range of essential information in these opening pages, we have hardly begun to tell you everything you will want or need to know about the exciting years of college that lie ahead. The college experience will help you make the transition from adolescence to adulthood only if you take some of the responsibility for making that change happen. Subsequent chapters in this book are by college professionals who want to help you succeed. Read their words carefully, and you, too, will join their ranks as former freshmen who took full advantage of all college had to offer and used that power to pursue a richer, more satisfying life.

This is the beginning of that pursuit. Read how Charlotte Patterson, a psychology professor at the University of Virginia, views the arrival of the freshman class each fall:

"You won't want to come into the office today. The freshmen are arriving, and it's a mess over here. . . ."

It certainly is a mess. Hundreds of station wagons packed with steaming students, their families, and their endless belongings seek nonexistent parking spots along a few feet of curb. Irritable mothers and fathers bicker about when, where, and whether to park. Campus police do what they can to direct traffic, but they know it is beyond their control; the rules will have to bend a little more than usual today. . . . It is the messiest day of the year, no doubt about it. It is also my favorite.

It makes me think of those slushy days in early spring when the snow is melting and one cannot step down anywhere without splashing. Even when I am cold and wet, I cannot hate those days; they presage too much. Freshman arrival is also a mess, but I cannot hate it either. They appear in town like young green shoots, sprouting up everywhere, looking for light. Their faces hang out the windows of dorms like tiny new buds on an old, old tree. Someone else may worry about the sun and the soil and the possibility of frost; for them, it is enough just to *be*.

Yes, today is the beginning of a new life. One day you're Mama's child, living at home; the next day, you're a freshman and on your own. The end of childhood. Instant adulthood. Or is it? *Freshman!* I like the word. The very label itself suggests the dilemma. Should it be pronounced with emphasis on the *fresh* or the *man*? It points both ways. It doesn't matter whether you think of adulthood as a journey or as an arrival; today it is clearly a step on the path. Freshman fantasies and freshman fears can be seen on every young face.

This is a day that I mark for myself also. Freshman arrival signifies that it is time to come out of my summer's hibernation; time to use the dreams of a long summer to breathe life into teaching again; time, as they say, to "cultivate young minds" again. I am never as conscious of how much in need of cultivation my own mind still remains. There are always regrets about manuscripts as yet unwritten, books as yet unopened, problems as yet unresolved, but there is no time now for regrets. It is a time for new students, new lectures, new discussions, new research. It is time to begin again.

And that is why I like this day. For all its obvious, outward specialness, it is really no different from any other day. We are always ending something, and we are always beginning something else; we are always cherishing hopes and hiding fears, always searching for a new life and a new birth. Freshman arrival is a reminder that we are always, as Gertrude Stein once put it, "beginning again and again"—that, insofar as we are fully human, every day is always fresh. Freshman arrival changes everything and it changes nothing; it makes us stop to look at what was always there for us to see.*

May your hopes and dreams for the future be realized in your new beginning.

Suggested Activities

1. Charlotte Patterson's essay offers many thoughts for contemplation. For example:
   a. How is the first day of the fall term like "one of those slushy days in early spring when the snow is melting and one cannot step down anywhere without splashing"?
   b. What does the author mean by the dilemma of the word *freshman*?
   c. What does she mean when she says that "it is time to begin again" for her as well as for the freshmen?
   d. Reread the last paragraph of the essay and, in your own words, express the author's message.
   e. Using this essay as a basis, write about your own experience on your first day on campus. It might be the day you moved into

Due Mon., page

* Excerpted by permission from "With Fall, a Fresh Start," by Charlotte J. Patterson, Department of Psychology, University of Virginia, and originally published in *The Washington Post,* September 1, 1980.

your room, the day you arrived for orientation, or the first day of classes. Try to convey not only what you experienced but also how you felt about those experiences and what you think you will remember about them.

2. Here is a list of the most common fears reported by freshmen during their first week of college. Check the ones you are experiencing or anticipate. Add others you may be experiencing—this list is by no means complete! Realize, finally, that such fears are normal among college freshmen.

_____ I will not have enough money to do all the things I want to do.
_____ I will not be able to manage my time for studying, sleeping, meals, and exercise.
_____ I will have difficulty making friends.
_____ I will have difficulty in relationships with the opposite sex.
_____ I will become depressed, and this will affect my ability to make good grades.
_____ College will be too difficult for me.
_____ I don't feel as if I should be in college.
_____ I will disappoint my parents, who are paying for my education.
_____ I will have trouble getting along with my roommate.
_____ I will get lost on campus and be late for important classes.
_____ I will choose a major that is not suited to my skills or interests.
_____ My homesickness will adversely affect my grades.
_____ I will not be able to develop proper study habits.
_____ I will have trouble understanding professors.
_____ Other students will see me as a boring person.
_____ I will be too shy to speak up in and out of class.
_____ I will be tempted to cheat to get good grades.
_____ I will not be as sophisticated as other freshmen.

Note: Of all these concerns, most freshmen say what they fear most is the lack of supervision. Freedom, in other words, seems to have its price (at least, initially). One way to get a head start in this respect is to learn the art of time management, discussed in the chapter on study skills, Chapter 4.

The College Experience: An Investment in Your Future

Hilda F. Owens

VICE PRESIDENT FOR ACADEMIC AFFAIRS
SPARTANBURG METHODIST COLLEGE

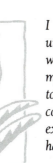

I can vividly recall my feelings of excitement, anticipation, uncertainty, and fear of the unknown during those first few weeks of my freshman year at East Carolina University in my native state of North Carolina. My school experiences up to that time had been pleasant and successful, but I was still concerned that measuring up to a new level of academic expectation and competition might be more difficult than I had expected.

New friends, competent professors, a developing comfortableness with the new environment, and satisfactory academic performance soon reassured me that I could still meet the demands of an academic environment and that college would be a challenging and pleasant experience. Time passed quickly, and graduation arrived all too soon. Little did I realize on that graduation day that college was only the beginning of a life filled with new learning experiences, new friends and associates, new and meaningful professional work, and a somewhat changed and emerging personality.

I found challenge, reward, and satisfaction in my years as a student. Each experience added something to the whole of who and what I am. I hope you will work to make your college experience as rewarding as mine was.

So you've decided to go to college! Few decisions will have as great an impact on the quality and direction of your life. In addition to increased knowledge and personal understanding, college not only can help prepare you to make intelligent decisions regarding career choices and educational options but also may affect your views on family matters, social issues, community service, political issues, health-care matters, recreation and leisure activities, and economic and consumer priorities.

The former president of a well-known Midwestern college used to begin his message to freshmen each year by saying, "Now that you have come to college, you can never go home again." His adaptation of the title of Thomas Wolfe's famous novel *You Can't Go Home Again* was not to say that students would forsake friends and family when they enter college but to underscore that the lenses through which they view the past and the future would now be ground by a significantly new set of experiences, acquaintances, demands, and expectations. Yes, with the decision to go to college, you've begun a course that can change your life for the better. This claim is not just an assumption; there is now adequate evidence that college students generally differ in significant ways from people who don't go to college and that individuals also change considerably while in college. Those differences and the impact of college will be discussed later in this chapter.

Changing Philosophies About College Attendance

As you look around at your fellow students, you may note considerable diversity. It hasn't always been this way in American higher education. From the founding of Harvard College (in 1636) until about 1862, American higher education had an aristocratic philosophy, and college students were primarily white males from the richer families. They studied the classics and prepared for the professions of theology, law, and medicine; they further prepared for positions of leadership in a developing democracy.

With the passage of the Morrill Act of 1862, the country began to develop a meritocratic stance with regard to college attendance. (By establishing the first land-grant colleges in America, the Morrill Act brought higher education within reach of more citizens.) This meritocratic period, which lasted through the 1950s, expressed the view that any person of merit—who had academic ability and a demonstrated commitment to collegiate study by successfully completing high school work—should be given the opportunity to attend college and to contribute to the increasing demand for an educated citizenry and a trained labor force. The curricula were expanded to include new options, and new kinds of colleges emerged. Although a more diversified student body enrolled, and the number of veteran, women, and black students increased, students' choices were still very much restricted by the society's expectations.

Since the mid-sixties, an egalitarian approach to higher education has enabled many individuals and even whole segments of society to become a part of the collegiate scene—people not accommodated earlier by universities. An egalitarian emphasis has encouraged a different type of student to continue formal education to develop personal and work-related knowledge and skills in accord with his or her own abilities. The junior college movement that had begun in the early 1900s flourished in the egalitarian spirit of the sixties, seventies, and early eighties. The "people's colleges," as the community and junior colleges are often referred to, expanded until in the mid-1980s one-third of all colleges in America were two-year colleges and about one-third of all students were served by these colleges. Over half of all college freshmen beginning their college careers today are in two-year colleges.

The egalitarian approach has brought many nontraditional and new students to America's college campuses. Cross (1980) defines *new students* as those who need help with basic skills, motivation, and guidance about how to make it in the educational system. They may be white or black, rich or poor, but they share the common experience of poor performance in school, and without special admissions programs they would not generally be considered college material. *Nontraditional students,* as Cross described them, are largely adult part-time learners who carry full-time responsibilities in addition to their studies. These students generally have been successful previously in high school and/or college, but other responsibilities plus their experience and maturity mandate special consideration with regard to schedules, curricula, and instruction if their needs are to be met. Perhaps you are a member of one of these new or nontraditional categories of college students who now join traditional students on campus.

Major Questions About Going to College

The historical development of higher education has brought us from a time when few students were served by a limited number of institutions for highly selective purposes to a time when higher education has over 3,000 colleges and universities serving approximately 12 million credit-earning students at a cost of billions of dollars per year to its students and supporters. At the beginning of the twentieth century, fewer than 2 percent of people of college age attended college; today almost 50 percent of Americans of college age formally continue their education beyond high school. Whether from a real desire to go to college or as a matter of necessity just to compete, you have chosen to be in the college-bound group. You have answered yes to the major question: Should I go to college?

Where Should I Go to College?

Once you made the decision to go to college, other important questions emerged. Where should I go to college? Should I attend a large or small college, public or private institution, single-sex or coeducational college, a comprehensive university, four-year liberal arts college, or one of the over 1,200 community/junior colleges? Because of the tremendous similarities among colleges, where you attend college will make less difference than some people think, but where you attend will make a difference in the impact college may have on your development and on related options available to you. Institutions differ in their goals and purposes, their predominant campus environment, the areas of student development that they emphasize, and available curricula and other educational options.

How Shall I Go to College?

The question of how to go to college is also important. Will you be a full-time or part-time student? Will you be an on-campus resident student, live in campus-provided facilities off campus, continue to reside with your family, or live in an apartment or other home of your own? Will you work part time in addition to your studies, or will you finance college by savings, loans, or scholarships? Will you have family and work responsibilities besides college-related activities? Will you have time to engage in extracurricular activities and use extra support opportunities, or will course work and required activities be your primary—if not sole—interaction with the college environment?

Decisions in these areas are important because studies indicate that student development occurs in varying degrees and in different areas depending on these factors. Resident students tend to develop in more areas and to a greater extent than do commuters; full-time students tend to change more than those who attend part time. Research indicates that students who become involved in the nonacademic areas of college and those who work part time (especially on campus) are more likely to persist in college, to be satisfied with college, and to be affected to a greater degree by the college experience.

What Shall I Study?

What to study is also a basic question. You should decide after a careful and honest appraisal of your knowledge and skill level in chosen and necessary fields and/or your ability and willingness to acquire prerequisite knowledge and skills. You should also consider your personality, interests, life-style requirements, and values in making this decision. What you study is too important for you to select a major because of what your parents want you to choose, what your closest friends have picked, or what strikes you as an "easy" major.

Your decision to major in business administration, education, religion, nursing, philosophy, biology, agriculture, journalism, data processing, music, engineering, or any one of hundreds of other choices can make a significant difference in your future life, personal happiness, and job satisfaction. Don't be afraid to examine options or reexamine previous choices; don't be afraid to admit if you are undecided about your major or career option. An acknowledged undecided student can probably receive more effective advice regarding choice of major and other areas of goal achievement than an undecided student who fakes a choice. Learn as much as you can about as many subjects as you can; whatever your choice, you'll find it valuable to develop good communication skills and good computation skills.

Your decisions regarding major and field of study will help open some doors to you and may close others, at least temporarily. These decisions may help you find challenge and satisfaction in your life and work or lead to possible frustration, and perhaps failure, in these areas. What you choose to study and to do will be a partial expression of who you are and what you value. Your work will consume a major portion of your life, so you should choose carefully and wisely. Your choice must fit *you* if it is to be a good one. Do keep in mind, however, that although this decision is very important, you can change or modify it later if circumstances necessitate it or if you want to change. You may have to back up some, and it may take you more than four years to complete your degree, but such action may be better than continuing indefinitely with a choice that is no longer the right one for you.

Impact of College on Individuals

By now you're probably asking, "Just how will college affect me? How will I change in ways that are different from persons who decided to work, join the army, or do something else rather than go to college?" Of course, some changes in knowledge, attitude, behavior, and skill will occur simply because of increased maturation and experience. You will also encounter some significant changes as you interact with others in the collegiate environment and participate in college life.

Many satisfying experiences will be yours during this higher education venture. But going to college can also be a stressful and frustrating experience in many ways. You should be consoled that facing cognitive dissonance (resistance to foreign ideas), creative tension, and crises are essential if you are to learn and develop further. If you believe that going to college is going to be all fun and games, you should know that for a full-time student college should be as demanding as a full-time job—maybe more so. Much learning will occur because of what you do to change your attitudes and behaviors; some learning will occur in spite of yourself if certain environmental factors are at work.

One of the most important legacies of the sixties and seventies was the recognition of the American college student as a subject of needed research and study. A number of these studies have greatly expanded our knowledge of the impact of college on students, how students change during college, and our awareness of their characteristics and concerns. Levine's book *When Dreams and Heroes Died: A Portrait of Today's College Student* (1981) has given us a contemporary portrait of the characteristics, concerns, and habits of college students, and others continue to seek new data that will lead toward greater understanding of college students. What follows is a summary of research findings regarding the effects of college on students.

Major Areas of Change

On the basis of his own extensive clinical studies as a psychologist and his assessment of the available literature related to the personal development of college students, Katz (1976) identified seven major areas of change for students: (1) authoritarianism declines, (2) autonomy grows, (3) self-esteem increases, (4) the ability to relate ideas to one another grows, (5) political sophistication increases, (6) esthetic capacity grows, and (7) theoretical issues are better understood. Katz also noted that many investigators found among college students an increase in political and social liberalism and a decrease in formal religious identification and religious activities. These findings basically still hold true. A recent trend toward more conservative positions with regard to political and social issues and religious identification in society is now beginning to be reflected in campus profiles. Although current college students may be somewhat less liberal than in the past twenty years, they will still differ by being more liberal than the society at large.

Brawer (1973), Bowen (1977), Astin (1977), and Parker (1978) stress (1) the importance of the impact of college on increased knowledge and cognitive development; (2) increased correlation between educational attainment, career development, and income; (3) increased self-discovery and changes in attitudes, beliefs, self-concept, values, and behavior; and (4) increased practical competence of students, especially in the area of family life.

Virtually all of the evidence to date suggests that the college experience generally has a strong positive impact on cognitive learning (content and thought process), as measured when comparing freshmen with seniors, college students with comparable persons not attending college, or alumni with comparable noncollege people. Significant increases in the level of substantive knowledge, intellectual sensibilities, intellectual tolerance, and an interest in lifelong learning are recognizable qualities of the typical college graduate. Colleges seem to do a good job at what they claim to do best—increasing the knowledge and development of their students.

Although academic achievement is the most heavily researched topic in higher education, the relationship between educational attainment and income level has been researched longer. Findings indicate that educational achievement and attainment, career opportunities, and income level are all positively related. Even in a day when educational critics are pointing out the number of people with college degrees who are unemployed or under-employed, you have only to look at the employment figures of high school graduates, high school dropouts, and people with less than a high school education to see that the competitive edge in job opportunity and income level still generally favors the person with the highest educational level. In a day when you may question the desirability of investing time and money in a college education, evidence still supports it as a good investment. As one well-known educator has expressed it, "If you think education is expensive, try ignorance; ignorance is more expensive almost every time."

Colleges claim to help facilitate total student development, that is, to educate the whole person. They often claim to have an impact on an individual's ability for personal discovery—who one is, what one knows and can do, believes, and values, and where one fits in the scheme of things—and for personalizing many attitudes, beliefs, and values picked up from others along the way. Colleges further contend that they give students the opportunity to clarify and improve their self-concept—their own view of their aptitudes, interests, values, commitments, and aspirations—and to positively affect certain skills, competencies, and behaviors. Significant evidence shows that colleges do affect students in these areas and that, generally speaking, these changes are in positive directions.

Students tend to leave college not only more competent but also more confident than when they came. They also tend to have a better sense of who they are, where they belong, and how they might make a difference in the world about them. The only changes that some persons might regard as negative changes are some decline of traditional religious values and some increase in hedonistic behavior (drinking, gambling). At any rate, college will influence your attitudes, values, behaviors, and self-concepts—with most changes, but not all, in positive directions. Note also that many of these changes are highly affected by your personal characteristics, the goals of the college you attend, the campus environment at your college, and your intentional and unintentional interaction with that environment.

A frequently stated goal of higher education is to prepare people for competence and performance in the "practical affairs of life." This goal often appears in college catalogs, but educators and political leaders haven't fully defined how the college experience actually achieves this goal.

Research shows that college graduates tend to be more adaptable and more oriented to the future, adopt more liberal views and more ideological thinking, develop greater interest in political and public affairs, are more likely than others to vote and to be more active in community affairs, and are less prone to ordinary criminal activity. Regrettably, ethical behavior and integrity have not been shown to be so positively affected by the college experience. Ethical behavior and integrity may be best taught and best learned in other social and learning environments, and some theorists say they may be essentially established much earlier in life than the college years.

From an economic standpoint, college tends to provide a labor force with needed knowledge and skill and tends to reduce unemployment. College further helps people develop the flexibility, mobility, and knowledge needed to adapt to the many changing demands of work, life, and relationships. It also seems to contribute to increased productivity and job satisfaction and to provide a reasonable financial return on the time, energy, and money invested in a college education.

Further, college is an important influence on family life. The stereotypical images of the appropriate roles of men and women in the family seem to change with increased education. As women earn more of the family income (over 60 percent of women in America work outside the home), matters of child care and household responsibilities are more likely to be shared or shifted by marriage partners. College-educated people tend to delay the age of marriage, to have fewer chidren, and to plan the timing of their children's births. They also tend to allocate more thought, time, energy, and money to child rearing. The divorce rate among college-educated people is slightly less than that among others, and the children of college-educated parents seem to have greater abilities and enjoy greater achievements of their own than do other children.

College-educated people are characteristically more efficient consumers, with higher financial returns from different levels of income. As consumers, they tend to save more of their money, take greater—but wiser—investment risks, and spend money in ways that reflect their personal values and tastes, including a high priority on home, intellectual and cultural interests, and the nurturing of children. As consumers and citizens, they are also more able to deal with the complexities of bureaucracies at all levels, the legal system, tax laws and requirements, and false or misleading advertising.

They also tend to exhibit a practical competence with regard to leisure activities. They spend less time and money on television and movies and more time on adult education, hobbies, community and civic affairs, and vacations. There is a difference in the amount of time college-educated persons spend in these areas and in the quality of these activities.

In regard to health care, college graduates are likely to be more concerned with prevention rather than just treatment of physical and mental health problems. Diet, exercise, and stress management influence the life span and number of disabilities. Attention to preventive health maintenance, which is generally a priority for college-educated people, is probably related to their increased self-concept and sense of personal worth.

A college education, then, has a positive impact in the areas of citizenship, economic productivity, health priorities and status, consumer behavior, and leisure activities. The largest impact, however, occurs in the increased emphasis on family life among college graduates and an increase in the quality of their family life.

—ııı—ııı—ııı—
On the Value of the College Experience

Although your many benefits from a college education are not all measurable, many people—including students, parents, educators, public officials, and the general public—tend to think of college primarily in terms of its relationship to employment and its effect on income. Bird (1975), one of the most articulate spokespersons against a college education for some people, argues that a college education is not a good investment. Freeman and Hollomon (1975) discuss the supply and demand issues related to a college education and note that the value of college is declining.

Such critics see college in terms of its monetary value only. Although employment and income are important factors in life and in a college education, many others believe that these aren't the best or only reasons for going to college or the greatest benefits from college. College can and should be much more than a place just to "process" someone into a higher wage bracket. College should help add meaning and purpose to life.

According to Frankel (1969), individuals can find meaning and purpose in their lives in three ways: (1) by what they give to the world in terms of their creations, (2) by what they take from the world through encounters and experiences, and (3) by the stand they take with regard to their human predicaments. College-educated people, according to research and the observations of many people, usually gain skills, attitudes, and behaviors during the college experience that enable them to develop more meaning and purpose in their lives—not always, but certainly frequently enough to conclude that college is an important experience in the fuller development of human potential.

Kingman Brewster, a former president of Yale University, identified the primary goals of a college education as the development of three senses: (1) a sense of place, (2) a sense of self, and (3) a sense of judgment. Brewster clearly argued for the broader and more liberating view of education when he concluded:

The most fundamental value of education is that it makes life more interesting. This is true whether you are fetched up on a desert island or adrift in the impersonal loneliness of the urban hurly-burly. It allows you to see things which the uneducated do not see. It allows you to understand things which do not occur to the less learned. In short, it makes it less likely that you will be bored with life. It also makes it less likely that you will be a crashing bore to those whose company you keep. By analogy, it makes the difference between the traveler who understands the local language and the traveler to whom the local language is a jumble of nonsense words [Cited by Davis, 1977, p. xv].

Eddy (1977) concluded that the real task of an educated person is to be able to articulate to himself and others what he is willing to bet his life on. These spokesmen join Astin, Bowen, Feldman and Newcomb, Katz, Sanford, and many others who feel that the real value of education greatly exceeds its monetary value. Its real value is that it most likely will improve the quality of life for students, their families and friends, and their world. Perhaps it is time for educators to explain more effectively to prospective and present students and to legislators and donors who fund higher education the whole story of the value of college. I welcome this opportunity to do so with you.

Your own characteristics, the characteristics of your institution, and the extent and duration of your interaction with your college will affect the extent of your development and change. Therefore, you and your friends won't all change in the same areas and to the same extent, but most of you will be changed substantially by the college experience. Tragically, some of you will not change but will graduate instead very much as you entered, only more so, because of your refusal to accommodate new knowledge, attitudes, and behaviors. Please don't waste this valuable opportunity for positive change in your life.

College is and should be, most educators believe, a place to learn much about how to earn a living. But more importantly, it's a place to learn some necessary skills and attitudes for building a meaningful life. You should be developing a philosophy that will help see you through future changes, both in you and your world. You are on a great voyage. What difference will it make? That will depend a lot on you. Is the college experience potentially worth your investment? You bet it is! Decide today to make the best of this great adventure in learning and living. Manage those changes to your own advantage.

Suggested Activities

1. Read your college catalog and student handbook carefully so you'll understand your institution's expectations of you and what you have a right to expect of it.

2. Visit the counseling or career-planning office to discuss your career aspirations, personal characteristics, and college major.

3. If you find a "misfit" between you and your selected college or major, begin to explore other options. A good place to begin might be with the career counselor on your campus.

4. Read further about the general impact of college on students and on the more specific impact of the peer group, the college environment, and selected programs and experiences.

5. Develop a good relationship with at least one faculty member who can help you through the academic maze and be your friend or mentor during this important phase of your life.

6. How do your aptitudes, interests, personality, and values match your stated major?

7. Is the college or university you've selected likely to maximize your development?

8. Is the fit between your characteristics and those of your institution such that you'll be compatible enough to be reasonably satisfied but at the same time have enough cognitive dissonance or creative tension to require new thought and behavior patterns?

9. Are you engaged in appropriate extracurricular activities to extend learning opportunities beyond the classroom and to work with other types of students?

10. Are you aware of the likely differences in impact that different types of colleges have on students? What kind of impact is your college likely to make?

11. Are you taking advantage of the various cultural, educational, and recreational opportunities available at your institution and in the local community?

12. Are you working toward clarifying your identity and your philosophy of life?

13. Are you identifying what you want to contribute to life as well as what you want to get from life?

References

Astin, A. W. *Four Critical Years: Effects of College on Beliefs, Attitudes, and Knowledge.* San Francisco: Jossey-Bass, 1977.

Bird, C. *The Case Against College.* New York: McKay, 1975.

Bowen, H. R. *Investment in Learning: The Individual and Social Value of American Higher Education.* San Francisco: Jossey-Bass, 1977.

Brawer, F. B. *New Perspectives on Personality Development in College Students.* San Francisco: Jossey-Bass, 1973.

Cross, K. P. "Our Changing Students and Their Impact on Colleges: Prospects for a True Learning Society." *Phi Delta Kappan* 61 (1980): 627–630.

Davis, J. R. *Going to College: The Study of Students and the Student Experience.* Boulder, Colo.: Westview Press, 1977.

Eddy, E. D. "What Happened to Student Values?" *Educational Record* 58, no. 1 (1977): 7–17.

Frankel, V. *The Will to Meaning.* New York: Plume, 1969.

Freeman, R. B., and J. H. Holloman. "The Declining Value of College Going." *Change,* September 1975, 24–31.

Katz, J. "Benefits for Personal Development from Going to College." Paper presented at the annual meeting of the Association of Professors of Higher Education. Chicago, March 6–7, 1976.

Katz, N., ed. *No Time for Youth: Growth and Constraint in College Students.* San Francisco: Jossey-Bass, 1968.

Levine, A. W. *When Dreams and Heroes Died: A Portrait of Today's College Students.* San Francisco: Jossey-Bass, 1981.

Parker, C. A., ed. *Encouraging Development in College Students.* Minneapolis: University of Minnesota Press, 1978.

Sanford, N. *Self and Society: Social Change and Individual Development.* New York: Atherton Press, 1966.

Sanford, N., ed. *The American College: A Psychological and Social Interpretation of the Higher Learning.* New York: Wiley, 1962.

3 Higher Education in the Western World: Some Contrasts

John Orr Dwyer

DEAN, COLLEGE OF LIBERAL ARTS
UNIVERSITY OF DETROIT

I entered Yale as a freshman in September 1956. I enjoyed university life so much that I have stayed in academe ever since—as a student, a teacher, and an administrator. For me, there can be no better work environment than a campus.

After finishing at Yale with a bachelor's and a master's degree, I began my career teaching history at a high school in Connecticut. Caught up in the optimism of the 1960s and inspired by our young president's words and thoughts and actions, I took my training to Uganda for a two-year stint as a teacher at a Catholic mission school.

To train for the teaching of African history at the college level, I returned to the United States to work for my Ph.D. degree at Columbia University, the second of my several campus homes. Dissertation research took me back to Africa; I was married by then and our first child was born while we were living on yet another campus, Makerere University in Uganda's capital, Kampala. I then took a job teaching at Pomona College in Claremont, California. This stop counts as six campuses, not one, because the Claremont Colleges are six in number, contiguous, cooperative, and collegiate, but proud and distinct in their traditions and their missions.

I took my first administrative position at a small liberal arts college, Centre College of Kentucky. There my family and I were able to experience campus life 168 hours per week, because with my deanship came a residence in the freshman men's dormitory. I moved quickly after that experience into academic administra-tion at my next campus, the University of San Francisco. USF is one of the twenty-eight Jesuit colleges and universities in the United States, and I came to appreciate the proud tradition of liberal education that the Jesuits have earned since the sixteenth century. When the offer of a deanship at yet another of the Jesuit campuses, the University of Detroit, came in 1983, I quickly accepted what I hope will be a long-term relationship with another fine campus.

If you are reading this chapter, you probably are a new or continuing student at an American college or university at the end of the twentieth century. These few pages will show how higher education has changed in Europe and America since it emerged in its present form about 800 years ago. Consider as you read: Are conditions significantly different or substantially the same for you and for the student of medieval times?

This account is restricted to the history of higher education in Western Europe and the United States. Educational traditions exist in all other parts of the world, and some have more distinction than the one we will describe. Universities have existed for centuries in Asia (China), Africa (Egypt), and Latin America (Mexico), and their achievements have been significant.

Is College Essential for Achievement?

A college campus provides much to delight and little to bemoan. Physically, a campus is usually a comfortable and an attractive place and will contain facilities from classrooms and offices and dormitories to gymnasiums, sta-diums, and auditoriums. Most important, it will contain a library. You cannot spend too much time in that hallowed hall, even if you are taking a nap with your head holding open the pages of Tolstoy's *War and Peace*.

The campus also contains, by definition, a high concentration of bright and interesting people. Some of these people will become your close friends for a lifetime; others you will admire from a distance as they dazzle the place with their charm and their learning. One definition of a university is "a place where people come together for the precise purpose of disagreeing with one another." College is not just the cornucopia of information and the labora-tory of research; it is also the arena of ideas.

Attendance at college or university, delightful though it can be, is not a prescription or a requirement for success, happiness, or prosperity. Many examples could be cited of persons who had those things without college:

powerful monarchs, talented authors and athletes, and Buddha, Jesus, and Muhammad, whose religions influence the lives of a majority of people on the planet.

College is not even a prerequisite for a life of intellectual achievement. It might be argued that modern thought has been most significantly influenced by Marx, Darwin, and Freud (try out that contention on your profs and peers), all of whom had some university education in the previous century. But consider the life of another nineteenth century intellectual, John Stuart Mill (1806–1873), who was educated exclusively by his father, James Mill (1773–1836), a noted English philosopher, historian, economist—and a strict disciplinarian. By 1816, when the younger Mill was only ten, his father had guided him through a considerable amount of history in English, and an astounding syllabus of readings in the original Greek: Aesop's *Fables,* Xenophon's *Anabasis,* all of the writings of the historian Herodotus, the satires of Lucian, and the writings of Diogenes, Isocrates, and Plato. Having turned ten, Mill now took up the study of Latin, the geometry of Euclid, algebra, and more history. At twelve he began his study of scholastic logic and read all of Aristotle's logical treatises. In the following year, at age thirteen, Mill turned to relatively modern times, studying the economics and philosophies of Adam Smith and David Ricardo.

A university curriculum probably would have had little to offer to Mill. One is reminded of the reply attributed to the great Shakespearean scholar

George Lyman Kittredge when a colleague asked him why he did not have a doctorate: "Who would examine me?" But John Stuart Mill, in not attending a university, was certainly deprived of a special kind of life. Formal disputations, late-night disagreements, intimate relationships with fellow adolescents and young adults, the multiplicity of mentors on a faculty, distance from his father—all these were denied to him.

Mill had a successful career as a civil servant, however, and was able to enjoy the life of the mind as well. In addition to his work at the India Office, Mill wrote some of the most influential works of the nineteenth century, including *On Liberty* (1859), *Utilitarianism* (1863), and his celebrated *Autobiography* (1873).

—III——III——III—

Historical Overview

Although students in Europe had been studying for centuries, there were new conditions in the Middle Ages that brought about the model of the modern university. A formal education, by which we mean a course of study that most students have in common, was becoming essential for training for the professions of law, medicine, and the priesthood. Societies of scholars, already learned, came together to share their knowledge, first with each other and then with students. They did this at Bologna, in Italy, in the middle of the twelfth century, and soon thereafter at Paris, in France, and at Oxford and Cambridge, in England. Patterns of study, reading, initiation, teaching, and vocation soon could be recognized at these institutions and others founded in Spain, Germany, and elsewhere from the thirteenth to the fifteenth centuries. One such pattern was the designation of the larger and encompassing institution as the *university* and the smaller components, the residences, as the *colleges*.

By the sixteenth century, European universities had assimilated both classical learning and the wisdom of the best minds of their time: the history and belles-lettres that Erasmus (1466–1536) called "polite learning," and the *eloquentia perfecta* that Ignatius Loyola (1491–1556) described as the code of communication needed for young men to be influential and persuasive as citizens and professionals. Liberal education had been born.

In America

Only nine colleges were founded in the colonial era of what was to become the United States. These were seven of the eight universities now in the "Ivy League" (Harvard, Yale, Princeton, Pennsylvania, Columbia, Brown, and Dartmouth; Cornell was not founded until 1865) plus William and Mary

The Gifts of Academe: II
A Reputation for Martin Luther

Martin Luther (1483–1546), a leader of the Protestant Reformation, studied at the University of Erfurt, a prestigious German institution. There he continued the pattern he had started as a boy of making close friends of other students and older people as well. He also became proficient at playing the lute and entertained others on breaks from their studies.

In classrooms and in disputations, Luther invariably wanted to extend the argument of the day. His conversations outside of class were long and serious. When he left the University of Erfurt in 1502 he had not yet turned 20, but already he was known as "The Philosopher."

and Rutgers. Harvard, founded in 1636, was the first and only American college for much of the seventeenth century. Indeed, Yale graduates have noted that one of the hardships of the early colonists was that Harvard was the only college they could attend.

In the early nineteenth century, as the country expanded westward, most towns wanted hotels, railways—and colleges. Many of America's small liberal arts colleges were founded (and some faltered) in this period. Many were affiliated with Christian denominations. Women were admitted at Oberlin and at Mount Holyoke in 1837 and at the state universities and various new women's colleges later in the century. The Morrill Act of 1862 allowed the expansion of land-grant colleges and state universities.

The twentieth century saw higher education in America expanded even further. No longer were places in college reserved for the few who were privileged by their birth or honored for their achievements. Now, as a character in Owen Johnson's *Stover at Yale* (1911) observed, "The function of college has changed. It is now the problem of educating masses and not individuals."

The Unintended Revolution

By 1940, though, the masses had not yet arrived on America's campuses. Only 1.5 million students, 60 percent male and 97 percent white, were studying with 110,000 faculty members in that year. It took World War II, and the returning veterans with their G.I. Bill of Rights to fill the campuses with men and women who had never had college expectations. The new goal of higher education for everyone who could benefit, the pressures of the baby boom, the challenge of *Sputnik* in 1957, and the new demands for research being placed on the universities by the government resulted in campus expansion and euphoria in the 1960s. Campus protests against the Vietnam War and the economic recession of the late 1970s took their toll, but the "unintended revolution," as Bonner (1986) termed it, had taken place. There were 1,500 more colleges in America in the 1980s than there had been in 1940, and, instead of the 1.5 million on our campuses then, there were 12 million in 1985.

Curriculum

Perhaps the most famous American college graduate of the 1980s is Brooke Shields, the actress who received her degree from Princeton in 1987. Surely she is the only alum to give her transcript to *Life* magazine. Here are the courses Ms. Shields took during her four years at Princeton:

- ☐ 4 in French language (her major)
- ☐ 5 in French literature

- ☐ 3 in acting
- ☐ 3 in cinema analysis
- ☐ 1 in dance
- ☐ 1 in contemporary English drama

- ☐ 3 in ceramics
- ☐ 3 in psychology
- ☐ 2 in English literature
- ☐ 1 in philosophy
- ☐ 1 in religion
- ☐ 1 in sociology
- ☐ 1 in geology

Brooke Shields graduated with honors, having earned grades of A or B in all her courses. And, although some commentators (see Koppett, 1987) are distressed that she had no math, computer studies, or lab science, no classical studies, geography, or history, and no American literature, government, or economics, this is probably not an unusual transcript. She has developed some skills, studied one subject in some depth, and has met distribution requirements in the traditional areas of science, humanities, and the social sciences. She also earned credit for directed studies not reflected in this summary.

Choice of Courses

How might we compare Brooke Shields's course of study at Princeton in the 1980s to the curriculum of her academic ancestors? One of the most obvious differences concerns *choice*. You and Brooke were presented with a college catalog listing more courses than you could take in several four-year student careers. Until the nineteenth century, there was virtually no choice. Most undergraduates studied the same subjects.

Although some students in twelfth-century Europe came to the university towns such as Bologna to study for a career in law, medicine, or the priesthood, many others came to places such as Paris to study the liberal arts with famous teachers like Peter Abelard, for example. These arts became formalized in the late Middle Ages into a curriculum recognized in all the universities of western Europe as the *Trivium* (grammar, rhetoric, and logic) and the *Quadrivium* (geometry, arithmetic, astronomy, and music). The "three philosophies" of metaphysics, ethics, and natural science were soon added, and the Renaissance contributed the study of Greek and Hebrew literature. Little changed until the nineteenth century.

The Gifts of Academe: IV
Relief from Boredom for Albert Einstein

Albert Einstein (1879–1955) did not enjoy his schooling as a boy in Germany. The life was rigidly disciplined and the teaching harsh and pedantic. Einstein felt himself to be a free spirit, and he did not fit. His grades showed it: They were poor.

Einstein received inspiration from his uncles rather than his teachers. They introduced him to the fascinations of mathematics and science, and, at age 16, Einstein wrote an essay that contained the seeds of what became, a decade later, his special theory of relativity.

The Federal Polytechnic Academy in Zurich, Switzerland, provided Einstein with the relief he sought from the boredom and intimidation of his schools. He studied physics and mathematics there before going on for his Ph.D. degree at the University of Zurich.

Faculty

Another contrast between early and modern curricula involves the delivery system: *the faculty.* You and Brooke can read dozens, if not hundreds, of professors' names in your college catalog. Most of them are available to teach only in the academic discipline in which they were trained; others may team-teach or offer courses in only one area. When today's teachers give small seminars and tutorials, though, they most often do so in the subject on which they have done the most research and writing. They are most comfortable—and most inspiring—when they are teaching the topics they "own."

The medieval master who agreed to accept a new student at Bologna, Paris, Oxford, or Cambridge was taking on a different form of faculty responsibility. He taught the students only one subject at a time, moving on to the next only when he believed them to be ready. He gave hour-long lectures and expected his students to read, memorize, and discuss their lessons. Logic was the most important of the studies of the young freshman because it was an essential tool of debate. The master would determine when the freshman had passed probation and was eligible to participate in the public disputations that were central to university life. The medieval master was the generalist who trained students for the transition from the passive form of education—reading and listening—to the active participation in formal debates using the recognized rules of logic.

The Gifts of Academe: V
Shocks of Recognition for Mary McCarthy

Mary McCarthy (b. 1912), the distinguished American writer, had a perfect preparation for college: good schools and lots of reading. She used her grandfather's library as a child, devouring the works of Dickens and Tolstoy, among others, and establishing the habits of a lifetime. She once wrote that she "reads with a certain gluttony which now and then overreaches itself." This is the best kind of addiction.

McCarthy entered Vassar College in 1929, and there she developed her skills as a writer. Her professors encouraged her obvious talent, and she enjoyed "the shocks of recognition that make us, in adolescence, elect what we are or shall be."

When, in 1640, Henry Dunster, a 30-year-old graduate of Magdalene College, Cambridge, became president of Harvard College in Cambridge, Massachusetts, students were offered the following subjects: logic, mathematics, physics, astronomy, Greek, Hebrew, Aramaic, Syriac, rhetoric, and divinity. The young president taught them all. Dunster and his seventeenth-century successors also acted as the admissions officers at Harvard, examining each applicant carefully and orally in Latin, Greek, and the classics. You and Brooke would be hard-pressed to find a faculty member today, let alone a college president, willing and able to take on such responsibilities.

Harvard's presidents gradually delegated some of their curricular tasks to teaching fellows who were also talented generalists. A fellow would meet with a group of freshmen, and, much as a medieval master, he would teach them one subject at a time throughout the normal undergraduate period of four years. This system continued throughout the colonial period in America (Morison, 1936a).

Freshmen entering Harvard in 1868 still had a prescribed curriculum (mathematics, French, Greek, Latin, elocution, and ethics), but improved secondary schools brought increased demands for admission, and the college was able to raise its standards (Morison, 1930). Tutors, masters, and professors were able to become more specialized in their curricular offerings, and students, having access to more subjects, were able to come to know many more members of the faculty. Faculty members, in turn, had better access to more students, and patterns of informal gatherings, both social and for study, emerged. Faculty members became more involved in extra-curricular activities as well (Morison, 1936b). You and Brooke enjoy the

The Gifts of Academe: VI
Vocation and Avocation for Martin Luther King, Jr.

Martin Luther King, Jr., (1929–1968) came from a family of preachers, but when he entered Morehouse College in Atlanta, Georgia, he did not intend to follow his father into the ministry.

His teachers at Morehouse changed his mind—and his life. Two of them, George Kelsey in the philosophy department and Benjamin Mays, the president, convinced King that a career in the church could be intellectually satisfying. King was ordained before he graduated and became an assistant pastor in his father's church in 1947.

Returning to Morehouse for his final year, King became active in the National Association for the Advancement of Colored People (NAACP), and thus he began both his ministry and his civil rights leadership before leaving college.

teaching of faculty members who have become more specialized in their studies, but, as counselors, mentors, advisors, and friends, they have developed more generalized interests in their students.

The Role of Books

In the 1980s, you and Brooke have access to books and other sources of information virtually without restriction. If a book is not in your library, it is probably in one nearby. If it is far away, it is probably available on interlibrary loan. If the information you seek is not in book form, it is usually retrievable by computer from some data base. The uncollected knowledge of your professors and your peers is available in conversation. The sources for Brooke's entire curriculum were almost certainly available to her on or near Princeton's campus.

It was not always thus. The beginnings of Western higher education as we have described it preceded the invention of movable type and the printing press, and books were rare and valuable items to the medieval student. He had to plan his schedule carefully to take advantage of the availability of books. Libraries existed, of course, but they could not always guarantee a volume to a student. There were no bookstores, not only because there were not enough books but also because if books were sold they would then leave the university with the departing alumni and would no longer be available to the scholars left behind. Students most often had to rent their books.

Technology to the Rescue

Type for printing was invented in China. Movable type, made from molds of the individual characters to be printed, was used in Korea before its independent invention in Europe in the fifteenth century. Credit for this extraordinary development has been given to Johannes Gutenberg, who may have made his type in Strasbourg in 1436 or 1437. His Mazarin Bible, printed about 1456 in Mainz, is believed to be the first book printed in Europe from movable type. It revolutionized the world for students as for everyone else.

Not only did the student have access to a wider pool of knowledge through the increased availability of books but his study habits were changed as well. He was no longer restricted to the rental of rare volumes for a limited time. He could now purchase them himself. Indeed, he could build his own library.

A Personal Library

By the sixteenth century, about a century after the invention of the printed book, some students, perhaps wealthier than others, were able to build personal libraries in their college rooms. At the University of Paris in about 1550, for example, a student might own about twenty volumes, whereas the young men studying to be Jesuit priests at the same time, with different demands being made upon them, might have about twice that number. The catalog of one student who was studying at the University of Toulouse up until his death in 1572 has survived, no doubt because it was unusual, not typical. The young man had more than 150 books, a library comparable to that of a professional scholar of his day. He probably managed his books as a lending library for his less affluent friends, for the catalog lists works that were being studied by other French students at the time. The student collector seems to have had little interest in science or theology, and owned no works in Greek (a student at a Jesuit college would have), but he was clearly very interested in his own times. Erasmus was his favorite, and he also had copies of books written by his own teachers. There were books of recent history and maps on his walls showing the European countries and the specific sites of contemporary battles (Davies, 1983). What could a future historian learn from reading a catalog of *your* library?

What will you read as a college student? Your class assignments, of

The Gifts of Academe: VII

Books for John Barth

John Barth (b. 1930), author of my favorite novel, *The Sot-Weed Factor,* laments that today's students don't read many books: "It's pathetic. They want to join a conversation that has been going on for millennia, and they want to join it from the top without having read all this stuff."

Barth admits that as a freshman at Johns Hopkins in the 1940s, "I decided I hadn't read anything, and therefore I would try to read everything." He didn't succeed, of course, but he was particularly inspired by Faulkner and Joyce—"both big revelations" (Barth, 1987).

There are revelations there for you, too. Read, then join the conversation.

course, plus the new works of writers you enjoyed before coming to college. Then you will receive a flock of suggestions from your professors and your peers, from reviews in newspapers and magazines (develop the habit of regular periodical reading if you haven't already), and from proposed reading programs. The best known of these latter is *The Great Books of the Western World,* a list compiled in mid-century by Robert Maynard Hutchins and others at the University of Chicago. The authors even propose a ten-year reading program in the great books, giving monthly chapter and page assignments.

If you confined your lifelong reading program to three volumes only, the Bible, *The Dialogues of Plato,* and *The Complete Works of William Shakespeare,* you could be content. So would your listeners be. But lists keep coming, occasionally from college deans such as Raymond Schroth (1983) of Holy Cross and John Schlegel (n.d.) of Marquette University.

A Tolerable Tension

One of the basic tensions in American higher education is one you may have felt yourself as you considered your future in college. It is the strain between what might be called classical liberal education, on the one hand, and a practical vocational education, on the other. The division is not new, and educators have been attempting to bridge the gap for centuries. A happy compromise at many colleges is some form of "core curriculum" in which

The Gifts of Academe: VIII
Opportunity for Ved Mehta

Ved Mehta (b. 1934), staff writer for *The New Yorker* and author of
several books, was born in India and has been blind since the age of
four. In 1952 he wrote in his journal, "I am the only handicapped
person at Pomona and the only Indian."

Mehta was a freshman at Pomona College in Claremont, California, that fall and, despite his blindness, succeeded in his studies and
in as many recreations as he could fit into his schedule. These
included (remarkably) bicycle riding and mudhole wrestling: "Generations of Pomona freshmen had fought the sophomores in the
mudhole, in order to prove themselves worthy of attending the
college—of sharing the turf. The mudhole was both the culmination
of the orientation program and an initiation into the life of the
college, and now it was our turn. I couldn't wait to get into the
mudhole and prove myself worthy."

Mehta wrote proudly, "I am finally not at an institution for the
blind but at a proper school, an ordinary college for normal people."
Pomona was certainly not ordinary, and it inspired Mehta: "I
wanted—I thought I needed—to learn everything the college had to
offer, even if it took twenty, thirty, maybe forty years" (Mehta,
1987).

students are taught the liberal arts before going on to major, or specialize, in
a particular academic discipline.

Although the tension exists everywhere in American higher education,
we can illustrate it historically by a glance at Harvard and Yale. The institutions are linked in many ways, but most fundamentally in the founding of
Yale, the younger of the two, in 1701. At that time, Cotton Mather, the
Puritan divine, was disturbed by what he deemed to be excessive tolerance of
religious dissent at Harvard. Mather persuaded a wealthy trader named Elihu
Yale to make a large donation to the fledgling Collegiate School in New
Haven, Connecticut. He did so, and the school was immediately named for
him. Under the supervision of Mather's co-religionists, Yale's curriculum
emphasized classical studies and strict adherence to orthodox Puritanism.

In 1828, Yale responded to a number of pressures on universities for
their curricula to emphasize practical arts rather than the classics. President
Jeremiah Day issued the *Yale Report* in that year; it was a strong defense of
the traditional course of study. The report helped to slow the introduction of
practical arts and sciences into American colleges, at least until after the Civil
War. Ironically, the great Benjamin Silliman, who taught at Yale from 1802

to 1853, made experimental and applied science respectable subjects for students. Silliman was the founder of the Sheffield Science School at Yale and *The American Journal of Science and Arts,* one of the first American journals of scientific research. At about the same time, Harvard's Lawrence Scientific School was founded; it, too, stimulated the growth of applied science in the country.

Charles William Eliot, president of Harvard from 1869 to 1909, made the university into an institution of national influence. He also began the debate about the kind of curriculum that forms "educated men and women." Eliot introduced an elective system to replace the old, rigid, classical curriculum. Undergraduates began to specialize in their own areas of interest. By 1894, the only required subjects for freshmen were rhetoric and modern language. By 1908, Yale also had set aside the Greek requirement and had begun to emphasize training in the professions.

By the 1940s, there was a discernible backlash from those who saw the elective system as academic anarchy. Irving Babbitt and others were calling for a renewal of classical liberal education. In 1945, the Harvard "Red Book" (*General Education in a Free Society*) gave support to the backlash and opposed allowing undergraduate specialization. The "Red Book" called for a return to basic studies in the humanities, social sciences, and natural sciences. But even these guidelines could be interpreted permissively by the faculty, and by 1970 a de facto elective system was in place again. Derek Bok and Henry Rosovsky, Harvard's president and dean, led the response to this laxity. In 1978, a new core curriculum required undergraduates to complete basic studies in five areas while pursuing work in their areas of specialization.

Other universities around the country are following suit in the 1980s, but no doubt the pendulum will swing again. Our examination of the evolution of higher education has shown that colleges and universities are constantly changing institutions. They reshape their values, their curricula, and their programs to meet new needs. You and Brooke would probably not be comfortable with the medieval curriculum of Greek and metaphysics; the scholars of old would probably not appreciate Princeton's offerings of the 1980s. It is the task of faculty members to maintain a balance for their times.

Suggested Activities

1. Read all you can about the history of your college or university. You may find that an official history has been published.

2. Seek out the college archives. Read records, ledgers, and correspondence for the month and year of your birth (or some other year if you are older than the college).

3. Make an appointment to visit and interview the official historian of your institution. If there is no historian (or archivist), ask your president to appoint one.

4. Visit and interview (by telephone, if necessary) your oldest living alumnus or alumna. Your alumni affairs director can help you identify this person.

5. Complete a chrestomathy and submit it to your alumni magazine for publication.

6. Ask your academic dean for a summary of your institution's position on the tension between liberal education and vocational training.

Suggested Readings

In addition to the resources used as references, you may wish to read in some of the following works.

Elmhirst, Willie. *A Freshman's Diary, 1911–1912.* Oxford: Blackwell, 1969.

Haskins, Charles H. *The Rise of the Universities.* Ithaca, N.Y.: Cornell University Press, 1957.

Horowitz, Helen Lefkowitz. *Alma Mater.* New York: Knopf, 1984.

Horowitz, Helen Lefkowitz. *Campus Life: Undergraduate Cultures from the End of the 18th Century to the Present.* New York: Knopf, 1987.

Stone, James C. *Portraits of the American University, 1890–1910.* San Francisco: Jossey-Bass, 1971.

References

Barth, John. "The Scheherazade Factor." *U.S. News and World Report,* August 31, 1987, p. 55.

Bonner, Thomas. "The Unintended Revolution." *Change,* September/October, 1986, pp. 44–51.

Davies, Joan. "Student Libraries in Seventeenth Century Toulouse." in *History of Universities.* Vol. 3. 1983.

Johnson, Owen. *Stover at Yale.* New York: Collier Books, 1968. (Originally published 1911.)

Koppett, Leonard. "Princeton: The Tiger Seems to Have Lost Its Teeth."
Buffalo *News,* August 18, 1987.

Mehta, Ved. "Personal History." *The New Yorker,* August 24, 1987, 34–59.

Morison, Samuel Eliot. *The Development of Harvard University Since the In-auguration of President Eliot, 1869–1929.* Cambridge, Mass.:
Harvard University Press, 1930.

Morison, Samuel Eliot. "The History of the Universities." *Rice Institute Pamphlet,* 23, no. 4 (October 1936a): 231.

Morison, Samuel Eliot. *Three Centuries of Harvard.* Cambridge, Mass.:
Harvard University Press, 1936b.

Schlegel, John P. *An Incomplete Reading List.* Milwaukee, Wis.: College of
Arts and Sciences, Marquette University, n.d.

Schroth, Raymond A. *The Holy Cross 100 Books.* Worcester, Mass.: College
of the Holy Cross, 1983.

College as Academic Blossoming

4 Study Skills: Mastering the Basics

Kenneth F. Long

COORDINATOR OF EXPOSITORY WRITING PROGRAM
DEPARTMENT OF ENGLISH
UNIVERSITY OF WINDSOR

I received a D on my first important university assignment. It came in my best subject, or at least what had been my best subject, and I was shocked. After a day or two of worry, I found some courage and, with an open mind, went to see the instructor. He was a crusty old veteran, authoritarian in class, and therefore a bit intimidating to me. That meeting turned out to be very significant. In a surprisingly understanding and considerate manner, my professor explained that the problem was not with "what" I knew but with "how" I had gone about the task. This was my first introduction to the importance of study skills. But it took me many more years to develop a full understanding of just how beneficial skillful study could be. After teaching and counseling for several years, I was asked to develop a study skills program for first-year students.

I learned that the skills I had developed as a student, however successful, were a patchwork of survival techniques born of commitment and perseverance, but not of wisdom. No one had ever told me that there were efficient and powerful methods based on science, and tested in the classroom, that could make study easier, more efficient and effective, and give the added bonus of truly free time left over to do just as you please. If I had only known then what I know now, I could have done better and had even more fun—and I did okay and had my share of good times.

These skills can become part of how you do in college. They are based on the science of human behavior faced with the tasks of listening, reading, remembering, and presenting new knowledge. The skills work. Thousands of students use them daily, and they do well, feel proud, and enjoy themselves.

In the next few pages I want to show you how to use some basic study skills. Use of one lends strength to the next, and together they provide a powerful strategy for achieving your goals at college.

—lll——lll——lll—

Time Management:
A Plan for the Way You Live

Time management is a way of planning your life. In college certain activities must take priority over all others, and these priorities change the way you live. The decision to attend college is a commitment to becoming a professional student for extended periods of time, called semesters or quarters, that range from ten to sixteen weeks. Any professional—whether an athlete, a doctor, a businessperson, or a student—attends to his or her professional responsibilities above all other things in life—in short, work before pleasure. For you as a student, time management requires clear identification of the right priorities and provides a system for living each day according to them. What are the right priorities and how do they affect your life?

Let me begin by telling you about Joe, a type of student whom I meet every semester. Joe is bright and well intentioned and he may even do well eventually, but he is in danger of failing his first semester. Joe complains about too much work and not enough time. If we could watch Joe, we would see that he fritters away sixty-five hours a week!

First, Joe socializes at the drop of a hat. He wants to be popular, so he is available when anyone calls. Sometimes he has so much fun that he stays out very late, even during the week. Then to be fresh for the next day, he skips his 8:30 class. He can make that work up later. Right! More often, Joe makes it to class, tired or not, and manages to take notes, usually from the back of the room. Joe's uncontrolled penchant for socializing is making study unnecessarily difficult.

Joe's strong potential shows in some other activities. He is a volunteer Big Brother and never disappoints his little friend. He has also undertaken to write an occasional column for the student newspaper. He makes his deadlines but often at the expense of study. This is when Joe complains about never having enough time. Actually he has exactly the same number of hours and minutes in each day as you or I. But Joe lets college life control him rather than the other way around. With his volunteer work and journalism activities, he puts preference ahead of responsibility. His socializing shows a lack of mature commitment to college.

Look around you! There are all kinds of Joes at college. They don't know that good time management skills, mixed with a touch of maturity, can put study first and leave time for other things, too. Time management invites you to become fully conscious of the right priorities and to plan accordingly. Here's how it's done.

The Master Schedule

The master schedule is mostly determined for you by the semester, your class timetable, test dates, and other regularly scheduled commitments such as part-time work. Make a visible picture of your master schedule: Fill in all important dates on a monthly planning calendar. As your classes progress, fill in the dates for tests and assignments. This visible picture helps you discover that a semester is a short, intense period of time with "bulges" of responsibility at mid-semester and at the end. This visible picture allows you to anticipate these bulges and work toward them from long range. For example, you may have to finish an essay early because it falls due right between two tests. It is awfully hard to study for tests and finish an essay at the same time. A detailed master schedule helps you to avoid this crunch, so make a good one and keep it where you can see it often.

The Weekly Schedule

A weekly schedule can be a pocket appointments calendar that you carry all the time or nothing more than a piece of paper with columns for the days and squares for the hours. It looks something like the master schedule, but its purpose is different. As you will learn later, some subjects require short daily study sessions, others require longer periodic review sessions, while tests and assignments require even longer periods of uninterrupted time. The weekly schedule allows you to see when to plan for the right kind of study time. For example, it enables you to reserve part of Wednesday evening to prepare for the Thursday morning quiz and to have a ready-made excuse for delaying your arrival at the latest party. It will enable you to work extra, or in advance, when you see a special social occasion coming. In this way, your work does not suffer and nothing else does either, because you have a device that allows you to control your time and portion it out in accordance with priorities.

The Daily Schedule

The daily schedule is simply a note that you write to yourself, usually the night before. It is based on consultation with your master and weekly schedules, but anticipates the regular and special needs of each day. Daily schedules can free the mind of clutter, create motivation and pace for each day, reduce waste and forgetting, and leave you with a strong sense of accomplishment.

Let's examine Lisa's daily schedule. Unlike Joe's spontaneous, disorganized life, Lisa is in control, but is doing all that Joe does and more. Lisa's schedule, and my commentary, will help you recall the skills of good time management and anticipate other habits of good study that we will discuss next.

LISA'S SCHEDULE—TUESDAY
7:00 a.m.—up

COMMENTARY
It is a good idea to schedule early classes and rise early. It gives you the jump on the day.

8–9:00—review psych & soc notes with Rob over breakfast.

It's helpful to warm up for listening in class. Rob is also an organized student—a good study partner.

9–10:00—psych lecture

10–11:00—soc lecture

11–11:30—complete psych & soc notes.

As you will discover, it is very important to review as soon after class as possible; this combats forgetting.

11:30–12:30—lunch

12:30–2:00—go to bookstore, get text, supplies, go to library for reference material.

Right after lunch is a fine time for miscellaneous activity. Paying attention is harder on a full stomach.

2–3:00—math class

3–3:30—practice math problems.

Math is studied best by short, regular practice sessions.

4–5:30—25 min. jog with Alice, shower, sauna.

Lisa knows that regular exercise is important. It actually aids study by promoting alertness. Alice is a new friend met while jogging.

5:30–6:30—dinner

6:30–7:00—free time

Schedule free time. It allows for flexibility.

7–9:00—study for geography quiz, read chapters for English, work on assign. for biology, write schedule for Wed.

It is best to schedule a variety of activities, with specific objectives for each, to cover an extended study session. You will learn more about how to do this.

9–12:00—reading or talking—whatever happens. I'm open! Another great day!

Most students are active throughout the evening. Many keep very late hours. Lisa's schedule gives her a choice. With all of the day's responsibilities taken care of, and tomorrow anticipated, Lisa can relax, socialize, or do light reading. The choice is hers. She has also planned for at least seven or eight hours sleep.

Every day's schedule is a little different. For example, if Lisa has an important midterm test in English on Wednesday, her schedule would read differently at 12:30, 4:00, 6:00, and 9:00. There is plenty of time for the extra work that major tests require, but the day's regular responsibilities are still taken care of. Good time management is flexible. It apportions time to conscious priorities and creates free time as well. Time management requires self-discipline, and the various schedules are merely devices that allow good things to happen.

■III■III■III■
The Classroom: Listening and Taking Notes

Let's look now at something that you and I and nearly everybody else is good at: forgetting. As a student, I was dismayed at having to study material over and over again, at having to reread chapters that seemed almost like new, at laboring over notes that were only a month old. Forgetting plagues us all and is likely the source of the axiom, "Goes in one ear and out the other." About ten years ago I learned something unforgettable about forgetting. I read about an experiment involving groups of students who were tested at various periods of time after listening to a lecture. This experiment showed that most forgetting takes place almost immediately after listening (more than half in the first twenty-four hours) and then tapers off. (You can read all about this experiment in Walter Paulk's book, *How to Study in College,* cited at the end of this chapter.) It follows logically that any effective study system must bring the phenomenon of forgetting under control, both with respect to classroom material and textbook material. Otherwise, a student can be overwhelmed by the sheer bulk of material; this problem begins when students enter the classroom without a plan in mind.

Let me tell you what I see from my side of the classroom. I see too many students who come to class prepared only to write a lot of words down on paper. It is as if they have a second self, a stenographer, whose only purpose is to capture everything that is said. A full notebook creates a false sense of security. In reality, this practice is inefficient because it leaves all of the learning for later and does nothing to combat forgetting. These students do not understand that every lecture, or teaching session of any kind, is a sophisticated intellectual encounter that requires active listening. These students should be searching for important ideas, for answers to questions, and for understanding. Their notes should reflect this. Lisa's daily schedule shows that she is preparing to be an active listener by warming up with her study partner for classes in psychology and sociology. As you will see, both Lisa and Rob have the kind of system that allows them to listen intently for longer periods of time, comprehend more, and create good notes that allow for a direct attack on forgetting. You can do this, too.

Your system begins by drawing a line to divide each piece of notepaper into two columns. (Looseleaf is a good choice; write on one side only.) The one on the left, approximately 2½ inches wide, is called the "recall column" and remains blank while you take notes during class on the remaining portion. Just what should you write down? Well, it varies with each instructor's style and purpose, but it is safe to say that every class is based on a few key ideas, rarely more than five, and frequently only one. Ask yourself, "What does my instructor want me to know at the end of today's session?" The answer is the main idea(s). It may be buried in detail, statistics, anecdotes, or in problems to solve, but the purpose of notes is to capture the main idea or ideas for later study. Not everything needs to be written down! First-year students, because of insecurity and inexperience, try to write everything. They stop thinking and the stenographer takes over. Don't let this happen. Be an assertive listener by always searching for main ideas, and after a few weeks' practice, as you get to know your instructors, you will have better and fewer notes.

When class ends, you don't stop working, not if you want to combat forgetting. Now the recall column, still blank, becomes important. In five or ten minutes, quickly review your notes and select key words or phrases (or make up some) that act as labels or tags for ideas and information. Write these in the recall column beside the material they represent. When you finish, cover the notes and use the tags in the recall column to help you recite a short version of what you understand from the class you have just participated in.

Why is this process so powerful? First, you are encountering the same material in three different ways: active listening and writing, reading and summarizing in the recall column, and finally saying aloud what you understand from class. Your whole person, mind and body, is involved. All of these actions promote learning; recitation is particularly effective against forgetting. Although the exact reason for recitation's power remains unknown, educational psychologists describe it as holding ideas long enough for the memory to grasp them. Strictly speaking, we never really forget anything, we just lose control of it somewhere in our minds. So having a good memory really means having an organized method of capturing and recalling whatever our minds encounter.

A student who does this with every day's class notes is actively learning on a day-to-day basis. Look back at Lisa's daily schedule. From 11:00 to 11:30 she makes recall columns and recites notes based on her two morning classes. She does this before forgetting takes place. The longer you wait, the more time it takes to make a recall column and recite. The recall column is also useful for warm-ups for class and, as we will see later, can help you study for exams. For now, let me summarize the past several paragraphs by identifying what you might put in a recall column if you had listened to this material as a lecture. My commentary is on the right, where your notes would be.

THE RECALL COLUMN	COMMENTARY
Forgetting—its significance	If you can use these tags to recite the main ideas of this system for listening and taking notes, then you know what I want you to know.
Active listening and a lecture—what are they?	
Note taking & main ideas.	Works nicely, doesn't it?
The recall column—what? how? why? when?	
Recitation, it's important.	

Reading Textbooks: A Special Kind of Reading

The technique for active listening and taking notes is based on scientific understanding of how the brain works to receive, understand, store, and retrieve information and concepts. This system adapts readily to the reading of texts. Make no mistake about it, reading textbook material is tough.

First, let's examine what happens when you set out to read those five chapters assigned for the next class, two days away. You plan to start reading at 7:00, but when 7:00 arrives you visit the bathroom (five minutes), make a quick call to a friend (six minutes), go get an apple (two minutes) and then sit down to read, but only after clearing your desk, sharpening pencils, and arranging some notes (five minutes). It is almost 7:30 and you haven't read a word yet! Sound familiar? Even when you do get started, another problem with attention span occurs. You know, you read along with your eyes but your mind has gone somewhere else and when you catch yourself, you have to flip back a page or two to find where to start reading again. Studies on the amount of time lapsed from when you first start to read until your mind wanders have shown that a typical first-year student's attention span for textbook material is only about five minutes. Not long enough! You will need at least three times that for academic survival and even more as you progress.

But don't despair. You can quickly and dramatically improve a short reading attention span. It's a lot like jogging. When you first start out it is difficult. A mile run is an impossibility. But with perseverance and a good plan, a mile run is soon only a warm-up. The following system for textbook reading helps to solve the problem of delay/avoidance and attention span. It also promotes better understanding, increases speed, and most important of all, facilitates later study for tests and exams.

The system is divided into two stages, each having two activities. In the first stage, you plan to read and to measure the reading assignment. Planning to read is an undemanding but important activity that can fit nicely into your delay/avoidance time. The purpose is to create "advance organizers" by quickly surveying the pages to be read and looking for headings or key words or sentences that suggest what the subject matter is about. Sometimes texts feature questions at the back of the chapter, lists of main points, or summary paragraphs. These are particularly useful in creating advance organizers. Understanding comes later. The purpose of your search is to warm up the mind and to create a map for the actual reading.

Measuring the reading assignment is an activity based on how long your attention span is and how many pages you can read during your span. For example, you might divide a forty-page chapter into four ten-page reading assignments, each to be done in ten minutes. For each, you establish some advance organizers and read each separately. You then apply the strategies of stage two.

Stage two is the actual reading followed by recitation, similar to the strategy for listening and note taking. The active reader must have a pencil in hand and be prepared to underline, circle, draw arrows, or write brief notes in the margin as material is understood. This helps you identify and condense important material, and you cannot do this unless you are concentrating. Once you work over a portion of text in this fashion, use the markings to cue a brief recitation of what you have understood. Repeat the procedure until you complete the entire reading assignment.

No student ever picked up a textbook and read all of it in one sitting because it was so interesting it couldn't be put down. Textbook reading is demanding and fatiguing. No one, not even a professor, does it well for much longer than an hour at a time. So you need a powerful but simple strategy to help you with this essential task. Transform your textbooks into a study aid. There is not enough time to make notes from reading, so your underlining and marginalia accomplish the same purpose. You do not have enough time to reread everything before tests and exams. By setting out to transform your text, you will quickly discover that you can read for longer periods of time with greater accomplishment. At exam time, the properly managed text will be a valuable aid for study.

Studying for Tests

The Essay Exam

Good time management, aggressive listening (leading to good notes), attentive reading (leading to well-marked texts), and regular recitation create an ideal situation for preparing for exams. But too few students accomplish this. Consider what is usually the case. A student has pages and pages of notes and several chapters of text, all bearing on a test. What can be done? The clean text pages all look alike. The only choice is to reread and perhaps make some notes. This will take a lot of time. The notes, some more than a month old, appear strange, like brand new material. They also will have to be reread. And worse, in each case understanding is not enough because it all has to be remembered, too.

So this student resorts to reading short sections and then turns away, closes her eyes, and asks her mind to silently restate the material. For a while this works. But after about an hour the mind grows tired with this demand and she never can tell for sure if she will remember or not. And to make it all worse, time begins to run out and feelings of frustration, insecurity, and possibly panic begin to take over. This student is not likely to do her best.

By employing good study skills, here's how you can handle this situation. First, because of a detailed planning calendar, you have seen this test coming for a long time and you have cleared out other responsibilities, leaving plenty of extra time on the day or two before the test. Your pages of notes all have recall columns and you have recited, so they are familiar but not enough for a test.

Here's what to do. Lay several pages on the desk in front of you with each page covering two-thirds of the one before so that only recall columns show. (This is why I recommend writing on one side of looseleaf only, remember?) Let the recall columns prompt a recitation, in your own words, of the material at hand. When you get stuck, consult the notes to boost the recall column and then continue to recite. This is how to study when you want to remember. Work through the text chapters in similar fashion by using your markings to prompt recitation. When you can recite, you know it, and you know you know it. So you have little reason for anxiety.

This method of study trains your mind to respond to the situation created by tests. The words in the test questions act like the words in recall columns to prompt recitation—your answer to the question. This is exactly what you have been practicing all along by looking for and marking important material and by reciting. So the exam is really nothing new. Moreover, this system of study can be adapted to meet the requirements of different kinds of exams. Another strong study technique is the practice of composing questions based on studied material. Solid comprehension must precede the ability to formulate questions, so your concentration increases and understanding is ensured.

The Cheet Sheet

Of course, I'm not really talking about cheating, so we will spell the term incorrectly to help us remember a special study technique. Sometimes you can predict what is going to be asked on an exam. Regular attendance at class lets you get to know what a professor likes. These and other clues allow you to eliminate a lot of material for study by deciding to know a certain few things cold. One good way to go about this is to make a cheet sheet.

A cheet sheet is like a giant recall column. As you study your notes and chapters, keep a separate piece of paper handy. As you master the recitation of material, make up headings for what you know. For example, you may want to reduce ten pages of notes to one page of headings and then use this one page for further review. Remember, accepting the task of producing a cheet sheet guarantees active, rather than lazy, involvement with the material. And cheet sheets are particularly useful for review in the last hours or minutes before an exam. It is impossible to work with books and notes at this time, but a good cheet sheet lets you review quickly and easily.

Here is a cheet sheet covering the past few paragraphs on how to study for tests and exams. It would be confusing without prior knowledge but because you have read carefully, you will see how effective it is for recall.

CHEET SHEET: HOW TO STUDY

3 {
Time Management = extra time when needed   How?
Good Listening   = notes & recall columns
Good Reading   = a marked-up text   Why?
}

How: lay out the notes
    use the text markings to recite

How do you know you know?

How is studying practice for an exam?

The Cheet Sheet Technique—What, When, Why.

The Multiple-Choice Exam

Studying for a multiple-choice exam requires a different approach, but one still based on good notes and well-worked texts. A multiple-choice exam can contain over a hundred questions that can touch on everything covered in a course. So you need a technique that permits light review of material several times before the exam. In this case, your notes and text markings, aided by regular recitation, let you move through large amounts of material quickly with good attention. Each multiple-choice question cues a response, and that response is reinforced or identified by one of the choices. You will find, with careful reading, that most of the right answers will be immediately apparent. But some questions will always be puzzles. Here's what to do.

First, skip over these puzzling questions as you work quickly through the exam, but mark them in some fashion so that you can find them easily later. When you are finished answering all of the obvious questions, return to the puzzles. You will discover that you now know the right answers to some of them. Why? Because a multiple-choice exam is a review and the material in question 46 contains, or suggests, the right answer for question 10. This technique lets the nature of the exam work in your favor.

For the few puzzles that remain, another strategy is required. Since you really can't find the right answer, try to find the answers that are clearly wrong. Usually at least one of the choices is farfetched, another unlikely, and a third a "maybe." In this way you can reduce the odds to their most favorable and make the best guess possible. Using these strategies can make a significant difference in your final score.

Three Errors in Strategy and Three Suggestions

Consistent daily study plus the right exam strategy is the surest way to real learning and strong performance. The study system recommended here is not about memorization. Too often, memorization reflects only a shallow understanding. The mechanics of this system require repeated, attentive application to material that insists on understanding. How else could you make recall columns or cheet sheets? But you need to adapt the system to meet the requirements of different situations, as in the case of multiple-choice exams. Here are three other suggestions that will help you avoid some common errors in exam strategy; they involve timing, focus, and organization.

Most exams offer some choice in questions, but not all questions will be worth the same points. Therefore, it is a good idea to quickly survey the exam and note the questions that are easiest for you. Answer the easiest first, as a confidence builder, and get yourself moving. But there is a danger here. Some students, knowing certain material very well, spend thirty minutes writing a brilliant answer to a question worth only ten points. Then, with time running out, they have too few minutes to spend on a really important question. This is certainly how to get a C when you are more capable of a B or A. Avoid this costly error in strategy by knowing the basic structure, point allotments, and types of questions on the exam ahead of time. How? Ask your professor. Explain why this information will help you study more effectively. Your professor is sure to be impressed, and you can be prepared before going into the exam room.

Many well-prepared students write fine answers to questions that really haven't been asked. This problem stems from either not reading a question carefully or from using a question as an excuse for hastily writing down everything that you know on a topic and hoping that the question is answered. This is a lot like shooting at a target and never missing, but also never hitting the bull's-eye either. I can tell you that such answers are frustrating to read, both for their lack of focus and lack of organization. A simple strategy with five steps will help you avoid this problem.

1. Read the entire question carefully.

2. Read it again and underline select, key words. (This forces you to focus on the question asked.)

3. Use the underlined words to make a short outline. (This promotes organization.)

4. Begin writing by restating the question.

5. Write the rest of the answer according to the outline. (If new or important ideas come to mind as you write, add them at the end.)

Here is a sample question and outline that has been worked up in this way. I provide some commentary on the right.

QUESTION	COMMENTARY
Modern educational psychology has discovered a great deal about how students learn and this has lead to the development of several powerful study techniques. Identify three such techniques and explain how and why they work.	The underlining is sparse but forces focus on the question.

OUTLINE	COMMENTARY
Modern educational psychology can show a student <u>how</u> to learn more efficiently. Define efficiency. Forgetting—the enemy.	A simple direct restatement with an emphasis on how. The answer will build on the concept of efficiency and the problem of forgetting.
4 Advance organizers (conc) 3 Recitation 1 Recall Columns 2 Cheet Sheets 5 Multiple-Choice Exams (conc)	The numbers on the left indicate a logical organizational pattern saving 4 and 5 for a brief conclusion that mentions, but does not explain in detail, study techniques beyond what is called for in the question.

Remember, adopting the right exam strategy, in this case taking the time to plan for a focused, organized answer, is the surest way to achieve the best grade possible. This whole study system is designed to help you learn as much as possible as quickly as you can, but you must also demonstrate what you have learned on tests.

—ııı—ııı—ııı—

A Final Note

Knowing how to do something and doing it are two different things. Each semester I look forward to teaching a class of first-year students. I tell them what I have told you here. Since it makes sense, most students try it and many succeed. But there are always a few who don't. Typically, they are the ones who miss several classes, who ask for extensions on assignments, and who write "shotgun" answers on tests. They often appear tired and disinterested. They are always slightly behind in their work. No one is there to make them go to class, and no one knows if they haven't done their reading. No one says anything about the assignment not completed. "So why bother to keep up?" they say.

College is a great and wonderful challenge. The challenge comes from the work to be done and from the freedom. If you apply the strategies described here, you will be able to meet both parts of the challenge. You will learn and be able to show what you know, and you will have time left over for yourself. Why bother to keep up? To learn of course, but also to offer proof of a mature and responsible individual who is in control and who will do equally well in the many walks of life that follow college.

The basic strategies I have described here can get you started and keep you in charge of college life. But there is a lot more to effective study. If you want to read more, I recommend either of the books below. Make one part of your personal library. Good luck.

Suggested Activities

1. Ask a fellow student to show you his or her notes. Are your notes clear and solid by comparison? Do you agree on what is important? Is your student colleague using a note-taking system?

2. Invite a fellow student for a coffee after class. Ask if he or she will listen to your recitation from your recall column. Together you can check on one another's level of understanding. This is a great way to complete a day's study and develop new relationships at the same time.

3. Check on your reading attention span by timing yourself. Remember, when your mind wanders, that's the length of your attention span. Now use the textbook reading system and note how much your span increases. You will be surprised.

4. After about three weeks of class, review all of your notes and make a "cheet sheet." Use the cheet sheet to recite. This is an effective way to periodically review.

Suggested Readings

Paulk, Walter. *How to Study in College.* Boston: Houghton Mifflin, 1974.

Walter, Tim, and Al Siebert. *Student Success: How to do Better in College and Still Have Time for Your Friends.* New York: Holt, Rinehart and Winston, 1981.

5 Decoding Your Professors

John N. Gardner

DIRECTOR, UNIVERSITY 101
VICE CHANCELLOR FOR UNIVERSITY CAMPUSES AND
   CONTINUING EDUCATION
PROFESSOR OF LIBRARY AND INFORMATION SCIENCE
UNIVERSITY OF SOUTH CAROLINA

I went off to college in 1961, at 17 years of age. I went 600 miles from my home in New Canaan, Connecticut, to the oldest college in Ohio, Marietta College. I was homesick for my family and my girlfriend. I turned in a miserable academic performance. When I went home at Thanksgiving (a holiday that, for me, was inappropriately named that year), the news of my midterm grades (three F's, two D's, and one A) had preceded me. The A was in Physical Education, an automatic A for participation in a varsity sport, lightweight crew. There were lots of reasons for my bad grades: I didn't know how to take notes; I lacked proper study habits; I did not seek out professors for help, and I didn't yet know how to relate to them or understand them. No one had taught me how to "decode professors." There isn't enough space in this brief introduction for me to even begin to explain how I turned myself around academically and became a very successful student and leader, but the most important reason for this about-face was my relationships with professors. They changed my life for the better and they can change yours, too—if you let them. So let my advice sink in, and you'll have a far richer college experience and a far better life after college.

From years of teaching college students, we have developed many insights into the relationship between student and professor. Little did we suspect, when we were college students, that our professors really had an interest in teaching us something or that they might have appreciated our dropping by for a chat. Office hours, we now know, are for students—and we've often wondered over the years why we weren't smart enough to take advantage of them. We also now know that freshmen who interact with professors outside of class are more likely to become sophomores.

College professors are supposed to be smart, yet some of the things they say and do in class make you wonder. They rush through pages of notes, so it's impossible to remember all the important details. They give too many quizzes and expect too much from you in return. It doesn't matter to them whether it's homecoming weekend, or the big fraternity/sorority rush week, or the day you just have to go home because it's your birthday. They still expect you to be in class, on time, and most importantly, *prepared*! In fact, many of them act as though their class is the only one you're taking.

Do your college professors really understand you? Sure they do (most of them), but if you expect them to act, think, or even dress the way your high school teachers did, you may be in for a rude awakening.

Furthermore, you might be surprised to know that many of your college teachers are extremely interested in your well-being and hope you'll earn high grades in their classes (and believe that you can do so). These same individuals, however, may be quick to disagree with your ideas, ready to correct you when you answer a question in class, and extremely demanding about the amount of work they expect from you. If that scares you as you begin your college career, hold on. Establishing a positive relationship with your college professor, in the way we're about to discuss, can be one of the most rewarding experiences not only of your college years but also of your entire life.

Teachers: People Who Once Were Freshmen

As you warily approach your professors during your first semester in college, remember that they are former freshmen. Your professors are also human beings who respond to many of the same kinds of needs, goals, rewards, aspirations, gestures, and praise that you do. While you need to generate some empathy for them, many of them—despite what you think—have even more empathy for you.

Your college professors are probably teaching because they love their subjects and love to communicate to others what they know best. They certainly did not choose their profession for the money! To find out what kind of people they are, you might begin by studying their offices. Usually you will find them decorated to reflect the interests and personality of each teacher, and you will most certainly find them filled with books. Professors read voraciously, and they like to talk about what they have read. Some may mention articles from the *New York Times* or the *Washington Post*. Others may quote from trade or professional journals, such as *Advertising Age* or the *Chronicle of Higher Education*. Some may speak of travels abroad, or to other parts of the United States, where they have lived, taught, or attended college. If you have lived in the same area most of your life, you can learn much from your college professors about the rest of your country and the world.

Differences Between Professors and High School Teachers

You might be surprised to learn that most of your college professors—unlike your high school teachers—have never taken an education course in their lives. Instead, they chose courses in their academic disciplines that taught them how to acquire new knowledge and to understand that knowledge. They did not learn how to communicate that knowledge to you, or how to entertain you as they did so. In fact, you might find a few professors who would much rather be doing nothing but research, but must teach to justify their salaries. Others have left careers in various fields in order to teach their professions to college students. You'll find lawyers teaching law, physicians teaching medicine, newspaper editors teaching journalism, and corporation executives teaching business management.

Professors who pursued several advanced degrees in graduate schools or spent many years working in a profession have learned the virtues of diligence, patience, and persistence. They know the value of being able to ask about, process, and handle enormous amounts of minute detail, so they'll probably expect you to do the same.

Your professors probably won't spend much time in class teaching you the textbooks, and they won't base their tests exclusively on them, either. If it were enough to teach you the book, professors would not need to work very hard. But your professors have their own ideas about their disciplines, or subjects, and one of their goals is to help you learn as much as you can. This usually means that a textbook is only a support for all else in the course, and you'll probably work harder than you ever did in high school to absorb all the material they give you.

In high school, your teachers filled you with knowledge and information accumulated by others. Their task was simply to pass it on to you. Naturally, your college teachers also want to pass on the knowledge accumulated by others, but many professors feel the need to create new knowledge of their own. At many schools, faculty can only earn tenure if they do such research (more about tenure later in this chapter). As a result, many of them will talk to you about the research they are doing, in the hope that you'll find this interesting and will want to learn more.

Your high school teachers perhaps checked your notebooks to see that they were neat, took attendance regularly, and checked up on you to make certain you were doing all your work. In college, some professors will take roll, but others never will. It isn't that they don't care whether you come or not—they do. But they also feel you should be treated as an adult. They hope, of course, that you're taking adequate notes, but they won't be checking to see that you do. And you do need to take adequate notes because many professors are far more likely to test you on classroom lecture materials than on text materials.

A Belief in Education and Interest in You

To college professors, a solid education is much more than a means of getting a degree and a job. Becoming an educated person is in itself something they prize, and they hope you'll take the same pride in education. Consequently, many professors will be idealistic and not as practical as you might like. You probably can't change that, but you can try to appreciate their zest for knowledge and to understand how vitally it affects their lives.

Many college faculty will take a personal interest in you as a student and as a person. These professors chose teaching because they genuinely wanted to help others. However, they may not take the initiative to ask you to come see them. You will have to do that. Faculty try to treat students as adults. They don't want to baby-sit, but they do appreciate a friendly visit. One of your greatest opportunities for learning in college will come from the kind of one-on-one interaction you can experience with a professor outside the class. As we said before, visiting with professors outside of class enhances your learning and chances of persisting in college. Unlike your high school teachers, professors are required to keep office hours, and that's the time to make an appointment to see them. Don't feel as though you're bothering them. It's part of their job to make time for you.

Why Professors Chose College Teaching

How does one explain what draws an individual to teaching on a college campus? The hours are long, the pay is only fair, and the frustrations are many. Perhaps it begins with a love of the college experience, when the professor was once a student, and a desire to someday return to that intellectually and socially stimulating environment. For some, it may involve a desire to learn more about a favorite subject while imparting that knowledge to others. Many professors love research and find it rewarding to uncover new ideas about people and the world. Others are talented in the arts—in writing or music or painting—and want to develop those skills further while helping others develop their skills.

Deep within nearly all college professors is the desire to use their knowledge and experiences to affect the lives of others in a positive way. After all, they were probably affected in the same way by certain professors while they were students. Some professors feel inspired to repay the debt of being helped by professors in their own days as college students. Ask several of your professors why they chose teaching. You'll find as many answers as the number of people you ask.

If your professors don't love what they're teaching, they're probably not very good professors. Often good professors love their subjects so much that in their enthusiasm they may speed up their lectures because they want to tell you so much, and you just can't keep up. That's when you should raise your hand and ask them to slow down. Just because they're rushing through the material doesn't mean they're not willing to listen to you. Many professors get carried away by their own thoughts and must be brought down to earth by a student.

What College Professors Do

One of the most common myths about college professsors is that they lead easy lives of quiet contemplation while teaching one or two classes every week. College professors do much more than go to class. In fact, the time they spend in classroom instruction takes up a relatively small part of a typical workweek. The average professor spends between six and fifteen hours in the classroom weekly, compared to the thirty hours or more a high school teacher spends. Yet that same college professor works from sixty to eighty hours a week.

Because they must remain current in their field, professors spend part of that time reading, reading, reading. That leads to additional hours during which they revise and update their class lecture notes. It takes far longer to prepare notes than to deliver them in class. Professors may spend time conducting experiments, reviewing manuscripts, and writing. They may be called upon to speak to community, civic, and professional groups or to assist such groups in the development of a project. They may do consulting for private corporations and government agencies for extra money. They may be writing books, book reviews, journal articles, or papers for delivery at conventions.

When they're not doing any of these things, you'll probably find them advising students. Many spend considerable time in individual and group conferences with students to help them plan their academic programs for the term, reach career decisions, deal with personal problems, or find ways to improve their grades.

And with the time that's left, your professsors are asked to perform administrative duties, serve on academic committees, or become involved in special college or university projects. A typical college professor may serve as chairperson of a college advising committee (to improve student advisement), be a member of an awards committee (to nominate and select outstanding students), serve as a faculty senator, or representative, in a university-wide governance system, and be called upon to participate in a special task force to evaluate the current student disciplinary system.

When not in the classroom or in the office, professors are still working: behind closed doors in committee sessions or at home grading papers and preparing for tomorrow's classes. To accept this sort of schedule willingly, they must feel strongly about the importance of the college experience.

Making the Most of the Student-Professor Relationship

Remember what we said earlier about professors being people who respond positively to the same things other people do, such as politeness, consideration, tact, a smile, attention, and compliments? If you will remember this, you can do a few simple things to cause your professors to think more positively about you.

First, come to class regularly and be on time. Many students don't do this, so your exceptional behavior will stand out. Take advantage of office hours and see professors when it's appropriate. Realize that professors are not people to be avoided at all costs and that you will not be criticized by your peers if you're seen talking with them. (It's likely that these same peers have already talked with them.) Use office hours to get to know your professors and let them make you a significant person in their lives, too.

What else can you do to make your professors think highly of you? Come to class well groomed and properly dressed. A sloppy appearance suggests you can't be very serious about their lectures and discussions. Read all the assigned material before class. Ask questions frequently, but not to the point of annoyance or distraction. Show interest in the subject. Remember, your professors are extremely interested in their subjects and for that reason they'll appreciate your concern.

Sit near the front of the class. A number of studies have shown that students who do so tend to make better grades. To your professors, this will indicate your heightened interest in their ideas. Never talk or whisper while professors are lecturing. They'll interpret this as an uncaring or even rude gesture, which indeed it is!

Finally, don't hand your professors a lot of "bull." They've been hearing this drivel for years, and can spot phony excuses a mile away. If you're sincere and give honest reasons for missing class or work, they're more likely to respect you for it and may even bend their rules about late work and grade penalties.

—Ⅲ——Ⅲ——Ⅲ—

Academic Freedom

Academic freedom is a condition and a right most college faculty enjoy at the majority of private and state-supported institutions. Simply put, it is the freedom to pursue intellectual inquiry and research, or to raise questions that are legitimately related to scholarly interests and professions. The concept of academic freedom allows professors to raise controversial issues without risk of losing their jobs. It doesn't give them total immunity from pressure and reprisals, but it does allow them more latitude than your high school teachers had.

Academic freedom is a long-established tradition in American higher education and has its origins in the development of intellectual history, dating back to the Middle Ages. Colleges and universities have found it desirable to promote the advancement of research and knowledge by giving their scholars and professors virtually unlimited freedom of inquiry, as long as human lives, rights, and privacy are not violated. This same assurance of freedom from political intervention and pressure is one of the appealing things to faculty about the collegiate life-style. It allows a professor to enjoy a personal and intellectual freedom not possible in many other professions and opens the door to less conventional thoughts and actions.

Such thoughts and actions may surprise and even anger you at times. Your professors occasionally may articulate some ideas and opinions that offend you. You won't like them because they'll be contrary to some of your basic values and beliefs. Professsors may insult a politician you admire, may speak with sarcasm about cherished American institutions such as the presidency, or may look with disdain upon organized religion.

Sometimes, they may be doing this just to get a reaction from you. They may believe that, to get you to think, they must disrupt and provoke you out of your "intellectual complacency." On the other hand, your professors may actually believe those statements you find outrageous. You need to realize that professors are highly independent, intellectually and personally, compared to the average American. Since college professors may be free thinkers, you may hear ideas from them that are at variance with many social conventions. This does not mean you must agree with them to get good grades. It does mean, however, that you must understand such views, examine them rationally, and be prepared to defend your own views if you still believe you are correct.

—|||———|||———|||—
Tenure

The notion of academic freedom is related to something called *tenure*. This is the award a college or university gives to professors once they reach a certain point in their professional development; it promises them lifetime employment. Although untenured faculty also have academic freedom, tenured faculty theoretically have more of it. Tenure, in effect, means that a professor may not be terminated from employment except for these extraordinary situations:

1. *An act of moral turpitude.* Such an act would be a gross violation of the legal code or of any code of conventionally acceptable behavior. As current standards for conventionally accepted behavior become increasingly more tolerant, the range of behaviors involving moral turpitude become narrower.

2. *Insubordination.* Since a professor enjoys academic freedom, it is very difficult to define, let alone prove, insubordination. Few professors, therefore, are terminated for this infraction.

3. *Incompetence.* Once again, who is to prove that the faculty member is incompetent? Obtaining the consensus of one's peers is virtually impossible, although complaints by students may be effective here.

4. *Bona fide reduction in staff.* If your college experiences severe financial hardships, the institution could decide to eliminate faculty positions, departments, or majors, and the reduction in staff might include tenured faculty.

You won't be able to tell if your professors are tenured just by looking at them. The existence of tenure is a support of the general climate of free expression and free inquiry into the pursuit of ideas, which makes higher education an uplifting experience for professors and their students.

—|||———|||———|||—
Rank

Not all professors are "professors." A subtle yet significant pecking order exists among college professors, reflecting enormous differences in power, authority, prestige, income, and special privileges. Here is how it works.

First, there are instructors and lecturers. Next come assistant professors, followed by associate professors and full professors. Most colleges have probationary periods of employment for faculty that they must complete before applying for promotion to the next highest rank. When promotion comes from assistant to associate professor, it may also include the award of tenure. Full professors generally teach fewer classes, have fewer students, and are more likely to be working with graduate students.

This pecking order may not be important to you at first, but it could become important if you should decide to seek advanced degrees. A recommendation for employment or graduate school from a senior professor can carry more weight than one from a lower ranking professor, especially if your senior professor is well known in the field.

—|||——|||——|||—
Academic Standards

Although it's difficult to generalize about college professors because they exhibit so many personal and intellectual differences, it's relatively safe to assume that most of them believe in the value of a liberal education.

Many people agree that a liberal education is important because it can make you more marketable when you're looking for a job. To your professors, its value goes far beyond that. The word *liberal* is a direct reference to the ability of education to free your mind. Indeed, the word comes from the Latin *libero,* a verb meaning "to free." The goal of a liberal education is to free you from the biases, superstitions, prejudices, and lack of knowledge that characterized you before you came to college.

To free you of these restraints, it may be necessary to provoke, challenge, and disturb you by presenting you with new ideas, beliefs, and values that differ from your previous perceptions. Keep that in mind the next time your college professors say something that surprises you. In college, as in life, you'll have to learn to tolerate opinions that are vastly different from yours. Note that you need not always accept them, but you should learn to evaluate them for yourself instead of basing your responses on what others have always told you.

Because your professors want you to grow intellectually, they'll probably demand more of you than your high school teachers did. You'll probably have to study more to get good grades, because your professors may be inclined to give fewer A's and more F's than teachers in high school gave. Most college professors believe students who enter college are woefully underprepared to do college work—many through no fault of their own. As a result, they'll challenge you to raise your standards to theirs, instead of lowering theirs to meet yours.

It often comes as a great shock to students who made high grades in high school with little or no studying to find that they must study for hours to earn a high grade on a college exam. As a rule of thumb, you may need to spend two to three hours preparing outside of class for every hour you spend in class. So if you're carrying fifteen hours a semester, you should be spending an additional thirty hours each week studying, for a total work-week of forty-five hours, which is similar to the amount of time you'll be working when you begin your professional career. One of the biggest adjustments high school students have to make in college is simply the greatly increased amount of time they need to spend studying to meet the demands of professors. So even if you think you are studying more now than in high school, it's still probably not enough. Keep trying to increase your study time gradually.

—Ⅲ—Ⅲ—Ⅲ—

What Professors Want from Their Students

Good professors frequently have students approach them at the end of the term to tell them how much they enjoyed the class. Professors appreciate that, but what they really want to hear is, "I really learned a lot from you and I want to thank you for it." Enjoyment should result from the positive learning experience; it shouldn't result from enjoyment for its own sake. Frankly, the pleasure of learning new ideas should constitute enjoyment in itself, and that is what your professors want to hear. Remember, they're not primarily entertainers but teachers. If they entertain out of proportion to teaching, they may be less than adequate in their profession.

Much has been written about professsors who don't really care about students, but are dedicated in their desire to teach them new ideas. It's difficult to see how these two ideas are consistent with one another. Some level of caring must exist before learning can be passed from one individual to another. If you doubt that your professors care about their students, ask them. The question may be revealing to them, and the answer may be revealing to both of you.

Finally, remember that professors will like you more, even though they may not show it, if you participate in class discussion, complete your assignments on time, ask questions during class, make appointments to see them, comment on lecture materials, or simply smile and say "hello" when you meet on campus. They'll appreciate you if you maintain frequent eye contact with them during class, share a story or anecdote, joke with them or the class, and show you realize the value of what they're teaching you.

During the remainder of your life, you'll meet many admirable, stimulat-ing, exciting, unique, remarkable, inspiring, perplexing, frustrating, and challenging individuals. Few will be more complex than your college pro-fessors. One or two of your college faculty may help counsel or guide you as you pursue your goals and may indeed affect your entire life significantly.

For that reason alone, it pays to get the most out of them during your four years in college, which is probably the most significant period of change in your entire life.

Suggested Activity

1. Interview one or more of your current professors to find out whether they fit the descriptions provided in this chapter. You might ask them how they chose their academic discipline, what motivated them to teach on a college campus, what they regard as the ideal student, and what irritates or bothers them most about college students today. To gain an even more complete picture of college professors, share your interviews with other students, and have them share theirs with you.

6 Getting the Most from Your Academic Advisor

Mary Stuart Hunter

CO-DIRECTOR FOR CONFERENCES AND ADMINISTRATION
UNIVERSITY 101
UNIVERSITY OF SOUTH CAROLINA

In retrospect, I now know that all of the ingredients for good academic advising existed when I was a freshman. Seventeen years ago when I entered Queens College in Charlotte, North Carolina, the college administration had done an excellent job of structuring and organizing its academic advising program. For me and each of my classmates, our academic advisor was the same individual who taught us freshman composition. So I saw that person at least twice a week in class and had the opportunity to get to know her well. What I didn't know back then was what an academic advisor was. Consequently, I missed the opportunity to really benefit from the academic advising relationship.

My advisor had all the qualities that make a faculty member an excellent advisor. But if she ever told me what her role as an advisor was, I either didn't hear it or didn't pay attention to what she said. I was one of those students who was in college because it was expected of me. Both my parents and everyone in my family had been to college. I really didn't know why I was there, other than the fact that it was what people did when they finished high school. The four years that I spent at Queens College were both educational and enjoyable. I learned a lot about myself and the world around me, and as an English major I was introduced to volumes of great literature. My liberal arts education has served me well in preparing me for the world of work and life in general. The critical thinking, writing, and problem-solving skills developed in college have transferred well into the various positions I have since held.

Only when I began working as an academic advisor did I truly begin to realize what an academic advising relationship should be. Although I'm no longer doing academic advising exclusively, I still enjoy the contact with the few students I advise. I am always ready to get on my soapbox to tell students how to get the most from their academic advisor during their college careers. If there is one thing I've learned over the years, it is that much of the truly valuable learning during college takes place outside of the classroom through interpersonal relationships; a great deal of this learning can occur during advisement.

—|||—|||—|||—

Probably one of the first people you met after being accepted at your college or university was your academic advisor. This person can be one of the most significant people in your life during your college career. It is crucial for you to understand who this person is, what sort of relationship you can develop with this person, and how to make the most out of the academic advising relationship.

—|||—|||—|||—

Why an Academic Advisor?

When you were in high school, there was probably no such thing as an academic advisor. The person in high school most similar to an academic advisor was your guidance counselor. Your collegiate academic advisor will play a much more significant role in your academic career in college than did your guidance counselor in high school.

Why is it important to have an academic advisor during your college career? In high school you had few options as far as your curriculum was concerned. You basically either chose a vocational track or a college preparatory track. Your few choices probably were those where you selected a preference within an area—such as whether you would take French, Spanish, or another foreign language. You probably did not have the choice of whether or not you would take a foreign language. In college, however, your range of choices is much greater. You now have the opportunity to choose among courses in departments that may not have even existed in your high school curriculum. And more importantly, you have a much, much broader range of alternatives in terms of curricular emphasis. At the college level this curricular emphasis is called an *academic major*. Whereas in high school you simply chose between college preparatory or vocational tracks, you now have a wide range of academic major areas from which to choose. Some courses and areas of study such as criminal justice, journalism, engineering, anthropology, international studies, philosophy, theater, marine science, and geology may be available to you for the first time. At some institutions you may have as many as 100 different majors from which to choose. The choice is going to be very important, not only to your college career but also to your initial career direction after graduation and ultimately throughout life. An academic advisor can help you make sound choices so that you will enjoy your time in college and also benefit from it.

What Is Academic Advising?

To make the most of the relationship with your academic advisor, first understand what academic advising is. Many academic advisors at colleges and universities around the country have given a great deal of thought and attention to their work.

Academic advising is an ongoing process rather than a single or isolated appointment or meeting. It involves a developing relationship between you and your advisor. It means that the relationship is meant to help you during your college career to achieve your educational goals, career goals, and personal goals. It means that academic advising is designed to help you accomplish those goals through an awareness of, understanding of, and use of all of the resources available to you both at your college and in the community where your college is located. It means that in the academic advising relationship, your advisor will help you identify and accomplish those goals by seeing that you acquire the necessary skills and attitudes.

Academic advising then is essentially a relationship between you and another individual on your college campus. The development and nurturing of that relationship is the responsibility of both you and your advisor. The association is much more than an expert/novice relationship where the advisor bestows great knowledge and information to you. Both you and the advisor will learn and develop as the advising relationship grows and matures. Remember that an advisor is just that—an individual to advise, counsel, and guide your development. The ultimate responsibility for a successful advising relationship *and* college career is yours. It is your job to initiate and maintain the relationship.

Who Is Your Academic Advisor?

At most colleges and universities your academic advisor is assigned to you when you first arrive. Institutions of higher education are organized and managed in many different ways. Thus, the organization and management of academic advisement systems will vary tremendously from department to department on the same campus as well as from institution to institution.

Who serves as your academic advisor is not as important as the ability and the interest that person has in establishing productive relationships with students and helping them choose courses and majors wisely.

Many academic advisors are faculty members. Generally, the primary responsibilities of faculty are teaching and conducting research; for professors, academic advising is one of their many added responsibilities. Depending on how interested faculty are in developing relationships with advisees, they may be highly motivated toward academic advising or they may consider it simply one more task.

Your institution may have professional advisors specifically hired to advise. They may also teach a limited number of courses, but they were hired primarily for advisement. Some institutions also use peer advisors, usually an upperclass or graduate student who has been trained to assist in academic advising for freshmen and sophomores. These students are generally under the supervision of either a faculty member or professional advisor. Peer advisors are most commonly found on large university campuses.

How long will you continue to see the same person for advising? That may vary. The person initially assigned as your advisor may continue to assist you till graduation. If your academic advisor only works with lower division students (students in the first two years of college), you'll need to change to another advisor when you reach the upper division, declare a major, or enter your junior year.

You may have the opportunity to personally choose an academic advisor, but usually an advisor is assigned by your college or academic unit. Whatever the assignment procedure is on your campus, it is important that you be satisfied with the person assigned to you. Your advisor must be someone you feel comfortable with; someone you feel you can talk to; someone who is receptive to your ideas, your concerns, and your problems; and someone who shares in the joy of your successes. If you find yourself assigned to an advisor with whom you are not comfortable, or who doesn't seem to have time for or interest in your development, find out the established procedure for changing advisors and talk to your friends, your favorite teachers, and your academic dean to determine an advisor who can be more helpful to you.

━ ❙❙❙ ━ ❙❙❙ ━ ❙❙❙ ━
What Makes a Good Advisor-Student Relationship?

A good advisor-student relationship involves two-way communication with the burden of responsibility on both parties. Certain characteristics foster a positive advisor-advisee relationship. Here are some things to look for in a good advisor:

1. Is your advisor in touch with today's students at your campus? Does your advisor regard you as an individual with unique needs and interests?

2. Does your advisor believe in the worth and dignity of all students and believe that all have potential?

3. Does your advisor help you understand the many facets and steps required to make good academic decisions?

4. Does your advisor allow you to express your thoughts and feelings, truly listen to what you are saying, and look at you when you are speaking?

5. Does your advisor give you the undivided attention you deserve during your appointments? Are your meetings private and uninterrupted by phone calls or people dropping in?

6. Does your advisor know the current job market and is he or she aware of the ever changing nature of work in society?

7. Is your advisor able to interpret your institution's catalog and explain the rationale for curricular requirements in a satisfactory way?

8. Can your advisor adequately and appropriately refer you to other resource people on campus for additional information and assistance?

9. Can your advisor answer questions about the mechanics of the advisement and registration procedures at your institution?

10. Does your advisor post and keep office hours and is he or she receptive to you when you seek advice?

Just as you can expect a competent and interested academic advisor to possess certain characteristics, you have certain responsibilities as a student. Here are several things you can do to enhance your relationship with your academic advisor.

1. *Get to know yourself first.* Think back about how and why you chose your college or university. Determine where you are in the decision-making process of choosing an academic major. If you've made a decision, think about what led you to that decision. If you are undecided, identify what you can do to help yourself make a good decision. Meanwhile, don't worry about it; many freshmen are undecided and that's okay for now.

2. *Get to know your institution and its academic environment.* This includes not only your options for academic majors, minors, and elective courses but also the rules and regulations in force. A thorough understanding and base of knowledge on your part will make the time you spend with your advisor productive. Your meetings can then address subjects more important than the basic information you can get on your own. There

will certainly be some specific rules, policies, or procedures that you don't fully understand, and your advisor will be able to explain them.

3. *Take the initiative to get to know your advisor.* When I advised, my pet peeves were the students who only came to see me when they "needed something" (like a signature on a form or a new catalog) and expected me to remember them and their entire academic situation. On the other hand, it was a pleasure to see the familiar faces of students who had taken the time to develop a relationship before they needed something. In a nutshell, the better your advisor knows you, the more productive your time together will be and, more importantly, the more you'll get in return.

4. *When at all possible, make appointments to see your advisor.* Most advisors have busy schedules and their free time is limited. If you make appointments in advance, your advisor will be expecting you and can give your concerns the attention they deserve.

5. *Prepare for your appointments with your advisor.* If you initiated the meeting, have your questions ready. A mental or even written agenda will help structure your meeting. You'll be less likely to forget something you intended to discuss or a question you needed to ask. If your appointment is for a specific purpose, such as scheduling courses for an upcoming term, have suggestions and ideas ready for discussion. Don't expect your advisor to read your mind.

6. *Don't lose sight of the entire academic experience.* Remember that your academic career is a complete program of study—frequently four or more years in length. When planning a semester's course work, think about the sequencing of courses and the balancing or combining of courses in a given term. In other words, consider your total degree requirements when planning your schedule so you have a healthy combination of courses every term.

7. *Familiarize yourself with other campus resources such as the career center and counseling center.* Regardless how helpful your advisor may be, additional people and programs on campus can enrich your academic and extracurricular lives. Don't fail to take advantage of these.

—ııı—ııı—ııı—
Resources for Enhancing Academic Advising

It is unrealistic to expect every student and every academic advisor to live up to the ideals we've just outlined. However, the closer you can come to fulfilling those ideals, the more useful the advising relationship will be for you. Additional campus resources can enrich your college experience.

The institution's bulletin or catalog provides an outline of all degrees offered and curriculum requirements for specific degrees, as well as information on admission to particular programs and individual course descriptions. It also provides more information concerning academic rules and regulations for your institution. If you do not already have a personal copy of this important publication, ask your advisor how you can get one. Get it and hold on to it until you graduate.

The career center on campus will have data on career fields, job market projections, and other information on specific careers. Career counselors can help you find what resources you need and help you make sensible career and academic major decisions.

Many academic departments publish departmental handouts of course descriptions for the current or upcoming semester. These handouts provide much more detail concerning course content, evaluation procedures, and requirements than is available in the catalog. Departmental offices often will also have major requirements sheets. These curriculum handouts will list all courses required for completion of the major and will frequently include a suggested sequencing of courses. These can be especially helpful in schedule planning.

The registration office will print a master schedule of classes for each approaching semester. This lists the courses scheduled to be taught. Remember that not every course listed in the institution's catalog is taught every term. The master schedule will list the professor, the schedule, and the location for each course to be offered.

The campus bookstore is an often overlooked resource. When you're deciding upon courses to take, a review of the textbook for a course can provide a lot of information about the course content.

And finally, other people can be a most valuable resource. Professors can provide information about their disciplines as well as about individual courses they teach. Other students can be a good source of information concerning specific courses.

You are in college for an education, but the total collegiate experience also involves the activities you become involved in outside of the classroom. Remember that campus resources, student organizations, and other activities can contribute to your development, too. Consider yourself a consumer of education, and make the most of *all* the opportunities offered at your institution. Your advisor can be a friend, an ally, a source of information and inspiration, and a mentor.

Suggested Activities

1. Think about your academic advisor and answer the ten questions in this chapter about the characteristics to look for in a good advisor. How does your advisor score?

2. Develop an agenda for your next meeting with your advisor. Call to schedule an appointment and initiate the meeting.

3. Develop a tentative four-year plan. Decide which courses you will include in your program of study and which term you will take each of them. Discuss your tentative plan with your advisor.

7 Becoming an Information-Literate, Self-Reliant Learner

Charles C. Curran

ASSOCIATE PROFESSOR
COLLEGE OF LIBRARY AND INFORMATION SCIENCE
UNIVERSITY OF SOUTH CAROLINA

I was bewildered by college. The shock of choice overload, requirement overload, and information overload was sudden, powerful, and personal. I was an easy target.

The main reason I was so confused was that I could not even describe my problem. There I was, a freshman in the Duquesne University Library. I had a major assignment and no strategy—no inkling that mine was an information management problem and no prior experience that would help me solve my information management problem.

Oh, I had experienced the standard assortment of library lessons that grade and high school students suffer, but that was the problem! I had scored somewhere between prodigy and genius on silly library skills tests, but such rituals provided no real plan for identifying the need for information, locating it, evaluating it, synthesizing it, organizing it, and communicating it. I was an information illiterate in the Information Age; that's no way to be.

Had I the opportunity to work with librarians, teachers, and professors who understood the crucial differences between library skills and information literacy and who recognized the former as a companion to the latter, not its equivalent, I would have been a less bewildered freshman year student.

Thirty years in the information business have convinced me that students who want to survive and thrive in the Information Age must have a good plan for dealing with information problems. I have developed a plan and tested it. It works. Now I share it with you.

Since the appearance of the first edition of College Is Only the Beginning, *I have had a number of opportunities to work with the Information-Literate, Self-Reliant exercise described here in my own freshman classes and as an invited guest in the classes of colleagues at the University of South Carolina. I have also presented my model for developing Information-Literate Learners at the 1986 International Conference on the First Year Experience, Newcastle Upon Tyne, England. What follows is my cookbook approach to learning how to manage information. I believe this approach works because I have seen the outcomes. I have observed the successes students have enjoyed when they have had the opportunity to communicate the results of a systematic search for pertinent information.*

▬ⅠⅠⅠ▬ⅠⅠⅠ▬ⅠⅠⅠ▬

Whether or not you become an able information manager will have a lot to do with whether or not you enjoy success in school and in the work force. You must understand what it means when people say we live in the Information Age, because right now the Information Age affects everyone in crucial ways.

It affects you now and will affect you even more when you graduate and start your career, for about 60 percent of college graduates will earn their living by producing or processing information. Where will the jobs be for all the history, English, economics, psychology, and computer science majors? Most of them will be in the information industries. A few short decades ago you would have looked forward to growing or producing things or to delivering or servicing them. Tomorrow fewer people will be involved in production, even though production, driven by automation, will continue to rise. More and more professionals will be involved in creating, transferring, retrieving, and analyzing information—the new commodity. What kinds of skills will people have to acquire to deal with the mass of information that continues to develop at a prodigious pace? How do we manage the information explosion? In four years you may well earn your living looking for and working with answers to these questions.

We begin by having a plan. We practice a systematic approach. We use a model that aims at making us *information literate.* Information literacy is a concept that includes several elements:

☐ knowing what to look for

☐ knowing how to find it

☐ knowing how to interpret it

☐ knowing how to organize it

☐ knowing how to communicate it

Practicing the following exercise should help you acquire the skills required for information literacy. In the process you will become a self-reliant learner and user of information systems. You will get some practice interacting with the librarians who manage the information systems, and this practice will give you a lifelong skill that is transferable from library to library and organization to organization.

The exercise that follows has four parts. The first involves selecting a topic for investigation. The second consists of establishing a framework for organizing and delivering the information found on the topic. The third part is the model for making inquiries of the information agency. It provides a step-by-step procedure for the retrieval of information. You match the retrieved information with the framework established in Part 2. If it fits, you have relevant information; if it does not, you have a miss and you will need to keep on with the search. Part 4 is the communication step—the delivery step. Here you transfer to other information users the information that you have retrieved, synthesized, and organized.

So you see this exercise is not one of those this-is-how-to-use-your-library routines that stops at retrieval. This is not a treasure hunt that ends with finding a prize. This exercise involves you in a finding activity, yes, but it goes several important steps further: Here you practice analysis and communication, which, along with retrieval, are the stuff of information literacy. In the Information Age, you've got to be information literate!

—‖‖—‖‖—‖‖—
Part 1: Selecting a Topic

If you are enrolled in a class that is pursuing the topics in this book, your instructor will be leading you in this exercise. Otherwise, you will be doing this exercise on your own. Both ways will work for you. If you are doing the project alone, make the acquaintance early on with one of the librarians whose job it is to help people searching for information. Often such a person will have the title Reference Librarian, and, most probably, he or she will have a desk in some prominent location. Go right up to the librarian and say: "Hi, my name is Fred, and I am working on a library project on my own and for my own personal improvement. From time to time if I have a question, may I come to you for help?"

This will accomplish two important things. One, it will provide you with a friendly contact in the library; two, it will alert the librarian, especially if you show your assignment, that you are working to become a skillful information manager.

So as you read this section, remember that if you are going this alone, you will have to interpret all the references to a teacher's role as instructions to you.

Your instructor is going to distribute some blank cards to you. On them place your name and your top three choices from among the list of topics presented here. Pick subjects in which you have some interest because these are the topics you will be investigating and reporting about. You will get a lot more out of this enterprise if you really want to know more about the topic you study. List your top pick first, your next choice second, and your third choice last. If you are doing this on your own, you need not list second and third choices—just your first.

THE TOPICS

Adoption	Love	Racism
Air Pollution	Mafia	Radio Astronomy
Autism	Militarism	The Reformation
Capital	Montessori	Recidivism
Punishment	Method	Sea Monsters
Care of the	Moral Majority	Social Class
Mentally Ill	Nuclear Energy	The Stock Market
Christian Virtues	New York City	Stress
Democratic Party	Oriental Philosophy	Management
Drug Use	Paranoia	Symbiosis
Electronic Data	Penology	Televangelism
Processing	Politicization of	Venereal Disease
Employment	the Olympics	Witchcraft
The Future	Pop Art	The Women's
The Great	Prejudice	Movement
Depression	Property Taxes	(Feminism)
Hypnosis	Protectionism	Woodrow Wilson
The Ku Klux Klan	Providence	Zoroaster
Legalized	Psyche	
Prostitution		

Your card should look like this:

Jackie Smith
1 Paranoia
2 The Ku Klux Klan
3 Occult

Your instructor will collect these cards and try to assign you a topic of your top choice. Chances are you will work in teams of two or three, so you will have some help on this project.

The project itself requires you to investigate the topic by searching for information in the library, putting it together in a coherent package, and preparing and delivering a five-minute talk to the class about your project.

This is an exercise in searching, interpretation, synthesis, and communication—the skills required for information literacy.

☐ Searching: You have to find stuff and examine it to determine whether it is relevant to your topic and whether it fits your outline.

☐ Interpretation: Determine meaning and separate the more important from the less important.

☐ Synthesis: Combine the interpreted information into five minutes of air time.

☐ Communication: Relay it to the class by presenting your findings.

And by *present* I mean *tell,* not read. Know your topic well enough so you can speak from the heart, assisted maybe by an outline or some key words on note cards. Practice to make sure you come in under the five-minute time limit and to enable you to talk convincingly from heart and memory, not from prepared notes.

Most of you will be a bit nervous about this. That's okay. Everyone gets nervous before a performance. Let your extra energy, which is a part of being nervous, work for you. Experts in the field of conquering stage fright advise us to imagine ourselves doing well. Make working to create this image of being successful part of your preparation for the five-minute presentation. (See Chapter 19 for advice on handling anxiety.)

━Ⅲ━━Ⅲ━━Ⅲ━
Part 2: An Outline for Your Topic

Now we establish a framework so you can determine whether retrieved information is relevant to your topic and your assignment. Here it is:

I. The topic identified and defined

II. Why this topic is interesting, crucial, or controversial

III. How my ideas about this subject have been clarified or changed as a result of this search

IV. The source categories that were most helpful and those that I found least helpful

This outline also becomes the framework for your presentation. You will begin by telling what your topic is about; be sure to define any words that anyone might really need to know to follow your talk. That's *Step I.* In *Step II* you give the *so what?* of your investigation. In other words, why is it important that society solve the problem, understand the issue, or recognize the danger associated with your topic? In *Step III* state your personal reaction. The literature may say one thing; what do you say? Do you agree? Are you as concerned as the people who write about your topic? Do you think they overreact? What do *you* think? In *Step IV* you tell what categories of information were most useful to you. For example, you may have found the books too technical or too out of date while the periodicals may have been easier to understand and more current.

You will be retrieving lots of information on your topic. Soon a sudden and consequential shift will occur. Instead of facing the problem of how to *find* information, you will have the problem of how to deal with this mass of information that you have found! Management will replace retrieval as your principal concern. You solve this problem by subjecting each retrieved article of information to this question: Does this item fit my outline? Does it help me define or explain (Step I), or does it help me understand and prepare to relay consequences (Step II)? So you manage this information by superimposing your model on it. Is there a fit? Yes? Then you have some useful stuff. No? Discard it.

By the way, you can expect lots of *no* answers, and you will also find that some categories of information sources are silent about your topic, or have old information, or present it in a way that makes it too cumbersome to deal with. That's why information management is so crucial a skill for you to learn. You have to learn to separate the useful from the less useful.

The useful from the less useful and the good from the bad: These are concepts that can give you some trouble, yet information managers must make these distinctions, along with distinguishing between anecdotal and empirical reporting. Suppose you are examining the smoking and health controversy and you encounter the true story of a 96-year-old woman who smokes two packs of unfiltered cigarettes daily, keeps house, and attends the square dance every Saturday night. How do you reconcile that with another verifiable event—a study of 12,000 smokers showing an association between smoking and lung cancer and other diseases? What is the quality or force of an argument for or against smoking that might be based upon one of these two reports, both absolutely verifiable?

If you want to demonstrate this problem for yourself, start a class discussion of this issue: Boxing should be banned. Now listen to the arguments advanced on both sides of the issue.

□ Boxing is immoral.

□ Boxing is a way poor people emerge from poverty.

□ Scuba diving is more dangerous than boxing.

□ The fighters know what they are doing.

□ Boxers never know when to quit.

- Ring deaths are too frequent.

- My uncle boxed and he isn't punchy.

- To deliberately strike another human being so hard that it jars his brain against his skull is wrong.

- Boxing puts money in circulation.

- Prize fighters have to be in good shape and physical fitness is very important.

- Promoter Don King has funny hair.

What about these arguments, some of them quite fervently believed and forcefully delivered? How do we evaluate them? What is the quality of the evidence? How "scientifically" are the conclusions reached? Are some merely stories? How verifiable are the reports? Does bias, maybe of an uncontrolled nature, creep into these arguments? How well-informed are the proponents of the various points of view? What are the credentials of the debaters? These are good questions to ask when you are evaluating the points of view that you will encounter in your search. An important part of information literacy is the ability to *evaluate* information.

Part 3: The Retrieval Model

Take your topic to a general encyclopedia such as *Americana, World Book,* or *Britannica.* Use the index volume to begin.

The topic I looked for _____

Name of the encyclopedia _____

Is this topic listed in the index volume?   Yes _____   No _____

The page of the index volume on which this topic is listed _____
The references to which the index refers (include volume and page)

Reference topic	Volume	Pages
_____	_____	_____
_____	_____	_____
_____	_____	_____

If you do not find your topic listed, check to see if there is a reference from that topic to a related one. For example: "Dogs, see Canine." Pursue that. If there is no "see" reference, report this to your instructor or ask a librarian to help you if you are doing this on your own. Tell the librarian what you are looking for and ask him or her to help you interpret what you have found in the index volume. The encyclopedia may be silent on your topic, you may have to think of a related topic on your own, or the encyclopedia may consider your topic under a heading you have not yet connected with your problem. For example, you may be looking for *pop art*, but your encyclopedia may present that topic under *mass culture*—with no reference from *pop art*. Maybe you will have to select another encyclopedia.

If you have found some information, read it. Now evaluate it. Does it fit your framework? Will it help with introduction, definition, or importance? If it will, you have found some *useful* information and you will want to refer to it. If it does not fit your outline, either because it is off target, out of date, too vague, or too technical, then you will want to discard it. In either case you have practiced information management.

As part of this exercise indicate whether the retrieved information is useful. How does it fit the outline?

Why This Information is Useful

_____

_____

_____

Now go to a *subject* encyclopedia. There are subject encyclopedias covering just about every topic: art, criminal justice, economics, education, philosophy, psychology, religion, science, and sports, among others. You will probably want to ask a librarian how to locate these, for they may be more difficult to find than the general encyclopedias, which are usually kept in one special reference area. The subject encyclopedias will usually be shelved with the other reference books in their subject areas. The librarians will be glad to help you. That's their job. If you are using this book in a class, your instructor has probably informed them that you would be asking for assistance. Your instructor may have supplied the reference librarians with your assignments, so they know exactly what you are working on.

Here are three examples of special subject encyclopedias: *The International Encyclopedia of Psychiatry, Psychology, Psychoanalysis and Neurology, The McGraw-Hill Encyclopedia of Science and Technology,* and *Encyclopedia of World Art.* There are hundreds more. Locate one that you believe is related to your topic.

List the topic _____

Name the encyclopedia _____

Index page _____
The references to which the index refers

Reference topic	*Volume*	*Pages*
_____	_____	_____
_____	_____	_____
_____	_____	_____

Read this material. Is it useful? How does it fit your outline? Again as part of this exercise, use the space below to indicate why the information is of potential value.

Why This Information Meets My Requirements

_____

_____

_____

The next step will be to find books that might help you put your five-minute talk together. This step has two parts. The first part involves making sure that the way you are describing your topic is the same way that the Library of Congress describes it. This is important because subjects in the library's catalog will conform to a master authority list, not necessarily to your description. You may call it *abnormal psychology*. They call it *psychology, pathological*. You could look for a hundred years under *abnormal* in the "A" section of the catalog and not find the library's books on abnormal psychology because they are listed in the "P" drawer under *psychology, pathological*. How do you *know* this? You don't. That's why we all have to start a subject search by consulting the official subject list. Ask the librarian for help in locating the *LC List of Subject Headings*.

Record the subject you are looking for: _____
Does the *LC List* indicate that this is an official term? Get some help from the librarian on this. Once you understand the value of using the *LC List*, both for verifying the legal (used) terms and also for discovering related terms that may lead to additional sources of information, you will have mastered a valuable retrieval skill. The librarian works with this important reference tool every day and can immediately clear up any questions you may have as a first-time user. If the book tells you that you must use another term, record that:

_____

Now that you have the legal or authorized term, locate two books in the subject catalog on your subject. To indicate "Location," see the following paragraph.

Book 1

Subject heading _____

Call number _____

Title of book _____

Location _____

Book 2

Subject heading _____

Call number _____

Title of Book _____

Location _____

The next part of this step will be to actually retrieve these books from the stacks. This may require you to check the call numbers against posted signs that will tell you locations for those numbers. Mark the location, such as "Ground Level," "Fourth Floor," or "Reading Room" in the blanks for Books 1 and 2 and go to those locations and check for the numbers you have recorded. If the books are available, check to see if they meet the requirements of your outline (definition, explanation, importance, and so on). If they do, tell why in the space below. If they do not, or if they are not available to examine, search for others in the catalog until you have your required two.

Book 1: Why This Meets My Requirements

_____

_____

_____

Book 2: Why This Meets My Requirements

_____

_____

_____

Your next step is to check for periodical or magazine articles on your topic. Special indexes provide you with subject access to magazines. An index such as the *Readers' Guide to Periodical Literature* provides subject access to many periodicals from the present time all the way back to the beginning of the century. Now check the *Readers' Guide* for your topic. You will find that different bound volumes cover different years. The most current coverage will be found in the small, green paperback issues. Again you will be looking for two articles, and you will be evaluating each on the basis of how it matches your outline. When searching terms, watch out for cross-references in the form of "see" or "see also" statements. A "see" means that the term you are using is not the one used by the *Readers' Guide*. For example, if you were looking for "Airplane accidents," you might find a message like this: "Airplane accidents See Aeronautics—Accidents." This tells you that in *Readers' Guide* "Airplane accidents" is not a legal (used) term; "Aeronautics—Accidents" is the subject's legal term. In this example, "Air pilots See also Astronauts," the message is that "Air pilots" is a used term and so is "Astronauts," so you can use both of them to find information on related topics. A librarian will be glad to explain this to you if you need some help in decoding the language found in the *Readers' Guide* or any library source.

Okay, now go to work and record your periodical choices.

Article 1

Date of *RG* _____

Term(s) searched _____

Title of the article _____

Name of the journal _____

Volume no. _____ Pages _____ Date _____ Call number _____

Article 2

Date of *RG* _____

Term(s) searched _____

Title of the article _____

Name of the journal _____

Volume no. _____ Pages _____ Date _____ Call number _____

Before, when you were identifying books, getting the call number was part of the process of checking the catalog. The call number accompanied the listing of the book. But now what you have is a reference to an article—just the citation. Now you need to get a call number for that periodical so you can actually locate it and inspect it. This requires an additional step, and you may need some help the first time you try.

The librarians will gladly show you how to do this. Chances are you will have to go to a separate list that may be on some kind of microform. All the library's periodicals might be on sheets called microfiche, which you load into a machine and search alphabetically for the name of the magazine or journal you want. Ask for assistance, get the call number, see on which floor the wanted items are shelved, and go get them. Then determine whether your articles meet your needs.

Article 1: Why This Meets My Requirements

_____

_____

Article 2: Why This Meets My Requirements

_____

_____

Again, if either article is unsuitable or not available, return to the *Readers' Guide* and resume your search until you retrieve and analyze the required two.

Now you are going to do the same thing with indexes that you did with encyclopedias. First you used general encyclopedias, then subject ones. Next you used *Readers' Guide,* a general index. Now ask the librarian to point out a subject index to periodicals that is applicable to your search. Here are some examples of subject periodical indexes: *Humanities Index, Business Periodicals Index,* and *Education Index.*

Find one relevant article.

Name of the index _____

Date of the index _____

Term(s) searched _____

Title of the article _____

Name of the journal _____

Volume no. _____ Pages _____ Date _____ Call number _____

Search for this article or another if this one is unsuitable or missing, and indicate why it is useful to you.

Why This Article Meets My Requirements

_____

_____

Chances are that your topic is or was in some way controversial and newsworthy. Get some verification of this by checking with the librarian or your instructor. If you get the go ahead, consult *Editorials on File* for opinion on your topic. In this source you will gain access to unabashed opinion, obvious bias, and point of view. For example, you may find fourteen different editors giving fourteen different views of some hot news event. Know that if ever you need to find out what people think about an issue, *Editorials on File* will fill that need. It will also supply another valuable finding for people looking for answers to some of life's tough and complex questions. *Editorials on File* and other sources of opinion can demonstrate how reasonable people can differ. If nothing else, these editorials can show that when five intelligent people can view the same event or circumstance and report five different explanations or viewpoints, readers ought to be on guard against believing everything they see in print.

When you approach *Editorials on File*, try to match that source with the year in which your topic was hot. You will find "Iran-Contra Hearings" in 1987 and not before. If you wanted to find references to the presidency of Gerald R. Ford, you would have to go back to 1974 and work forward from that year.

Date of *Editorials on File* that helped _____

Term I consulted in index _____ page _____

Page I was referred to _____

Why This Editorial Meets My Requirements

_____

_____

Do the same for the *New York Times Index*.

Date of *Index* I consulted _____

Term I used _____

Reference I was given _____

Ask the librarian to help you interpret this code, for it is the key to your next step, which is to get the reel of microfilm containing the issue of the *New York Times* that you need. You will have to go to the library's microfilm area, request or retrieve the film, and load this into a reader and find the needed article. If the article you found is relevant, tell why; if it is not, say so.

Why This Article Meets My Requirements

_____

_____

If you have now found two encyclopedia references, two books, three journal or magazine articles, and perhaps some information from either *Editorials on File* or the *New York Times,* you and your team of searchers are ready to put together what you've got and divide the speaking assignments so that you can do your presentation in the allotted five minutes.

Another important thing you have accomplished is that if you have interacted with the library staff, you now know how to put them to work for you. And they know that you are a serious student who is well on the way to becoming an information-literate, self-reliant learner.

—‖‖—‖‖—‖‖—

Part 4: Communicating the Information

Whether you are working as an individual or as a team with one or two other students, your next task is to sift through the retrieved information and select what is relevant to your purposes. Remember that your job is to:

1. Define and explain.

2. Give reasons and evidence that this is an important topic or issue. (What will be the consequences if this problem is not solved? What's the *so what?* of this issue?)

3. Tell how your or your group's attitudes have been modified, if at all, after evaluating the retrieved information.

4. Tell which kinds of sources were helpful and which were not.

Here's an example. Suppose your topic was "the farm crisis in the United States." Your first job would be to define your terms. What is actually meant by this expression? What kinds of farms are being talked about, and what is the nature of the crisis? What's the problem? That's Part 1, definition and explanation.

Next you would elaborate on the crisis, perhaps by explaining the plight of farmers who find themselves in debt and unable to get out from under because farm prices are low. Give some figures on what you mean by low prices. Tell the rate at which farmers are losing their investments. Relate the consequences for them and for American consumers if the crisis is not solved. This is all Part 2, reasons and evidence.

Part 3, attitude changes, gives you a chance to say what *you* think. If there are three of you, one might be sympathetic for the farmer, another might blame the farmer for letting himself get too far in debt, a third might assert that the government should step in and halt the losses being suffered.

Finally, Part 4 requires you to evaluate your sources. You might have found that encyclopedias and magazines were very helpful in supplying information about the issue, but that books were less useful. You might also have found that the opinions expressed in *Editorials on File* really helped the group form some conclusions, although you disagreed on what those conclusions should be.

Determine how and who will deliver what information. If there are three of you, you might assign Parts 1, 2, and 3 to be presented by a different member and share Part 4.

You have probably discovered already that it is necessary to narrow your focus to one aspect of your topic. A broad topic such as *nuclear energy* may have to be narrowed to *peacetime use of, use for public utilities,* or *nuclear disasters*. I advised you earlier that your information problem would shift from one of *how to find* to one of *how to manage what has been found*. Paying careful attention to your outline, narrowing your topic, and talking this over with your team members should help you manage.

After you have sifted the information, placed it in its appropriate outline category, and made presentation assignments, try at least one practice run to make sure you come in under the five-minute time limit. If you go over, cut. Do not try to solve the time problem by talking faster. This seldom works and it's no way to manage information. You will just have to make the decision to excise the less important and keep the more important.

Make some notes. Plan to *talk* to your audience, not read to them. That's why you should not write out the whole talk and thus increase the temptation to read—or worse, memorize. If someone were trying to convince you that you should believe what he believes, you would be more persuaded by arguments delivered from the heart than by those read from some paper. That's true in the home, the classroom, the office, and the shop. So practice talking from conviction, not paper. And look people in the eye when you do your presentation. Find a couple of friendly faces in different parts of the room and alternate your eye contact with them. If your knees shake, deliver your little talk while seated. If your hands shake, grip a podium or clasp them in front of you on a desk or table. The last thing you want in your nervous hands is a rattling sheaf of paper. You'll fan your audience to death or, at least, distract them. Remember, as part of your preparation, imagine yourself doing a good job. Do not waste any valuable time worrying about being nervous. Of course you are going to be nervous; if you weren't nervous, you'd be comatose. Go get 'em.

Note to Instructors: If you decide to use this exercise, you will probably need about three class periods to explain the assignment, work in the library with your teams, and conduct the presentations. You really must alert the librarians about this, and as a courtesy, give them a copy of the assignment and a list of topics. Be there in the library with your students for one full period. They will have questions about sources, the quality of information, and other matters. Chances are that the students will need more than one hour to retrieve their sources, so explain to them that they will probably have to come back to the library on their own to complete that process.

If your college or university has a program in library and information studies, make the acquaintance of one of the instructors in that program. Explain what you are doing and you may be able to recruit some students who are training to be information officers/librarians to help with this project. They can be stationed at the various stops—encyclopedias, *LC List,* card catalog, indexes, *Editorials on File, New York Times Index,* and film cabinets—to work with teams as they progress from source to source. If you start your groups at several different stations, they will not all bunch up at one stop. Twenty-five students at the encyclopedias at one time is too many to work with.

Make this a required assignment that must be accomplished in order to pass the unit or course. This requirement will plug into the students' value systems. Listen to their reports and create an atmosphere where their classmates also listen. If time permits, ask a few questions of your presenters. Acknowledge the good performances, especially the ones that are well delivered and information rich.

You are about to be pleasantly surprised by the quality of student performance. This exercise works. It arms students with a genuine survival skill and it helps to prepare them for the real world of the Information Age.

I repeat that it is vital to keep the librarians informed about what you are doing. Since they, too, may engage in some form of library instruction program for freshmen, they should know that what you are doing is an assignment in synthesis and communication as well as a lesson in library procedures. If they do not fully understand your assignment and its special objectives, and especially that these objectives differ from those that normally guide library lessons, they may get the mistaken idea that you are trying to do *their* job. You want to avoid this misunderstanding, and the way to avoid this is—communicate.

References

I wish to acknowledge the contributions of several persons whose work has influenced my thinking about information literacy. Two articles that are especially relevant are:

Brevick, Patricia Senn. "Putting Libraries Back in the Information Society." *American Libraries* 16 (November 1985): 723.

Tuckett, Harold D., and Carla J. Stoffle. "Learning Theory and the Self-Reliant Library User." *RQ 24* (Fall 1984): 58–66.

8 Private Writing for Public Success

Carolyn Matalene

ASSOCIATE PROFESSOR OF ENGLISH
UNIVERSITY OF SOUTH CAROLINA

Late one night—well after midnight—in the study room of my dormitory, my new friend Judy approached me, somewhat aggressively, and said, "All right, Carolyn, tell me something. Just how do you be smart?"

I wasn't the right person to ask at the time; I was spending long hours studying, but I could seldom predict whether or not my efforts would be effective. It took me a long time—most of my first two years at Northwestern—to become a real student, knowing how to learn and how to use what I had learned.

Along the way I discovered that my greatest asset was writing well. That's what impressed my professors. But I didn't really understand much about writing or myself as a writer. After my first year in graduate school at the University of Pennsylvania, I suddenly had my own class of freshmen to teach—the freshman English course. Now I really didn't know what I was doing! And it was my job to know.

So I have been studying and thinking about how to be smart and how to be a writer and how to teach writing for the past twenty years. I have taught freshman English again and again, even directing the program for a while, and I teach a rigorous (but popular) advanced composition course. Lately, I have been teaching adult writers on the job—especially journalists—and studying the many kinds of writing required in the world of work.

The amount of writing required in an advanced industrial society such as ours is staggering—the Air Force alone, for example, turns out 500 million pages of writing a year. Indeed, having a job that requires a college degree is likely to mean being a writer. Thus, helping writers to become the best that they can be seems to me an exciting and an important task. (Sometimes I can't believe how much I like what I do.)

The more I learn about writers and writing, the more convinced I am that being smart and being a writer go together. Thinking and writing can't be separated like the hardware and the software of a computer; instead, they are inextricably connected—like the dancer and the dance.

So at last, I am beginning to think that I know how to respond to Judy's late-night question. Here's my answer—for you.

—\|\|\|—\|\|\|—\|\|\|—

Better Grades Through Better Writing

If you take this chapter seriously, you can raise your grade-point average by half a point, maybe even a whole point. You can watch disheartening C's change to encouraging B's. If you already know how to get B's, you can turn them into triumphant A's and start enjoying all of the glories A's seem to entail. And the effort involved will be less than you might think. You won't have to spend many more hours studying; you will just use some of your study time differently—engaging in *private writing*.

By private writing, I mean writing that you undertake as a way of learning, writing that you practice as a technique for studying, writing that only you see because it is not intended to communicate knowledge or information to anyone but yourself. Private writing works as a medium for you to communicate with yourself as a learner, asking your own questions about what you read and hear, questioning your own answers, and eventually becoming fluent in the language of a discipline. Of course, you will also have to engage in public writing—the essays, examinations, research papers, or critical analyses your professors assign. Public writing—what English teachers call "academic discourse"—is writing you present to your professors to show that you have learned; it must go through the process of revision and editing; it must be finished and polished. Private writing, by contrast, can remain unfinished, exploratory, inconclusive, a way of remembering facts and terms even if their meaning is not yet clear to you. In this chapter, as well as explaining how to practice private writing, I argue that private writing is a powerful way to become a better learner, to become a more effective public writer, and to raise your grade point. Your love life will probably improve, too. But more on that later—after grade points.

A Few Words About Grade Points

What is a grade point anyway? It is not just the translation of letter grades into a numerical average. A grade point indicates—approximately perhaps but not arbitrarily—a student's ability to use language. Some students are a lot better at this than others, and, as you may be angrily aware, how long or hard a student studies may not relate at all to the grade that student earns. It hardly seems fair. But one of the terrible truths that every college student must face is that in college, effort doesn't automatically count. Only achievement. That is, merely reading all of the assignments and listening in class isn't necessarily enough; what matters is your ability to talk and write about a subject. Thus, spending days doing research for a paper or studying hours for a test may or may not pay off. Of course, as a general rule, study ghouls are less likely to flunk out and are more likely to graduate than the party people who don't buy their books, let alone open them. But still, time spent is just not directly proportional to grade earned. Sorry. One of the sad truths of the college experience for many students is that by the time they learn how to study effectively, they are ready to graduate.

Language, Learning, and Your Future

Private writing, I am convinced, can help you get smart sooner. Here's why: Being smart means being skillful in manipulating language. A college degree is essentially a certification that the recipient is more skilled in using language, more capable of understanding and contributing to the specialized language of a particular discipline, than is the person without a degree. Whether the words are explaining biology or philosophy or history or finance, the medium is still language, and the skills—among them comprehending, synthesizing, organizing, analyzing, and evaluating—are the same.

Being smart in or with language is not, of course, the only way to be smart. Contemporary psychologists believe that there are several different kinds of intelligence—multiple intelligences. Howard Gardner, a Harvard psychologist who studies how people learn, suggests that as well as linguistic and logical-mathematical intelligences, human beings also possess musical, spatial, kinesthetic, and personal intelligences. These are distinct mental abilities that can be used to solve problems, to create products, and even to create new problems. When Jack Nicklaus hits a golf ball, for example, he is clearly exhibiting some extraordinary brain power, in this case kinesthetic or bodily intelligence. But it can't be measured by the SAT.

In fact, our educational institutions of higher learning are based exclusively on recognition of only two kinds of intelligence, verbal and mathematical. College admissions officers look at ACT or SAT verbal and SAT math scores; there is no SAT spatial or SAT musical test. And for most of us, it's good news that they look more closely at verbal than at math scores. We seem to be more likely to get by with a good verbal and a low math score than the other way around. So we're back to language skills again. If, as this book's title asserts, college is only the beginning, it is the beginning of an adult life lived in language, its success measured by success in using language.

When employers complain about the new graduates they have hired—and they do complain—their complaints almost always have to do with language skills. "The young people we get just can't read and write." "They aren't literate." Or, "They can't think." And the kind of thinking that most enterprises depend upon is once again verbal intelligence. Conversely, when exceptionally successful people explain how they rose to the top, they are likely to emphasize their skills as communicators. "I could write better than anyone else, and the boss liked that." "I was the only person who could explain things simply." Again and again, the essence of the success story is being an effective speaker and writer, being able to explain issues clearly and to convince others.

Being an Active Learner

What college is about then is not filling your head with the facts of a particular field but, rather, mastering the language of the field so you can become an active participant, a contributor, not just an onlooker. And that's where private writing comes in. You can become a more effective and more competent language user only if you actively practice using the medium that you are going to live your life in, the medium of language. Jack Nicklaus was born with athletic gifts, but he got smart as a golfer by practicing his medium endlessly, spending hours and days and months and years on the practice tee and the putting green, not by watching others play.

You must *actively practice* the medium you are trying to master. And that means writing, not just reading. Writing and reading are the systole and diastole—the inhaling and exhaling—of learning. Superior students, those who make Phi Beta Kappa and graduate cum laude know this. Average students think learning means reading and studying means memorizing. They think they can passively watch or soak up what others have learned. But they can't; passive learning leads to intellectual anemia, and anemic students get C's.

Good students practice active learning. As a reader, that means engaging with the text, questioning, making connections and comparisons, evaluating—thinking, in a word. But being a passive reader, as we all know, takes less energy. You no doubt have had the experience of reading a page in a textbook once, twice, even a third or fourth time without any of the content lodging in your brain. Or perhaps you have painstakingly underlined all of the important points in a chapter only to leave them all where they already were—on the pages of the book. That won't raise your grade point. Here is what will.

Writing and Reading

Private writing, writing in response to your reading, will require you to be an active reader, an engaged learner. For each of your courses, get a notebook with two or three divisions in it. Use one of the sections in each notebook only for reading notes. You might start this way. Take your sociology text, for example, and read a portion, perhaps a chapter. Don't underline or highlight every other sentence. Instead, read thoughtfully and then close the book. Now, in your reading notebook, write a brief summary in your own words of what you read. What is the chapter really about? Next, write some of your own reactions, comments, thoughts. What does this chapter make you think of? What can you relate it to? What examples from your own experience can you think of that would help the author prove the major points? Or what examples can you think of that would disprove those points? What questions do you have? What seems strange? What seems unclear or hard to understand? If you could ask your professor some questions about this material, what would they be?

Write. And write some more. Don't worry about spelling or crossing out; write as fast as you can—remember, no one is going to read this but you. As you write, you will have more ideas as the words you write bump together on the page. That's the fun of writing, the infinite creativity language allows its users. Enjoy it. Read another chapter and write again. If you hate the text, say so. Say why. By writing, you are now painlessly increasing your chances of remembering the material, really remembering because you are involved in it. You are also practicing literacy in the field you are reading about; you are making the language of the subject your own. You are engaged. And that is the essence of what any professor wants from any student—not agreement—but *engagement with the subject.*

The question that breaks the hearts of professors, the one that makes us want to quit and take up cab driving, is the one from the back row at the high point of the lecture, "Do we have to know this? Is this going to be on the exam?" No. You don't have to know anything, we want to say. You can go home and watch television and be a turnip. But if you do want to know something and to be someone, instead of just taking up space, then get involved and engaged. Jump into the language of the course and start manipulating it yourself, instead of just processing it as a private reader or turning it yellow with a highlighter or copying down sentences that don't belong to you.

Comparison

Here are some other approaches you can use as you respond to reading by writing: "What this chapter seems to be saying is *like* what we studied last week in this way. . . ." Or, "This chapter is *different* from what we have studied so far in these ways. . . ." Now you are comparing, and comparison is a powerful learning tool, perhaps the most powerful. Some learning specialists think that comparing is the basis of all learning, that new understanding results from matching—or comparing—the unfamiliar with the familiar, or new information with information we already have. (We can't avoid comparing, it seems, a new friend with an old, this teacher with that one, tonight's dinner with last night's.) Another good reason for thinking in terms of comparison is that comparison questions frequently turn up on exams. Compare the economic development of Chile with that of Argentina. Compare Wordsworth's theory of poetry with Pope's. Compare treatments for dyslexia.

Cause and Effect

In some courses—especially history—thinking in terms of cause and effect is important. This caused this. These were the major causes of World War I. These were the major effects of Roosevelt's domestic policies. Focusing on cause and effect is also a common and powerful way to structure our experience. Human beings are human partly because they are always asking, "What would happen if—if we mixed nitrogen and glycerine?" or "How could we get that to happen—how could we get to the moon?"

Narration

Another important form for writing in any course that is historically oriented is getting the order of events straight. This is what happened. Writing that presents a sequence of events is called a narrative, and of all of the different ways of structuring writing, the narrative seems to be our favorite. "Once upon a time" always engages our attention and makes us anticipate a good story.

Theories and Opinions

In a course that involves learning the theories of major thinkers, say Marx or Darwin or Freud, do some writing in which you explain what the thinker thought—in your own words. This is what Freud thought about infantile sexuality. This is what Marx thought about surplus value. And then, feel free to write down what you think. This is my interpretation of Nietzsche's statement, "God is dead." Or this is my opinion of Churchill's foreign policy. You will also discover that sometimes your professor will disagree with the author of a textbook. Write about that. Samuelson says this, but my instructor disagrees and says this instead. But I think they both are wrong because. Now you are getting practice in keeping straight who thinks what or which ideas belong to whom. And that, of course, is what academic discourse is all about.

You don't have to be serious all the time either. You might write about what would happen if Freud went to Jung for treatment or what Matthew Arnold would say about the poetry of e.e. cummings or how Mozart would react to the Beatles or Beethoven to U2. Or write a letter to your mom telling her how complicated or strange or interesting or unusual your philosophy course is and how you feel about that.

Explanation and Argumentation

One of the best ways to make sure you understand a principle, theory, or historical event is to write a pretend letter to someone who is not in your course; explain clearly to this open-minded but ignorant person what the issue is, why it matters, why any truly educated person should know about it. You will start to sound like an expert, and sounding like an expert is also what academic discourse requires. Experts are often convinced that their version or solution is the right one, and that is another useful writing response that you can practice: arguing. This is what ought to be done. This is the best course of action.

Writing to Learn

Writing after you read is probably the best study habit you can develop. Do you see why this kind of informal writing is such a powerful intellectual tool? You, yourself, are on the golf course, judging the distance to the trap, checking the wind and your lie—and suddenly realizing here's the shot you practiced for an hour yesterday until the grip and the stance and the timing felt as natural as breathing. When you write in private, you are not just watching someone else. You are doing the learning. And you are gaining ease and fluency in the medium you will be judged in: language. When exam time comes, you will have a headful of words, phrases, sentences, thoughts, opinions, and conclusions about the content of the course; they will be right there in that extraordinary floppy disk called your brain, ready to be part of the file named "answer."

Furthermore, when you write after you read, you will need to be seated at a desk or a table with pen and notebook, in the position traditionally assumed by people who are at work. Lying in bed supported by pillows is the position traditionally assumed by those who are sleeping. During your four years of college, learning is the job you have accepted. Stay vertical. And when you read, write.

—|||——|||——|||—
Writing and Listening

The most important part of any course is obviously the time you spend in class, listening to the teacher. But many college teachers are amazed at how few students bother to take notes while listening. It does seem odd, a sort of intellectual suicide, since the professors are there to explain their expertise, their approach to the field, their thoughts, findings, interpretations. The words of the professor are at least as important as the words of the text; most professors would say more important. And some professors, this one for instance, have a tendency to ask exam questions about material presented only in class. So not taking notes in class means that when it is time to bone up for the final, there is nothing in the cupboard to gnaw on. Not taking notes also allows you to keep your mind in neutral rather than engaged with what is happening—a surefire way to miss what matters.

Taking Notes

Take your class notes in one of the other sections of your notebook; keep them separate from your reading notes. You will need to develop your own note-taking system with your own shorthand for the important terms or ideas that keep recurring. As an English major, I had professors who were always talking about "literature," so I used the Greek letter lambda, Λ, instead of writing out the word *literature* all of the time. And in philosophy classes, Φ (phi) stood for *philosophy*. Make up your own. A few well-chosen symbols will not only speed up note taking but they will also mean that your notes will be useless or at least cryptic for would-be borrowers. (Let them take their own notes or lose someone else's.) You will also want to develop your own signs for indicating really important ideas as opposed to semi-important. Some students draw keys for key ideas; some use stars or draw wiggly lines or underline one, two, or three times. Just keep your system straight. And if you manage to write down what the professor says word for word, use quotation marks to show that.

The smartest young woman in my undergraduate class used a system of double-entry note taking. On every page of her class notebook, she used a ruler to draw a straight line right down the middle. On the right side she wrote her class notes; as exactly as possible she summarized what the professor said. On the left side and after class she wrote her own notes, what she thought, what questions she had, what she didn't agree with or didn't understand. She did this faithfully after every lecture—instead of just cramming before the final like the rest of us. She was engaging with learning every day—like a real student. And it paid off; she made straight A's and graduated with all the best prizes.

Double-entry note taking can be used when you take reading notes as well. You write down the important concept or theory on one side of your note page and your own responses and thoughts on the other. Get in the habit of using quotation marks to indicate when you are quoting word for word. Remember, who said what and who gets credit for which idea is extremely important in academic writing, as important as who owns which car in the parking lot. You wouldn't want the guy who entered with a VW to drive off with your BMW; don't drive off with the hard-earned ideas of others.

Being Philosophical

As you write privately about your reading or about your classes, you will be developing what has been called "the essayist attitude." That is, you will be engaging in musing, in thinking about what you are perceiving. Writing about what happened in class today or what you learned from the discussion or what you didn't understand or what changed your mind will help you to examine your life as a student, to become more comfortable with the philosophical approach. As you learn to adopt the essayist attitude, you will probably get better at writing the essays required in freshman English. And all the while you will be getting smart.

Writing and Studying

Some students form study groups to prepare for midterms or finals. This can be effective, depending, of course, on how good the other students in the group are. Are they really interested in learning and understanding the content and the approach of the course? Or are they just participating so that the other students in the group will do the learning for them? As a general rule, learning, like writing or exercising, is lonely. You've got to work up your own sweat.

Writing to Prepare for Exams

One way to get ready for exams all by yourself is—you guessed it—to *write*. Use the third part of your notebook for study notes. You might start your review by jotting down individual words—all of the special words or terms used in the course, such as *manifest destiny* or *mutual assured destruction* or *epanalepsis* and *anadiplosis*. Write down all of the new words that this course has taught you. Then write a paragraph about each one; define the term, explain it to your mom, give some examples. By doing this you are preparing yourself for that favorite exam mode of so many instructors, the "ident." "Briefly but adequately identify any ten of the following," they are fond of asking. If you are studying for a literature course, write down all of your (or the professor's) favorite lines or phrases from the works you have read. "Call me Ishmael." "Do I dare to eat a peach?" "Let me not to the marriage of true minds admit impediment." (If you can't remember any such lines, go back to your books.)

After you have warmed up on some terms or lines, try writing a summary of the entire course for that pleasant but ignorant person you wrote to before. Explain what this course was really about, why it matters, what the essence is, why everyone should take it. Next, try to "psych" the prof. What questions are obviously and inevitably going to be on the exam? What questions did the professor say would appear on the test? Write them down. Then write the answers.

Writing to Organize

Write the answers? "That's going too far. I'll do that in the exam but not now," most students say. I certainly did. Actually writing the answer to a tough essay exam question is not a lot of fun, just too grim a way to study.

Probably your creativity and spontaneity would suffer if you wrote the answer down ahead of time; then your answer would sound boring, you say. Okay. But at least get in the habit of *outlining* the answers to some of the exam questions you have imagined. Then you will be ready to outline the answers during the exam before you start to write.

Outline? Do I have to? Surely the outline ranks as the most despised study tool and least-liked preparation for writing ever required of innocent students by sadistic teachers. (Anyone who likes outlines or outlining is probably not to be trusted.) For the moment, I will talk about planning instead of outlining, but whatever the word, the issue is organization. And organization or structure is the essential transformation that must occur between the writing you do for your own learning and the writing you do to show that you have learned. Your examination answers will be read and judged by someone else—a reader who is an expert—and that is public writing.

From Private to Public Writing

Public writing terrifies many students. Some are so fearful of having to write that they will actually refuse to sign up for courses that require papers. Actually, they should refuse to take courses that don't require papers because how professors assign and respond to your writing reveals how much they care about *your* learning, as opposed to their own. We all know that we learn more about a subject by having to write about it than by any other way. So not being asked to write means that you are being shortchanged as a student.

Your Composing Process

Why do so many students hate writing with such passion? Usually because they don't have a composing process that works for them; usually they don't even know what a composing process is. The *composing process* simply means the stages a writer goes through to achieve writing that is ready for a reader. Private writing can just flow, following the stream of your thoughts, wandering out of the main channel, stopping and starting. But public writing, because it must provide readers with a structure, doesn't happen so easily. For most of us, public writing is hard work indeed, perhaps one of the most complex mental tasks that we attempt. The history of literature shows that writing can drive you crazy or to drink or gambling or spouse abuse. (Shakespeare quit after he made some money.)

But it needn't drive you crazy, if you are aware of the stages you have to go through as a writer to achieve successful writing. The more conscious you become about your own composing process, the more efficient and self-confident and effective you will become as a writer. You might even start to enjoy writing if you don't already. The history of literature also shows that writing can be the ultimate adventure, the path to glory. (Few have been revered as much as Shakespeare.)

So far, in explaining and arguing for private writing, I have been concentrating on the first stage of the composing process, *invention*. During the invention stage (some call it prewriting), writers concentrate on thinking, on questioning and connecting and generating and gathering and analyzing and evaluating. Of course, private writing also means drafting as words and sentences do appear on the page, but the drafting is fast and free and involves little concern for form. When you engage in public writing, however, the drafting must yield more structured discourse; somewhere along the way, either on paper or in your head, planning must occur. Planning and drafting—in some combination that is probably yours alone—you get your pages filled or your file lengthened, and at last you have a first draft.

However, writers seldom achieve their best efforts in first drafts. Amateurs often think they do (especially at two in the morning); professionals know they don't. So the next stage of the composing process is called revision. When you revise, you rewrite your first draft—sometimes changing almost everything—so that the reader can get your message with ease and enlightenment and even delight. Professional writers of both fiction and nonfiction insist that the energy and pain and effort devoted to revising—not the rare flashes of inspiration—make up the heart of writing. Or, as one of my colleagues puts it, "If you are lucky, you are born with some talent, and then you work very, very hard." Just like Jack Nicklaus.

The final stage of the composing process is editing, or editing and proofreading. Here you make smaller changes than when you are revising, mostly changes at the level of the sentence or the word. And here—if you really want an A—you correct the errors. All of them. Professional golfers, the saying goes, "drive for show and putt for dough." Editing and proofreading are like putting. Even with the insights of a genius, you can come across as an illiterate if you use *their* when you mean *there* or spell *summary* with an *e*.

Planning for Public Writing

Moving from private to public writing simply means adding more stages to your composing process. And to repeat, the first and most essential addition (the difference between C−'s, and B+'s) is structure. If you have been studying all along—and studying, I hope you now agree, means reading *and* writing—then you have been practicing invention all along. When exam time comes or when the paper assignment is given, you have available an abundance of content. The time has come for form. A successful piece of public writing must have a big plan, an organizational principle, a structure so clear that a reader could outline it if some tedious teacher insisted.

Focusing on Structure

The obvious technique for success in public writing—but one that many students never figure out—is to look for the tip-offs to an appropriate overall structure in the question or the assignment itself. Are you being asked to *compare* or to *explain* the effects or to *summarize* the theory or to *relate* what happened or to *interpret?* You might be asked to *describe* (this is how something looks) or to *analyze* (these are the parts of) or to *argue.* Focus on the structure words in the question or the assignment and do what they tell you, not something else. The next step is to write a plan (an outline) that corresponds to the task. In an essay exam, you will need to write the plan quickly, but a plan here is very important to help you focus on the question asked instead of drifting; it will also help you budget your time. For a term paper or a critical analysis, you might spend a major portion of your time on the plan. Figuring out what you are going to say and how you are going to say it takes trial and error and perspiration.

Some writers, however, cannot or will not or do not plan before they write. They just plunge in writing sentences—the same way you do in private writing. Their writing grows from the top. This is not my favored mode—because if my idea or plan or project fails, and sometimes it does, I would rather throw away a plan—a page with some words and arrows and circles on it, than throw away a draft, pages of hard-won sentences. But writers who do not plan, who write by drafting—and some excellent writers proceed this way—tell me that, no, they don't really throw away sentences; it only looks that way for a while. Eventually, everything gets used, but maybe in a different place.

Whether you plan before you write or plan while you write doesn't matter in the long run if you are accomplishing effective writing. What does matter—and matter a great deal—is that the writing you hand in goes through the transformation from private to public and has a clear structure apparent to readers. Maybe you are not quite sure about what the word *structure* really means when applied to writing. Don't be alarmed; you're not alone, because structure is hard to explain. When applied to writing, structure means the conceptual skeleton that holds the writing together.

In carefully structured discourse, each sentence relates to the main idea of the paragraph, each paragraph relates to the idea of that section, each section relates to the plan of the whole. Think of structure as a hierarchical or pyramidal diagram, like the flowchart of a corporation or the chain of command in the military. Readers expect writing to be structured hierarchically. They also expect—and insist upon—writing that moves up and down the different levels on the pyramid, from abstract to concrete, from general to specific. Readers find such writing both readable and convincing. When writing stays all at the same level, readers fall asleep.

In fact, levels of generality is what our unpopular friend the outline is all about. An outline is a diagram that shows hierarchical structure; some points are general or abstract, those that follow the I's, II's, III's and IV's. They are supported or proved by less general or more specific statements marked A, B, C, and so on. These in turn are supported by even more specific information under the 1's, 2's, 3's, and even further down the abstraction ladder are the little a's, b's, and c's, the specifics or the details that make writing believable and colorful and memorable. So stop hating the outline; instead try to keep its structure in your mind's eye as you write, a way of remembering that good writing moves between the abstract and the concrete, between the general and the specific, between making assertions and proving them.

—III—III—III—
Drafting

Drafting, that is, writing it down, may be the stage in the composing process that holds the greatest terror. Those of us who plan before we write, do so not because we are virtuous but because planning makes us feel braver as we face the blank page or the empty screen. Panic, it seems, is part of the process for most writers, and like the fear you feel at the top of the ski run or on the high dive or at center stage, you have to learn to deal with it. Many would-be writers intensify their own panic to the level of paralysis because they try to do two tasks at once, two tasks that can only be achieved separately. They try to get it down and get it right at the same time. Thus, every thought the right brain sends out, the left brain leaps on and says, "That's stupid! You dummy! Nobody would want to read that!" The writer writes a word, then crosses it out, then writes a sentence and crumples the page. It's called *writing block*. The internal editor functions as a nagging and judgmental critic at the wrong time, too soon. That editor must be put to sleep, that voice told to be quiet for a while. With great firmness, say to your negative critic, "Shut up! I don't have to listen to you. I will call on you later. Right now I need to take some risks, and I am too inspired to worry about your misplaced concerns."

As John McPhee, a professional writer of great talent, says, "You've got to put bad words down. And then massage them." He means his first draft and your first draft will probably be terrible. That's okay. Get something written, something on paper; you can massage it later. Perfectionism applied too early in the process prevents many talented people with intelligent things to say from ever becoming capable or competent writers. Indeed, an important reason for engaging in private writing is that writing for yourself, fast and furiously, will make you feel easier about drafting. You will be unembarrassed to try outlandish ideas on paper; you will be comfortable letting sloppy words hang out. Sloppy words can always be tidied up, revised, and edited. Blank pages can't be turned into anything.

—|||—|||—|||—

Revising and Editing

After you have completed the first sloppy draft, it's time to undope your editor. Try to read what you have written as a reader, rather than as the writer. Of course, if you are writing within the time constraints of an examination, you must speed up the entire composing process. You can't revise your answer; there isn't time. (That's why the plan matters so much.) The best you can do is to proofread carefully, add a few words, correct the obvious errors, and turn it in. But essay exams are only one kind of public writing—a special, hurried kind that requires you to turn in first drafts. Many college students don't seem to understand this and turn in first drafts as final versions for all of their writing assignments. They tend to get C's— or worse.

If you want to get A's on your papers, you have to hand in final versions, not first drafts. That means putting your sloppy draft through the process of revision, making it better, clearer, more carefully organized, more tightly packed, more interesting and lively. That means making your writing work for a reader, a reader who is in fact an expert, your professor. Some professors will offer to read a draft of your paper and offer suggestions before the final version to be graded is due. Never, never fail to take them up on this. The criticisms and suggestions they offer are the blueprints for your A.

Revising, getting the big plan right, and *editing,* tinkering with the words and sentences to make them do what you want them to do, are essential parts of the writing process. Professional writers invest extraordinary amounts of time and energy in revising and editing. So, as an amateur, you should certainly invest some. Actually, revising can be rewarding; turning a fairly average paper into a highly respectable one feels good—though it usually feels best after you have finished. And editing, changing gangly sentences into powerful ones and searching for just the right word, offers pleasures, too.

Some writers give their first drafts to someone else to read, an editor. The truth is, everybody needs an editor. Professional writers have professional editors. Finding a good editor for your own writing, though, can be tricky. Your roommate or your boyfriend or your mom may like you so much that they are too kind. You need an editor who reads well and who has the courage to say to you—in a kindly way and only when asked—"No, I can't follow your argument. No, it doesn't make sense." You want an editor who doesn't gush or flatter, but who can be an honest critic, someone who wants you to succeed but who knows clarity from chaos, good writing from bad. Of course *you* are this kind of person—when you are sane. But most writers, when they have just finished the terrible struggle with a first or second draft are not sane, not sane enough, that is, to criticize their own work.

Most of us, after finishing a first draft, often even after finishing a final draft, have little ability to judge our own writing with any consistency. We tend to overestimate or underestimate its worth. We give the piece an F if we are pessimists or an A if we are optimists, and lifelong optimists may turn into gloomy pessimists late at night. Writing, after all, is one of the most complex mental tasks we try. Not surprisingly, we aren't always good at judging our own creations. The friendly editor who didn't experience the pain or the pleasure you invested in your draft may be a better judge than you are.

When you think your draft is as good as it can get in the time available, summon up the English teacher editor from your subconscious. Let this purist worry about punctuation and spelling. If you are writing at a word processor—and you certainly should be—run the spelling check to catch the typos. (Not being able to type in the late twentieth century means you can't use a computer; that's like not being able to drive. Quick, take a typing course!)

When at last you hand in your great work, you probably will feel it still isn't perfect. That's okay. Nothing ever is for long. Even the person who wins the Nobel Prize for getting something right only got that something right for a particular time; someone doodling on a pad or engaging in private writing will come up with a new theory that will make the old one look silly. That's the way knowledge is—always changing. So, even if your draft is perfect, it isn't perfect. The point is not the *product* anyway, but the *process*. What has this piece of writing done for you? How have you changed because you wrote it? As Robert Pirsig concluded in his novel about maintaining a motorcycle, "The real motorcycle is a cycle called yourself."

Writing, private or public, is finally not about grade points. Writing is really about you, about the richness of your life lived in language, about the fullness of your participation in your community and in your culture, about the effectiveness of your efforts to achieve change. The person attuned to the infinite creativity that language allows us leads a richer life. And naturally, that person has a better love life, too. So can you.

9 The Liberal Arts and Critical Thinking: Building Blocks of the Educated Person

H. Thorne Compton

ASSOCIATE DEAN
COLLEGE OF HUMANITIES AND SOCIAL SCIENCES
UNIVERSITY OF SOUTH CAROLINA

When I started college I had a clear idea of what I wanted to be, but little idea of what I wanted to study. I wanted to be a journalist, and I imagined that I would take a lot of courses that would teach me to write exciting, perceptive, investigative essays for newspapers, and that would be my college education. Instead, after my first advisement session I found myself taking required courses in European history, logic, French, biology, and English—nothing that seemed even distantly related to what I wanted to do. I was frustrated, even angry, but when I confronted my advisor about this, he had no sympathy. "How are you going to be a writer," he said, "when you don't know anything to write about?" When I wanted to argue about the relevance of French and biology, he told me to see him at the end of the year, if I still felt they were irrelevant. He ended the session by telling me, "If you want to write about insects, you study insects; if you want to write about human beings, you study the human species. That's what the liberal arts are about."

That was the first time I had really paid attention to the phrase "liberal arts," and I had no idea what it meant. By the end of the year, I wasn't so sure what was "irrelevant" anymore, and the more I explored in the liberal arts, the less sure I became of who I was and what I wanted.

While I was learning what to think about, I was also learning how to think in a very different way. Some of my teachers seemed to challenge everything I had been taught, and in other classes I found it impossible to take notes—the whole class was spent in a dialogue and the teacher never told us which answers were the right ones. It took a while to adjust and almost three years to see the relationship between what I was learning and how I was learning to think about it.

While I eventually changed my career goal, I never gave up needing to understand the human species. Today, as a teacher of literature and academic advisor and administrator, I spend a lot of time talking to students about this important part of their college education. The liberal arts are for some students a part of their professional training; for others they are the whole focus of their education. For all students the liberal arts are the firm foundation for a lifetime of learning.

━Ⅲ━━Ⅲ━━Ⅲ━

Thinking about the Liberal Arts

Most of us have heard the phrase "liberal arts college," or we may have known someone who majored in "the liberal arts." In many colleges and universities there is a set of "liberal arts requirements" that all students must complete. What are these liberal arts? Where do they come from, why are they "liberal," and why are they considered so important in a time of increasing complexity and specialization?

The "liberal" in "liberal arts" has nothing to do with politics—it comes from a Latin root word *liber*, which means to free (*liberate* comes from the same root). An art (from the Latin root *ars*) is a skill, an ability to do something. The liberal arts are those *skills or abilities or understandings that set us free*. We are liberated by understanding ourselves, and to do that we must understand our culture and our environment. The liberal arts, then, are those studies that give us an understanding of ourselves, our culture, and our environment. These subjects focus on, among other things, how human beings think, behave, and express themselves within their cultures and their planetary environment.

This focus is certainly not a new trend in higher education. The liberal arts college is the ancestor of all modern colleges, universities, and professional training programs. It is only in recent times that training in law, medicine, engineering, and even business administration has been separated from a broad liberal arts environment. The liberal arts core is still central to a college or university education. As we shall see, the part of our education that gives us an understanding of ourselves, our culture, and the physical environment provides the context for all other kinds of education.

The liberal arts program is normally organized around several groups of disciplines that integrate knowledge from a variety of perspectives. These usually include:

1. *The Arts*, which study human thought and behavior through the creative works of people from the earliest appearance of humans until today. Subject areas include music, theater, art, and dance.

2. *The Humanities*, which study human experience through the written record of what people have thought, felt, or experienced in a variety of

cultures. Subject areas include languages and literatures, philosophy, history, and religion.

3. *The Social Sciences*, which study human beings and their behavior from a variety of perspectives: as individuals (psychology), groups (sociology), within cultures (anthropology), or as economic or political entities (economics and political science).

4. *Quantitative Studies*, which create systems for describing the physical world or human behavior in abstract or mathematical terms. Includes mathematics, statistics, and computer science.

5. *The Sciences*, which study the physical world and the symbolic relationships within it: chemistry, biology, and physics, for example.

While colleges and universities are normally broken up into subject departments, such as the Department of History, or the English Department, these subjects are actually all closely interrelated. Psychology is the study of human behavior, but to study human behavior, we must understand and appreciate the creations of the human mind—such as literature, the visual arts, music, or drama—that are the most significant examples of our inner behavior. We must also understand something about human biology, about the social systems regulating human behavior and how those systems evolved. In other words, to understand human behavior, we must understand culture, the human environment, and the scientific and social forces affecting humans. A liberal arts program implies study that integrates a wide variety of disciplines.

Why Is This Integration of Subjects Important?

The integrated nature of the liberal arts is, of course, a result of the enormous complexity of studying the human species. To understand literature it is as essential to know something of astronomy and theology as it is to know psychology and literary theory. Historical events are often as influenced by scientific phenomena as by political conspiracy. The medieval outbreaks of bubonic plague killed thousands of people, radically changed the population centers of Europe, destroyed the power of some nations to make war, and inflicted psychological scars on entire national cultures. As a result, one might argue that the flea (which carried the disease) was a more significant factor in European history than any royal dynasty. By focusing on the integration of all of these studies, we can begin to get an understanding of the complex variety of things relating to us.

Because so much of what we learn in any one field depends on a broad understanding of the human context of that field, most schools require a core of liberal arts courses during the freshman and sophomore years. This core, or foundation, transmits certain essential communication, thinking, and research skills that are the tools for learning in these areas.

Even the so-called professional degree programs, such as business administration, journalism, engineering, and nursing, often require a broad liberal arts background. These professionals ultimately have to live in our culture with other people. They have to communicate effectively and be able to respond to changes in their environment. For these reasons, the professional schools themselves have started to demand more and more from the liberal arts component of their degrees.

━Ⅲ━Ⅲ━Ⅲ━
Thinking in College

One of the difficult adjustments for some students when they come to college is that college teachers seem to have far different expectations than high school teachers have. One of my students put it this way: "In high school, when the teacher asked you a question, he knew the answer and wanted to see if you knew it, too. In college, they ask you questions that *no one* knows the answer to, just to see what you will say." Although that may be a slight exaggeration, it is essentially true. In our earlier education, in elementary and high school, we were building a knowledge base. We needed to learn facts and concepts and their applications. To make sure we were learning the "facts," we were most often tested on what we *knew*. Unfortunately this process also taught us that there was a "right" and a "wrong" answer, that being wrong was bad, and thus when in doubt about an answer, we learned that it was best just to *keep quiet*.

In college, professors assume that you have the fundamental knowledge base, the tools for learning, and while you still have a lot of facts left to learn, the emphasis is on *using* the knowledge as a foundation for new ideas and concepts. That's why teachers do ask questions "no one knows the answer to"—they are more interested in students learning the process of generating new ideas than in rehashing old ideas.

The Courage to Think

The problem for many freshmen is that they have been trained not to be "wrong," and they are afraid to take risks in thinking and learning. The psychologist and philosopher Rollo May tells us in his book *The Courage to Create* that creating anything new implies risk and destruction. Just as a bird must painfully tear its way out of the egg, destroy what has been its security and protection, and emerge completely vulnerable in order to grow and finally to fly, so we must be willing to risk and even to give up our secure womb of ideas and self-concepts in order to grow and learn. That can be frightening, especially in a situation as filled with pressures as college is.

We can combat these fears by doing two things in our thinking process: We must acknowledge what we do know and learn to use it, and we must learn to analyze and think critically.

Suppose for a moment that you have been trapped in a nuclear power plant that is in the midst of a fuel meltdown. Everyone else has evacuated the plant, trying to escape from the inevitable catastrophe. You stumble into the control room and approach the control panel, desperate to do anything to save your own life and the lives of many thousands in the area. You know absolutely nothing about nuclear power or the functioning of this plant, but you know you have to do *something*. On the control panel are two switches and two dials. The switches are labeled "Containment Grid" and the dials are labeled "Temp. Stress System." One of the switches is up, the other is down. One of the dials is turned all the way to the right, the other all the way to the left. What do you do?

Before you panic, stop and think about what you *do* know. You may know nothing about nuclear power, but you do know some simple things that may help. You know, for instance, that in your experience switches are normally *on* when they are up and *off* when they are down. This tells you that on the containment grid (whatever that is!) something is turned off that perhaps should be turned on (or vice versa). Dials are normally on when turned to the right, and off when turned to the left. Again, something is off that perhaps should be turned on. You might decide to turn all of the switches on or turn all of them off. Or you might decide that if what is happening now is bad, maybe if you reversed the switches something good would happen. Suddenly, you have a lot of options. You might proceed from this point (if you have time) and try to figure out what the labels on the switches and dials might mean. Of course, none of this may work, but since you *have to do something*, you have started a course of rational action based on what you know. The key is acknowledging what you do know and letting yourself think.

Thinking in Classes

You already know that different situations require you to speak or dress or behave differently. Similarly, different disciplines require you to think and reason differently. What is common to all subjects is the *dialectical process*. This simply means that when two different ideas come together, a new idea is produced from the interaction of the two. You should be familiar with this process because it is really a metaphor for a basic way in which things behave in nature. When one idea, the *thesis*, meets another idea, the *antithesis*, a third idea, a *synthesis*, is produced. The synthesis may be a combination of the thesis and the antithesis (a kind of compromise), or it may be something completely different, but it would not exist except through the interaction of the thesis and antithesis.

Within the processes of thinking are some strategies for effective reasoning. These help us reach valid conclusions through the use of observable facts or information. The two most familiar strategies are deductive and inductive reasoning.

—⫿—⫿—⫿—
Deductive and Inductive Reasoning

Remember how Sherlock Holmes amazed Dr. Watson and his clients by using a variety of small, seemingly unrelated facts to reach a general conclusion? For instance, when he met Dr. Watson, Holmes looked him over and immediately guessed that Watson was recently returned from Afghanistan. He later told Watson that he was able to guess this by noting details about Watson indicating that he was a military doctor, recently wounded in an eastern country. Given these facts, Afghanistan was the only country that seemed reasonable. Holmes reached these conclusions through "the science of deduction," which we call *deductive reasoning*. When we reason deductively, we take a number of isolated facts and generalize a large conclusion from them. Most of us do this all the time without really thinking about it.

Inductive reasoning works the other way around. We have a large conclusion, and from the conclusion we reason some of the individual facts that produced this conclusion.

Different strategies of reasoning are generally appropriate in different situations. For instance, in our history courses we often find ourselves using the inductive strategy. Historians often know the final result of a dispute, but little about what led up to the result. Reasoning backward, or inductively, tells them where to look for information. Some of our science courses, on the other hand, require us to reason from a number of isolated phenomena and construct an explanation or a theory that fits all of the facts. This is deductive reasoning.

This distinction is important, because if we allow ourselves to think, and to use these strategies, we can sometimes achieve beyond what we "know." Let's say a pop quiz in history asks you to comment on the importance of labor unions in the United States from 1900 through 1950. You somehow missed that portion of your text, but instead of panicking, you react as you did in the nuclear plant, and start reviewing what you do know. You know that, for a long time, strong laws have governed labor conditions in the United States. You know that we have health and safety regulations, child labor laws, and minimum wage requirements, most of which have come into being during the twentieth century. From your political science class you know that in modern American politics most laws have resulted from strong constituent demand. You know from your economics course that the average wage of industrial workers went up sharply and steadily in the first four decades of this century. You reason that since most legislation is the result of constituent demand, and since employers seldom raise wages except in response to economic pressure, it is reasonable to assume that somehow workers were able to pressure their government and employers for reforms. The rise of labor unions into an important political and economic force in the twentieth century seems to be a reasonable explanation.

—ııı——ııı——ııı—
Analysis and Critical Thinking

These strategies are a part of a thinking process called *analysis*. Analysis, as a scientific term, means to separate a chemical or compound into its constituent parts and to study the individual parts and how they form the whole. The term means the same thing when we apply it to thinking. When we analyze an idea, we first must understand the parts of the idea and then see how those parts interact to form the complete idea.

If someone alleges that the rise in the number of violent crimes is caused by the increase in violence in TV programs, this seems like a rather simple idea with which we could either agree or disagree. When we begin to analyze the statement, however, we find that things become very complicated.

Our first step is to define our terms. Are crimes considered "violent" only when physical harm occurs, or is it enough for there to be fear of physical harm? Does destruction of property count as a crime of violence? These are important questions because, under one definition, graffiti writing might be considered a crime of violence, while armed robbery would not. What does "violence" consist of on a TV show? Does it have to involve actual physical aggression in which bodily harm takes place, or can it be psychological? Under one definition the National Basketball Association play-offs might be considered harmfully violent while Alfred Hitchcock's classic thriller *Psycho* would not be.

Our next step is to examine the ideas on which the statement is based, the *premises*, and determine whether they are true. Once we define "violent crimes," we have to find out whether these crimes have really increased. Have they actually happened more often, or are they simply more often reported? Has there actually been an increase in violence on TV, or has television just been more closely watched for such things in recent years?

After determining whether the premises are true, we now need to examine the logic of the statement itself. The statement is only logical if we realize that we must accept some hidden assumptions. The first assumption is that there is an actual causal link between what we see and what we do. The second assumption is that the same people who watched the "violent" TV shows committed the "violent" crimes. The first assumption *might* be true, but can only be proved through scientific experiment and probably the use of statistical data. Even if it can be proved true, we might argue that people who are naturally violent watch these TV programs, and thus the programs are a reflection, rather than a cause, of the crimes.

This kind of analysis, or critical thinking, is an essential tool for learning in college—no matter what field we choose to study. Sometimes what gives us trouble in thinking in our courses is not the process but that the ideas with which we are working are abstract and seem difficult. In mathematics, we try to simplify this by using symbols to represent complicated concepts and ideas. This is helpful unless we focus on the symbols and miss the ideas. If we let our learning of mathematics simply become a memorization of formulas, then we will never be able to proceed beyond the last formula we learned. In thinking about math and philosophy, remember they use symbols and models of ideas; we should focus on the ideas and concepts rather than on the models and symbols.

In the arts, students sometimes feel completely at a loss, because the process of reasoning seems totally subjective and abstract. How can a poem "mean" something beyond what the phrases in it say? How can an abstract painting mean anything at all? When we talk about an artistic experience, we are usually talking about something on the border between the objective and subjective response. We are most often talking about how we respond to a work of art, what ideas it gives us, and how it does that. In a piece of abstract art or of music, it is much more difficult to describe where the idea comes from than with a novel. Still, the process of analysis is important, even if what it tells us is more about the observer than the piece of art. If I were to ask you why you fell in love with a particular person, you could probably give me a number of "reasons," but if you tried to show by analysis why these reasons applied only to this person, you would soon find yourself giving up pure logic in favor of describing your emotions. Studying art tells us a great deal about ourselves and about that line between where we end and the world begins.

—|||—|||—|||—
Where Do We Go from Here?

While you accumulate knowledge, allow yourself to think, to actively seek to understand. The result of your college education should not be simply a data bank of useful knowledge, but an integration of knowledge and understanding that allows you to think and create independently. Your diploma does not certify that you know all you need to, but it indicates that you have the tools and the knowledge to begin to learn, to grow, and to create.

Because courses in college generally last for a term, we tend to think of what we are learning as temporary. Some courses are designed to teach basic skills that you will use in more advanced courses, but most of what you learn in college has a permanent impact on how you think and feel, on what you do and how you do it, on who you are in your life beyond college. Because liberal arts courses are broad, sometimes abstract, and may not seem immediately "useful," you may ask, "What good are those courses going to do me when I get out of college and into the *real* world?" Remember that college, too, is part of this "real" world!

The Liberal Arts Beyond College

Most jobs in our economy require that you work with people and depend on people as consumers or clients. As the president of a large bank told me, "Banking is not a money business, it's a people business." Knowing how the society works, knowing the cultural conceptions of the people with whom you work, and knowing how to communicate effectively are essentials in almost any kind of job you do.

In recent years, the high-tech occupations have become glamorous. Several years ago *Time* magazine featured the computer as its "Man of the Year." At that time it was predicted that the home computer would become as ubiquitous, and as essential, as the dishwasher. A number of huge companies, with fantastic technology and extensive market research, sank millions of dollars into the home computer market. The product was truly remarkable and was produced at a reasonable price. Yet within two years, many of the companies were either out of the home computer market or out of business entirely. The difficulty was not with the product; rather it was that attention to the human dimension had not kept up with the technological innovations. While the personal computer was a remarkable machine, it didn't do anything in the home that most people needed done or that they couldn't do more easily themselves. Most people had to decide whether buying a computer was more important than buying snow tires or getting the heater fixed—not whether it would be nice to have a computer. Many computer companies have now hired people with liberal arts backgrounds, both to figure out how to sell the product and to develop ways of using it in a way that makes it accessible and attractive to the great majority of nontechnical humans.

The World Beyond the Workplace

Just as the workplace has grown more complex and demanding, so has living and coping outside the workplace. You will be required to make an enormous number of hard decisions after you leave college. As a citizen you may be asked to vote on issues such as the siting of toxic waste disposal facilities in your community. To make a good decision (and the results of a bad decision may be catastrophic), you must synthesize a large quantity of often contradictory information presented by scientists and experts on both sides of the question. As a parent, you may have to decide whether your child should go to school with children who are infected with AIDS. Again, you have to separate real information from hysteria and decide who or what to believe. Such issues are extremely complex because they involve scientific and technical problems and because the human dimension, the political and social consequences, is significant and difficult to assess. You will have to make these decisions, and having the kind of broad education that sees the relationships among the scientific, social, political, cultural, and human dimensions gives you at least a foundation on which to base your choices.

Thinking the Unthinkable, Expressing the Inexpressible

Just as we will face difficult choices, so we will also discover much about ourselves and our lives, which we will spend a lifetime trying to understand. We will have failures and tragedies that seem overpowering and inexplicable. Putting these problems into a context, knowing that people over the centuries have endured the same tragedies and uncertainties, being able to experience these feelings through the arts, or seeing them examined by thinkers in psychology, philosophy, or theology connects us to other people, to our culture, and to our species. This removes the sense of isolation and empowers us to "take arms against a sea of troubles."

Knowing Who You Are

When we are growing up we are told again and again to "just be yourself!" Being yourself is easy; it is finding out who "yourself" is that is difficult. Each of us is descended from literally billions of humans in countless generations going back thousands of years. The singular genetic pattern that makes each of us unique was determined by a multitude of ancestors whose lives, in turn, were the product of their own genetic pattern and world. To know who "we" are, we really must understand who each of those ancestors were, what their world was like, how they lived, loved, died, and thought

Such a task is impossible, but by studying the lives, the culture, the art, the wars, and even the deaths of the civilizations that preceded us, we can begin to understand who we are. Scientists tell us that we are also a result of how we interact with the physical world, that we are composed of elements that make up all other organisms. What we do in the physical world affects all other organisms, and we are affected by anything that touches the other organisms on our fragile planet.

Finding clues to who we are requires synthesizing a universe of information about the human species. And humans have spent most of their time on earth trying to do just that. The earliest evidences of human creations, from cave paintings and primitive rock carvings to myths, have been an attempt to understand the universe and to know who we are. Literature, art, music, and drama are still centered on the same basic questions of human birth, life, death, identity, and meaning.

Studying the human species is not just an academic pursuit preparing you for a particular job. It is a continuous process of self-discovery that is essential for us all.

—ııı——ııı——ııı—
Creating a Self to Be

Most of us think that when we finish college we will find a job—a challenging and satisfying job in which we will work with interesting, creative people, a job that makes us feel that we are making a significant contribution. Although most people will find jobs and careers that bring satisfactions, a significant part of our working lives is going to be spent doing the routine, frustrating, repetitious tasks that are a part of every job. We will spend a lot of time worrying about making mortgage payments, getting teeth straightened, and generally carrying out the dull, gray responsibilities that are the stuff of adulthood. When this happens, it is important that something occupies your head besides what you *do*—that there is an aspect of yourself that is what you *are*.

You may know what a "dedicated word processor" is. It is an office machine with only one function: It processes text. You turn it on when you get to the office in the morning, work on it all day, and turn it off when you leave for the evening. All night it sits silent and impotent on your desk until you turn it on the next day. You may also know people who are like that—who seem to function only for work and have no identity or ideas outside of work. Most of us don't want to end up that way. Your college education, especially in the liberal arts, should help you develop a self that transcends your job skills and allows you to be a thoughtful, creative, and fulfilled person outside of the work environment. That's a good goal to think about and work toward while you are in college.

A friend of mine is a social worker whose undergraduate major was history. I asked her once if history was a good major for social workers; she said it was, "because it gives me something to think about when I'm going crazy." That may seem like a very limited use for your major, but it could become an important one.

You may never become a famous artist or a poet or a musician, but painting or writing or playing the piano may become an absolutely essential way for you to communicate with yourself. Even if no one ever sees your creative work, the process of self-expression is a means of growing and coming to self-understanding.

Liberating yourself from ignorance, superstition, and prejudice is the beginning of real growth. Freeing yourself from the narrow view of one culture, finding an identity that transcends a single time and place, discovering a voice to communicate the contents of your heart and mind is the process and purpose of a life of learning.

Suggested Activities

1. Choose an important historical event (World War II, American Revolution, Vietnam War) and research and discuss the culture—art, music, literature—created in response to the event. Does the artistic response give you an objective view of the event? Why? Why not?

2. We think of artists, especially poets, as being outside the "real world," yet two of America's most famous poets—William Carlos Williams and Wallace Stevens—worked in traditional professions. Williams was a physician and Stevens was a corporate lawyer and vice president of a major insurance company. Most of their professional friends did not even know they were poets. Try to find others who pursued both artistic and professional careers.

3. Discuss with professionals and businesspeople you know the importance of the liberal arts disciplines to the way they live on and off the job.

4. Choose three advertisements, examine their premises, and discuss the methods they use to persuade.

Suggested Readings

Bloom, Allan. *The Closing of the American Mind.* New York: Simon and Schuster, 1987.

Booth, Wayne C. *The Knowledge Worth Having.* Chicago: University of Chicago Press, 1967.

Jarrell, Randall. *A Sad Heart at the Supermarket.* London: Eyre and Spottiswoode, 1965.

McPeck, John E. *Critical Thinking and Education.* New York: St. Martin's Press, 1981.

Sagan, Carl. *The Dragons of Eden.* New York: Random House, 1977.

10 How Rational Thinking Affects Student Success

Foster E. Tait

ASSOCIATE PROFESSOR OF PHILOSOPHY
UNIVERSITY OF SOUTH CAROLINA

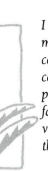

I wasn't born rational and neither were you. Being rational means being able to reason correctly. I became interested in correct reasoning when, as an undergraduate, I took several courses in logic and philosophy and discovered just what a poor reasoner I was. I saw that I'd been guilty of a number of fallacies in my thinking and in papers I'd written. Even my valedictory address to my high school seemed riddled with thoughts that didn't properly support one another.

In graduate school, I majored in philosophy and took additional courses in logic. The more I studied these subjects, the more aware I became of the problems I had in reasoning. It was then that I started applying the rules of logical reasoning to all my work. After receiving my doctorate, I went to teach at the University of South Carolina. There I found students who couldn't write any more coherently than could I as an undergraduate—and I began to emphasize the fact that we all need structure in our writing as well as in our general approach to life. I taught concepts of logic even in courses not specifically designated as logic courses. I emphasized correct reasoning as a means of establishing continuity in one's thoughts. Because of this, I now have students who write better papers and can state a thesis and defend it. I'm still learning as well and hope to improve the logical consistency of my own writing and reasoning.

What follows is a guide to avoiding commonly found errors in reasoning. Writing a proper paper, discussing ideas in class, and not just surviving, but flourishing at a college or university require that you understand the difference between correct and incorrect reasoning. Thinking, as well as writing good term papers, requires that you make the proper connections between your thoughts. You can do this only by following the rules of valid thinking and avoiding the use of common fallacies.

The Need for Correct Reasoning

Successful students generally become successful and productive people in society. This isn't surprising, since the habits and talents of successful students are similar to those required in business and professional life. If you can't understand what you read—or remember what you've read or heard— you're not likely to succeed at any demanding kind of life. The same is true of minimal mathematical skills and a knowledge of the basic principles of grammar—you can't succeed without them.

Such conditions are necessary for success in school and in society, but they're not all you need. Most teachers know students who can write crisp, nicely formed sentences, do mathematics and read well but who still can't write a logical paper or answer essay questions properly.

What's the problem? In many cases, the students can't relate one idea to another, or put ideas together to form a central theme, or thesis. In other words, they haven't learned the basic rules of reasoning—the rules that enable you to connect your thoughts in a logical fashion. The words may be appropriate and the grammar perfect, but what emerges is a lot of independent thoughts or sentences, not a cohesively written report, quiz answer, essay, or term paper.

Connecting your thoughts properly is more an art to be learned than an inherited characteristic. While the ancient Greeks defined human beings as "rational animals," they didn't believe people were rational from birth, only that they had the ability to reason correctly.

What is correct reasoning? The answer isn't easy. We'll begin our discussion by looking at examples of correct reasoning. Next we'll discuss the value of having a thesis upon which to base your comments, the importance of correct methods of argumentation, and how you learn or fail to learn through arguments. Finally, we'll examine how you can recognize and use correct reasoning so that your term papers, essays, test answers, and classroom participation improve—and your grades go up!

Reasoning: Correct and Incorrect

Most famous scientists and mathematicians probably made lucky guesses at one time or another about the truths they're credited with discovering. But the reason for their fame is that they were able to prove their discoveries to others. You may experience an important insight, but unless you can prove to others that it's new as well as valid, few people are going to accept it. Insights, no matter how profound they may be to those who experience them, must be backed by evidence. Basic college geometry, for example, is modeled on that developed twenty-three centuries ago by Euclid. He defined his terms carefully and proposed statements that were readily acceptable to the scientific community of his day. Based on these statements, Euclid was able to arrive at some very useful conclusions. Every carpenter and mechanic today recognizes that the sum of the angles of a triangle must equal two right angles and must total 180 degrees. The applied science of surveying is based in great measure on such truths.

The astronomer Edmund Halley, for whom a comet was named, observed his comet in 1682 and recorded data concerning its motion through our solar system. Based on this data, Halley concluded, in a work published in 1705, that the comet would return at approximately seventy-five-year intervals. Indeed, Halley was able to infer from his own observations, together with the work on gravitation published by the physicist-philosopher Isaac Newton, that the comet would return sometime in December 1758. Halley died in 1743, but fifteen years later, on Christmas Day 1758, the comet appeared. What a success, and what a triumph for reason! Halley's observations, coupled with Newton's theory, taken as axioms and postulates, allowed him to calculate a prediction accurate to one month in seventy-six years. Thus, the motion of comets, which had previously been considered erratic and even mysterious, was resolved to a system of laws that could predict their behavior.

—ııı—ııı—ııı—
The Logic of Correct Writing: The Thesis

The examples in the preceding section have several things in common. First, they state a thesis, which is something to be proved. (You've probably already heard your English teacher refer to "the thesis statement.") In Euclid's case, the thesis was actually a large number of statements, known in mathematics as theorems, which he was able to prove. In Halley's case, the thesis was the prediction that the comet would return at a specified time. A thesis, then, refers to something you want to prove. In any paper, the thesis is the central point—it represents what must be proved within the context of the paper. A paper without a thesis would be like a geometry with no theorems, or a work on astronomy that maintained only that a certain comet might or might not return. Such a paper would be useless. Science requires more of its practitioners, and so do teachers in any subject you can name. A paper of any merit always states a thesis. The thesis is always expressed as a statement, and it must be proved by correct, logical reasoning.

When you present a thesis and then give reasons why it should be accepted, you almost always ensure that your sentences and paragraphs, indeed your entire paper, will progress logically. To many college professors, the most poorly reasoned papers they receive are those where nothing is being argued and a simple comparison is made. If you do make comparisons between two authors, you should do so within the context of a thesis that states what you are comparing and why that point is important to an understanding of one or more works of the authors. You should then defend the thesis, which means introducing evidence to support it.

━ⅠⅠⅠ━ⅠⅠⅠ━ⅠⅠⅠ━
The Logic of Learning

You can think of a thesis as a conclusion. Reasoning works through argumentation, and each argument must have a conclusion. The conclusion, or thesis, is then defended by providing evidence in its favor. The evidence, in the form of basic statements, or premises, must be readily acceptable to your audience. If it's not, you should prove to your audience that the premises are acceptable to experts in the field. This applies to all theses: the main thesis as well as any minor theses that might exist. (These minor theses may serve as premises for the principal thesis.)

In establishing a thesis, not only should the premises used to support it be considered true but the steps you take in reasoning from the premises to the thesis must also be correct. At this point, the science (or art) of logic enters the picture, because this discipline, which stems largely from the Greek philosopher Aristotle, is concerned primarily with connecting evidence (premises) to conclusions (theses).

Aristotle presented rules for inferring conclusions from premises. When used correctly, these rules will lead you from true premises to true conclusions—not to false conclusions. Euclid and other mathematicians have used such rules for centuries. Halley, Newton, and all other recognized scientists have used some version of these rules. Indeed, calculus, which holds needless terrors for many students, is basically an application of logic and its rules to mathematics and science.

━ⅠⅠⅠ━ⅠⅠⅠ━ⅠⅠⅠ━
Learning Through Arguments

An *argument* is a process of reasoning that takes us from premises to a conclusion. An argument in this sense is certainly not an emotional "happening," where somebody gets bruised or bloodied. Newton, Copernicus, Einstein, and other famous thinkers were known for their powers of reasoning, not for their physical prowess.

So what is an argument? An argument is one or more premises together with one or more conclusions. As arguments are communicated from one person to another, they exemplify the use of reason. But not all arguments are good ones. Some are missing the proper connection between premises and conclusions, and others don't support, or lack acceptance for, their premises.

Arguments whose conclusions follow closely from their premises, and whose premises are well established, lead to increased knowledge. If we accept the premises as true, or correct, then logically correct arguments, such as those of Euclid, force us to accept the truth of the conclusions. If we accept the truth of the premises, but don't accept the conclusions, then we commit a contradiction, such as admitting that the sum of the angles of a triangle is equal to two right angles, yet not equal to 180 degrees.

The acceptance of contradictions is known as "being irrational," since we know they're false. It is inconsistent to believe something is true when we know it's false. For centuries, consistency has been considered the primary condition for being rational. Your teachers will certainly demand consistency in your essays and papers.

Let's look at an example of a correct argument, where the conclusion follows from the premises:

1. Either truth is purely subjective or it is objective in at least some sense.

2. If truth were purely subjective, it could be true that $2 + 2 = 5$, simply because someone believed it.

3. But it is not true that $2 + 2 = 5$. Consequently, it follows that:

4. Truth is not purely subjective. Thus we see from these premises, as well as from the fact that:

5. We all know that just wishing to make something true, such as wishing that there were actually a Santa Claus, is not enough to make the belief true; that:

6. Truth is objective in some sense.

In this example, the statement (6) that truth is objective in some sense is the major conclusion, or thesis, of the argument. Let's go through the reasoning process in this argument: Sentences (2) and (3) function as premises for (4), which might be termed a preliminary conclusion or a preliminary thesis. Sentence (4), together with sentences (1) and (5) provide evidence for the principal thesis (6). Note how the use of expressions such as "consequently it follows that" and "thus we see that" help show us that we have an argumentative structure—that a process of reasoning is occurring.

Such expressions, commonly known as "argument indicators," help tie sentences together so we can see a logical progression. The use of such indicators can help assure your reader or listener (or the professor grading your paper) that you are not producing a mere collection or jumble of sentences but that there is some determined meaning behind their arrangement. A long paper should normally include a number of supporting arguments for the principal conclusion. It will ordinarily also propose arguments against opposing points of view. Just remember that your arguments have to be clear and logical if they're going to support your views and discredit conflicting views.

Now let's look at an argument that is not correct because the conclusion does not follow logically from its premises. The premises represented by sentences (1) and (2) are true, but the conclusion, sentence (3), is false.

1. If Charleston were in North Carolina, then it would be in the Carolinas.

2. Charleston is not in North Carolina. Hence it follows that

3. Charleston is not in the Carolinas.

Please remember that an argument that can lead to false conclusions when its premises are true is not logically correct. Proper arguments carry the truth of premises through to the conclusion.

━ııı━ııı━ııı━
Failing to Learn Through Arguments: Some Common Fallacies

We've seen that in defending a thesis (conclusion), we need two things: (1) accurate evidence to serve as our premises and (2) correct reasoning from our premises to our conclusions. You might not agree completely with the premises, but, given those premises, the conclusions follow.

Most people—including you probably—are a little better at collecting evidence for premises than in using that evidence correctly to establish a conclusion. The reference librarian can help you find the data you'll need to put together premises. Please use this person and her or his valuable skills if you don't know where to find the information you need for a project! (See Chapter 7)

Unfortunately, libraries aren't equipped with resident Newtons or other logicians who can help you reason from your data to correct conclusions. So it might help you to enroll in one or more logic courses during your first semesters at the university or at least to have a logician look at your arguments. Most universities have people in the philosophy or mathematics departments who are trained in logic. Look for the names of these people in your catalog and arrange an appointment.

Now, let's look at some common ways that people go wrong in reasoning from premises to conclusions. These methods of incorrect reasoning have been recognized for centuries. Using any of them will never help you support your thesis.

Argument Directed to the Man: *Argumentum ad Hominem*

When you attack other people's positions, make sure it's their arguments you're attacking and not the individuals themselves. When very controversial questions, such as the legalization of abortion, are at issue, and strong emotions are involved, people often get caught up more in their arguments with the character or reputation of their opponent than with the content and meaning of the opponent's argument.

If you're arguing for a woman's right to have an abortion, and you're arguing against someone like Claire Boothe Luce, who gave many talks opposed to abortion on request and artificial means of birth control, don't say something like, "We all know where Mrs. Luce stood on these issues because she was a Roman Catholic." Such a statement has no bearing on your task of proving her wrong, but it might influence your audience, listeners, or readers, depending on their biases.

Appeal to Force: *Argumentum ad Baculum*

The famous seventeenth-century physicist and astronomer Galileo adopted the Copernican theory that the earth was not the center of either the solar system or the universe. With the aid of the telescope, which he had developed, Galileo was able to prove some of the views held by Copernicus. Copernican theory, however, contradicted centuries of church teachings, which held that everything revolved around the earth. For this reason, Galileo was condemned for heresy by the Inquisition and threatened with burning at the stake if he didn't change his position. The argument used by the Inquisition was basically: Your ideas are wrong, and you must see that this is the case or we'll kill you. Galileo did change his position, but the argument posed against his views was hardly a legitimate one. It appealed to force.

Your parents may have reasoned this way at times; they may have made you admit they were right on some issue by suggesting that unless you did this or that, you might not receive your allowance for the month or the car on Saturday night. Students use such arguments against teachers when they threaten to give them a poor evaluation. Teachers use the argument on students when they threaten to fail them for not agreeing with them.

Teachers can also use these techniques more subtly; for example, they might pick on certain students who don't agree with them. And students use this reasoning when they talk, read a newspaper, or work on an assignment for another class while the teacher is trying to lecture. This behavior is intimidating to most teachers because they want to communicate with their students, and they frequently see such behavior as a rebuff. Nothing you do can ensure a teacher's dislike more than practicing this sort of behavior. (See Chapter 5.)

Appeal to Pity: *Argumentum ad Misericordiam*

"Please, officer, don't give me a ticket because if you do I'll lose my license, and I don't deserve to lose my license because I have five little children to feed and won't be able to feed them if I can't drive my truck."

At issue here is whether or not the driver deserves to lose his or her license. None of the driver's statements offer any evidence, in any legal sense, as to why he or she shouldn't be given a ticket. The driver is making an appeal to pity. This isn't the way to reason with your instructors in your papers—and it's not a proper way of reasoning when a question of guilt is involved.

Either you did something or you didn't. If the "something" is a crime, then no matter how unfortunate your position and the circumstances involved, you either committed the crime or you didn't. Once the crime is established, some appeal to pity may be appropriate to lighten the sentence. If you can't finish an assignment on time, be honest and tell your teacher why. If you have problems in your family, state them. But don't say it's not your fault the paper is late because, poor you, this and that has happened. Instructors may get together and discover that the same student has had a maternal grandmother die two or three times in the last year. Admit fault, but also explain truthfully the circumstances that prevented completion of your assignment. Be frank and honest. Never, never say, "I don't deserve to be punished for such and such." Always try to communicate your problems to an instructor before an assignment is due. Teachers are usually understanding, and in those rare occasions when they're not, other methods of appeal may be open to you.

Appeal to Authority: *Argumentum ad Verecundiam*

An incorrect argument occurs when you hold that your position is correct and you base your claim on the authority of someone who quite possibly isn't an authority on the topic. And even if the person you cite is an authority, most people would rather learn your reasons in support of your claim rather than those of another.

Advertising abounds with *ad verecundiam* reasoning. Sports stars who are not doctors, dieticians, or nutritionists appear before us daily, urging us to eat a certain cereal for breakfast. Glamorous women who aren't mechanics tell us that a certain transmission will help our cars run better. Don't fall for this kind of advertising or this kind of argument. The expertise of most of these people is irrelevant to what you might be concerned with, be it nutrition or a better transmission.

Students frequently fall into the *ad verecundiam* trap by putting great weight on what other students say about teachers or courses or by consulting a friend about proper answers for a class assignment. The best person to consult about courses is your academic advisor. If you're having problems in a course, the best person to consult is your instructor. Please don't forget that the "stuffy" professor a friend told you to avoid might just possibly teach you more than most of your other professors.

Appeal to Popularity: *Argumentum ad Populum*

You've never seen a fat man model a bathing suit. You've never seen a woman with very heavy or very thin legs model pantyhose. Why not? The answer is easy! People want to associate with the people who tell them to buy things. So advertising looks for the "beautiful people" in a society—those who have looks, financial success, or sports fame. Studies by psychologists indicate that people generally listen more to popular people than to others. In other words, we believe more what we're told by successful and attractive people than what we're told by those who aren't so successful or attractive.

One of the worst kinds of reasoning you can follow is to imitate the commercials and base your arguments on a person's popularity. Establish your conclusions on facts, not on beauty, wealth, or fame. Students frequently choose their classes on the basis of such irrelevant things as a teacher's looks or popularity. Some teachers need to be popular; they want to be stars. They'll provide lively class sessions, but you may not learn much.

Argument from Ignorance: *Argumentum ad Ignorantiam*

A common argument takes the form: "My position is correct because it hasn't been proved incorrect." Go to a bookstore and you'll find dozens of books detailing close encounters with flying saucers and beings from outer space. Almost all of these books describe the person who has had the "close encounter" as beyond reproach in integrity and sanity. And, the description goes on, although they've had their statements questioned by the military or by unrelenting reporters and editors, these critics could not disprove the claims of the witnesses. Therefore, the events really occurred. Even in science, few things are ever proved completely false, but evidence can be discredited. Outside the realms of pure mathematics and logic, complete or demonstrative proof for the truth or falsehood of claims is seldom, if ever, possible. If you go to your instructor and argue that your claim is correct because he or she hasn't proven it false, the instructor can turn the tables on you by using the same fallacy. *Ad ignorantiam* arguments work both ways, and both ways are incorrect.

False Cause

Frequently, we think that just because one event was followed by another, the first event must have caused the second. This reasoning is the basis for many superstitions. The ancient Chinese once believed that by striking a large gong they could make the sun reappear after an eclipse. They knew nothing about eclipses, but they did know that on one such occasion the sun reappeared after a large gong had been struck. Today, we realize that the sun reappeared because eclipses are only temporary. Yet we also commit the same fallacy frequently.

You go shopping and an inconsiderate person blows smoke on you in an elevator. You become ill that evening and place the blame on the smoker in the elevator. Yet the blame might be based more properly on the deviled crab you ate at that charming little restaurant on the dock. It's difficult to establish causal relations, and some scientists maintain it can never be done. A single encounter with something isn't sufficient for assuming a causal relation.

All too often, students tend to put the blame for their failure on a teacher. Yet students often cause their own failure. If you don't read your notes after class, don't ask questions, and don't take notes while you read, chances are you won't do well in a course. Don't blame your failure on your instructor; to do so would be to commit the fallacy of false cause.

Hasty Generalization

Statisticians realize that no accurate generalization about the real world can be made on the basis of one or even a few samples. If someone selected one green marble from an urn containing 100 marbles, you wouldn't assume that the next marble would be green. After all, there are still ninety-nine marbles in the urn, and you know virtually nothing about the colors of those marbles. Given fifty draws from the urn, however, each of which produced a green marble after the urn had been shaken thoroughly, you would be much more willing to conclude that the next marble drawn would be green—a fairly large series of random samples has produced the same results.

So please, don't jump into hasty generalizations on your papers. And don't assume that just because one course you took in sociology or biology was boring, all courses in those subjects will be boring. Don't assume that just because you did poorly in one course in a particular subject, you'll do poorly in others. Frequently, the least interesting and, in some respects, most difficult course in a subject is the introductory one.

Correct Reasoning and How to Accomplish It

We've examined examples of correct and incorrect reasoning. What distinguishes them? Correct reasoning won't lead you from correct evidence (premises) to false conclusions. Correct, or valid, reasoning preserves the truth of your premises in the inferences made from them. Incorrect reasoning, as displayed in the fallacies we've just examined, is a haphazard affair that frequently will lead you to infer conclusions that are false and irrelevant to your premises. A thesis can't be defended by fallacious reasoning, and a paper that uses such reasoning can't display the proper logical progression and connection between its ideas. To test your reasoning, ask this of your arguments: If the conclusion inferred from my premises is false, isn't it likely that one or more of my premises is also false? If you're convinced the answer is yes, you probably have a proper argument. If your answer is no, try another argument, for the chances are you've committed a fallacy in your reasoning.

In writing a paper, always state the thesis representing your principal argument as early as possible. Provide evidence for your thesis and relate the evidence to the thesis by means of correct arguments. If there might be any doubt about the evidence for your final conclusion, you must provide arguments to establish the truth of that evidence. Be sure of the reliability of any source you use for your evidence, thus avoiding the fallacy of *argumentum ad verecundiam*.

Above all, never forget that correct reasoning, the ability to move from premise to a logical conclusion, is a key factor for success in college and in life.

Suggested Activities

1. Select a topic that interests you. Such a topic might deal with busing to achieve racial equality, a woman's right to abortion, or the reasons,

moral or practical, for imposing the death penalty. State your thesis (basic position to be defended). Find evidence for your thesis and argue for it from your evidence. Try your arguments on some of your friends and ask a teacher to look at them. Avoid using fallacies!

2. Consult a text in logic, such as Irving Copi's *Introduction to Logic,* 6th ed. (New York: Macmillan, 1982). Examine what the author describes as correct and incorrect forms of reasoning. Look carefully at Copi's discussions of uses of language and fallacies of reasoning.

3. Identify the name of the fallacy or fallacies in the following examples. (Examples of all of these fallacies appear in this chapter.)

    a. I do not deserve a D on this paper because it will mean that I will not make a grade higher than C in the course. If I do not make at least a B, I will lose my scholarship and will not be able to continue in school.

    b. I know that I deserve a higher grade than I received on my history paper. One of my best friends also took the course and said that my paper deserved an A.

    c. One just cannot receive a good grade in a course taught by a graduate student. This must be true since I just received my third C in a course taught by a graduate student.

    d. I should learn a lot from this course because the teacher is very attractive and she helped to write the book we are using.

    e. I failed my English course simply because my professor was a boring person who seemed to care more about literature than teaching students.

    f. I know that I am a better student than my grades indicate. The teachers who have given me poor grades have never proved, at least to my satisfaction, that there was anything wrong with my work.

    g. Why bother to take a course in the psychology of learning? After all, the professor who teaches the course is not even a citizen of the United States. Who knows, he might not even be a Christian! If he is neither an American nor a Christian, I doubt there is much he could teach me.

    h. I think my professor will be a little more understanding when it comes to grading my papers and tests. I explained to her at considerable length that my father, who is on the board of trustees at this university, takes a dim view of teachers who criticize students when the teacher herself has yet to receive tenure.

11 Choosing a Major, Planning a Career

Linda B. Salane

DIRECTOR, UNIVERSITY CAREER CENTER
UNIVERSITY OF SOUTH CAROLINA

Barbara G. Alley

PRESIDENT, EFFECTIVE SYSTEMS, INC.

Over the years Barbara and I have done a lot of things, held many different jobs, and seen our goals change. When I was young, I always wanted to be an actress or a dancer— something glamorous and exciting. No one talked to me about career planning or helped me explore my dreams, my skills, my potential. I had to figure it out for myself. What was I interested in? People and why they behave as they do. What was I good at doing? Making presentations and really listening to people. I'm a crusader—I believe in all the issues concerned with equality and quality of life: civil rights, feminism, consumerism. At the same time, I valued the home, family, and community and wanted roots. I wanted to change the world to reflect my values, and so I held many jobs to this end: social worker, residence hall director, women's center director. And through all this, I grew to appreciate my strengths and to understand that many jobs would meet my interests, values, and skills. Finally, I decided to help others learn this, to help others explore their career potentials.

Barbara has been working since she was thirteen years old. She began teaching dancing classes and moved on to modeling for local groups. Eventually, though, she decided to go to college and major in elementary education. She chose this field because she knew she had the skills, liked children, and would be able to get a job—lots of teaching jobs were available in the late fifties. Besides, it was "normal" then for a woman to be a teacher, and this was important to her since she'd always been criticized for being different. Barbara has learned over the years, though, that life is too short to spend your time doing things you're not interested in and don't enjoy. She became a teacher and loved it, but gradually her interests changed—and she followed them: full-time mother and homemaker, real estate agent, organizational development consultant, and administrator in higher education.

We've both achieved our individual dreams and find our lives filled with excitement, meaning, and creativity. A young friend of Barbara's, Josh, recently summed it all up: "Mommy," he said, "when I grow up I want to be just Josh." We believe the career-planning process can enable you to identify career fields that will give you the joy of being "just you." And we hope this chapter helps you begin to put it all together.

━Ⅲ━Ⅲ━Ⅲ━

When most people think of career planning, they think of choosing among career fields, deciding whether or not to take a job offer, or deciding whether to change employers. These are important issues, but college students face more immediate decisions. Choosing an academic major, selecting elective courses, and deciding which activities to get involved in at college are also career decisions.

There are no right or wrong choices. You'll decide what's right for you. If you make your decisions with a full understanding of your personal priorities and of the realities of the job market, your decisions can lead to an array of exciting career fields. You'll understand why you made the choices you did, and you'll realize that you can change your career direction as your priorities change. Begin to establish those priorities now, as you read this chapter.

Just as college is only the beginning of the rest of your life, so choosing a major is but the first step in planning your career. For some of you, choosing a major is a simple decision, but most of us enter college not knowing which major to select or which career we're best suited for.

If you find yourself facing such decisions right now, stop and ask yourself the following questions:

□ What kind of work do I want to do?

□ Which career fields offer opportunities for this kind of work?

□ What role will college play in my future career plans?

□ Are there specific things I can do to enhance my chances of getting a job when I graduate?

□ Do my career goals complement my life goals and work values?

Career planning involves the exploration of these questions to discover how they relate to one another, and to find the answers you'll need to make effective career choices.

Workplace and Work's Place

The reward of career planning is that it can help you find your place in the world of work. You've probably met people who tell you how much they love their jobs and even marvel that they're being paid to do something they enjoy. You've probably also met people who dislike what they do, count the days until Friday, and are always looking for another job. We might say that the latter group has a place to work while the former group has work that has a place in their total lives. Career planning can help you identify the kind of work that will fit or have a place in your life.

The career-planning process stresses the importance of knowing enough about yourself, specific career fields, and your personal values system so that you can consciously and intentionally make the decisions involved in choosing a satisfying career. This process has all the potential for helping you find work that is both interesting and uses your abilities and skills. It can also help you to examine your values (what is important to you) in relation to your work and personal life and to explore ways of meeting needs based on those values.

If your goal is to identify work that will be a vital part of your life, you need two kinds of information. First, you'll need information you can obtain from self-assessment: your personality type, interests, values, aptitudes, skills, and goals. Second, you'll need information you can obtain through career research: information that will help you determine which career fields can provide opportunities for exploring your interests, exercising your values, demonstrating your aptitudes, using your skills, and fulfilling your personal goals.

Before you actively begin the career-planning process, though, let's explore some false assumptions that may keep you from making a sensible career decision.

The Major Myth

Most college students think a matching academic major exists for each specific career field, and that it's impossible to enter most career fields unless they choose that matching major for undergraduate study. This is not true!

The relationship of college majors to career fields varies. Obviously, some career choices dictate that you choose a specific undergraduate major. If you want to be a nurse, you must major in nursing. Engineers major in engineering. Architects major in architecture. There's no other way to be certified as a nurse, engineer, or architect. However, most career fields don't require a specific major, and people with specific majors don't have to use them in ways most commonly expected. For example, if you major in nursing, history, engineering, English, or many other majors, you might nevertheless choose to become a bank manager, sales representative, career counselor, production manager, or a number of other things. Your awareness of the relationship between career fields and college majors can play a vital part in your choice of academic major, minor, and elective courses.

Going Beyond Your Major

In most cases, a college major alone is not sufficient for getting a job. The increased number of college graduates has produced more competition in the job market. To be competitive in today's market, you need the experience and competencies related to your chosen career fields. Internships, part-time jobs, and extracurricular activities can provide numerous opportunities for you to gain experience and develop the competencies required by your career choices.

Therefore, you should plan your college curriculum so that you can study what you enjoy learning about, what you can do successfully, and what will serve as groundwork for the future you want for yourself.

The most common question college students ask is, "What can I do with my major?" Career planning can help you focus on a different question: "What do I want to do?" This question leads you to explore yourself and career fields that provide opportunities for you to achieve what you want, not only from your college major but from life as well.

In attempting to answer what you want to do, you'll find that the choice of an academic major takes on new meaning. You're no longer concerned with the prescribed route of specific majors. The search becomes one of finding the best academic program for your chosen career goals. We can compare this process to mapmaking. You actually begin to chart your college career, using your career goals as the basis for decisions about your academic major, minor, elective courses, internships, vacation jobs, and extracurricular activities.

Map Reading and Mapmaking

Map reading can be appropriate if you're looking for the shortest distance between two points, or if the scenery and experiences along the way are the ones you want. Many people tend to look at academic majors as maps. They choose a major, read about what other people with the same major are doing to earn money, and, without further thought, decide to look for the same kind of job when they graduate. How many times have you heard someone say, "I'm majoring in English so I guess I'll teach"? If you question that person further, you might learn that he doesn't like anything about teaching except the subject matter. Obviously, this person began with the question "What can I do with my major?" and chose to follow someone else's map. Such behavior is typical of map readers, those who view academic majors as maps.

In contrast are the students who view the choice of an academic major as one part of a map they're making in order to reach their chosen career goals. Mapmakers know what they want to do and where they want to go, so they make decisions that will help them get there. They're ready to begin the journey.

The remainder of this chapter is designed to help you make that map for the journey to your career choice.

—ııı—ııı—ııı—

Career Planning and You

Before you begin a journey—whether to the beach for spring break, or home for the weekend—you quickly assess what you have and what you'll need to make the trip a good one. You automatically determine whether there's enough gas in the car, where and when to meet your ride, what clothes to take, and so on. As you do this, you automatically begin to set priorities. You may have a closet full of clothes you could take, but you pack only what you have room for.

The same processes of assessment and decision making are the major components of career planning. Instead of considering factors such as gasoline, distance, money, and weather, though, you evaluate important factors about yourself: your interests, skills, aptitudes, personality characteristics, life goals, and work values.

You are a unique and complex individual. You bring to college a maze of different characteristics forged by your previous experiences. You have developed and will continue to refine a picture of who you are—your self-image. Some people have a very definite and complete self-image by the time they enter college, but most students are in the process of defining (or perhaps redefining) themselves. The complexity of all these factors makes the assessment a difficult task. Often, students see themselves as puzzles.

To begin understanding this puzzle, consider each factor separately and then consider the impact each has on the others. Let's begin.

Interests

Interests develop from your previous experiences and from assumptions you formed in the context of the environment in which you have lived. For example, you may be interested in writing for the college newspaper because you did it in high school and loved it or because you'd like to try it even though you've never done it before.

Throughout your lifetime, your interests will develop and change. Involvement may lead you to drop old interests and add new ones. It's not unusual for a student to enter Psychology 101 with a great interest in psychology and realize halfway through the course that psychology is not what he or she imagined.

How do you identify what you're interested in? First, you can take many standardized personality inventories or tests through the counseling services at your school. You can also help identify your interests by doing the following:

1. Read through your college catalog and check each course that sounds interesting to you. Ask yourself why they sound interesting.

2. Make a list of all the classes, activities, and clubs you enjoyed in high school. Ask yourself why you enjoyed these things.

Skills

Skills are things you do well. To claim something as a skill, you must have proof that you do it well. You can't claim to be a good writer, for example, unless you write well. You can measure your current level of skill by your past performance.

Note the reference to "current level of skill." Skills, like interests, can be developed. You may be a poor writer now, and you may choose to work on that skill. By using resources available to you at college and by practicing, you can become a better writer.

Use the list in Figure 11–1 to help you determine your best skills. First, check the skills you think you presently have. Then, identify the five skills you are most confident about, those about which you could say to anyone: "I am good at this." Circle those five skills. Finally, place an X next to the skills you would like to develop while you are in college.

Aptitudes

Aptitudes are inherent strengths. They may be part of your biological heritage, or they may have emerged from your early learning environment. Aptitudes are the foundation for skill development. High aptitudes generally produce the potential for higher skill levels. In discussing skills, we said that through practice and the use of available resources, you could improve your writing. Now we can add that if you have an aptitude for writing and couple

Figure 11-1 *Skills Checklist*

- writing
- reading
- conversing
- reporting information
- interviewing
- being creative
- making machines and mechanical things work
- applying technical knowledge
- building things
- repairing things
- operating tools
- observing
- listening
- coming up with ideas

- cooperating
- being tactful
- socializing
- making a team effort
- explaining
- helping others
- teaching
- entertaining
- public speaking
- being sensitive
- learning
- analyzing
- evaluating
- handling money
- planning
- problem solving
- scheduling

- following through
- getting results
- being neat
- keeping records
- being accurate
- asserting self
- taking risks
- negotiating
- selling
- winning
- being friendly
- motivating
- managing
- directing others
- adapting
- encouraging
- other

that aptitude with practice and the use of resources, you'll probably become a better writer than someone who doesn't have a strong writing aptitude.

Having an aptitude for something doesn't ensure success. But aptitude coupled with high motivation and hard work breeds success. At the same time, high motivation and hard work alone may not be able to compensate for low aptitude. A student may study calculus for hours and still barely make a C.

Each of us has aptitudes we can build on. It makes sense to build on your strengths. Strengths are clues to those areas where you will be most successful. Check the following aptitude areas that you believe are strong for you. Strike through those you know are weak areas. Put a question mark by those you are not sure about. Then identify your strongest aptitudes. Are they in the same family as the skills you previously checked?

- Abstract reasoning
- Verbal reasoning
- Spatial relations

- Mechanical ability
- Clerical speed
- Clerical accuracy
- Language usage

- Spelling
- Numerical ability

Personality Characteristics

What makes you different from others around you? Obviously, each of us is physically unique. But we're all psychologically unique, too. The personality characteristics you've developed through the years make you *you*, and those characteristics can't be ignored in the career-decision process. The person who is quiet, orderly, calm, and detailed probably will make a different work choice than an aggressive, outgoing, argumentative, and witty person. Many psychologists believe that working in an occupation consistent with your personality can make you feel more successful and satisfied with your work.

What ten words would you use to describe yourself? Using the list in Figure 11–2, place a checkmark next to the adjectives you think best describe you. Then ask your parents, your brother or sister, and a close friend to write down ten words they would use to describe you. How do the lists compare?

Figure 11–2 *Adjective Checklist*

___ academic	___ cool	___ honest
___ accurate	___ cooperative	___ humorous
___ active	___ courageous	___ idealistic
___ adaptable	___ curious	___ imaginative
___ adventurous	___ daring	___ independent
___ affectionate	___ deliberate	___ individualistic
___ aggressive	___ determined	___ industrious
___ alert	___ dignified	___ informal
___ ambitious	___ discreet	___ intellectual
___ artistic	___ dominant	___ intelligent
___ attractive	___ eager	___ inventive
___ bold	___ easygoing	___ kind
___ broad-minded	___ efficient	___ leisurely
___ businesslike	___ emotional	___ light-hearted
___ calm	___ energetic	___ likeable
___ capable	___ fair-minded	___ logical
___ careful	___ farsighted	___ loyal
___ cautious	___ firm	___ mature
___ charming	___ flexible	___ methodical
___ cheerful	___ forceful	___ meticulous
___ clear-thinking	___ formal	___ mild
___ competent	___ frank	___ moderate
___ competitive	___ friendly	___ modest
___ confident	___ generous	___ natural
___ conscientious	___ good-natured	___ obliging
___ conservative	___ healthy	___ open-minded
___ considerate	___ helpful	___ opportunistic

__ optimistic	__ reliable	__ tactful
__ organized	__ reserved	__ teachable
__ original	__ resourceful	__ tenacious
__ outgoing	__ responsible	__ thorough
__ painstaking	__ retiring	__ tolerant
__ patient	__ robust	__ tough
__ peaceable	__ self-confident	__ trusting
__ persevering	__ self-controlled	__ trustworthy
__ pleasant	__ sensible	__ unaffected
__ poised	__ sensitive	__ unassuming
__ polite	__ serious	__ understanding
__ practical	__ sharp-witted	__ unexcitable
__ precise	__ sincere	__ uninhibited
__ progressive	__ sociable	__ verbal
__ prudent	__ spontaneous	__ versatile
__ purposeful	__ spunky	__ warm
__ quick	__ stable	__ wholesome
__ rational	__ steady	__ wise
__ realistic	__ strong	__ witty
__ reflective	__ strong-minded	__ zany
__ relaxed	__ sympathetic	

Life Goals and Work Values

Most people want two things from life: success and satisfaction. Each of us defines these words in our own way, and one person's perception of success and satisfaction may be the opposite of another's. Defining these concepts is complex and very personal.

Two things influence our conclusions about success and happiness. One is knowing that we are achieving the life goals we've set for ourselves. The other is finding that we value what we're receiving from our work.

Figure 11–3 is a list of life goals some people have set for themselves. This list can help you begin to think about the kinds of goals you may want to establish for yourself. Read each goal and check the ones you would like to have as part of your ideal life. Next, review the goals you have checked and circle the five you want most. Finally, review your list of five goals and rank them by priority (1 as most important, 5 as least important).

The chart in Figure 11–4 includes typical work values, or reasons people say they like the work they do. This list can help you begin to think about what you want to receive from your work. Read each definition and check the items you'd like to have as part of your ideal job. Then review the items you've checked and circle the ten items you want most. Finally, review your list of ten items and put them in order of importance (1 as most important, 10 as least important).

Figure 11–3 *Life Goals Checklist**

My life goals include:

___ the love and admiration of friends.

___ a healthy life.

___ lifetime financial security.

___ a lovely home.

___ international fame.

___ freedom within my work setting.

___ a really good love relationship.

___ a satisfying religious faith.

___ recognition as the most attractive person in the world.

___ a happy family relationship.

___ complete self-confidence.

___ an understanding of the meaning of life.

___ success in my chosen profession.

___ a personal contribution to the elimination of poverty and sickness.

___ a chance to direct the destinies of a nation.

___ freedom to do what I want.

___ a satisfying and fulfilling marriage.

___ other

Figure 11–4 *Work Values Chart†*

___ *Help society:* Do something to contribute to the betterment of the world.

___ *Help others:* Be involved in helping other people in a direct way, either individually or in a small group.

___ *Public contact:* Have a lot of day-to-day contact with people.

___ *Work with others:* Have close working relationships with a group, as a result of my work activities.

___ *Competition:* Engage in activities that pit my abilities against others where there are clear win-and-lose outcomes.

___ *Make decisions:* Have the power to decide courses of action, policies, and so on.

___ *Power and authority:* Control the work activities or (partially) the destinies of other people.

___ *Influence people:* Be in a position to change the attitudes or opinions of other people.

___ *Work alone:* Do projects by myself, without any significant amount of contact with others.

---

* Adapted from Human Potential Seminar by James D. McHolland, Evanston, Illinois, 1975. Used by permission of the author.

† Figler, Howard E. *PATH: A Career Workbook for Liberal Arts Students,* Cranston, R.I.: The Carroll Press, copyright © 1979. Reprinted by permission.

___ *Knowledge:* Engage myself in the pursuit of knowledge, truth, and understanding.

___ *Intellectual status:* Be regarded as a person of high intellectual prowess or as one who is an acknowledged "expert" in a given field.

___ *Creativity (general):* Create new ideas, programs, organizational structures or anything else not following a format previously developed by others.

___ *Supervision:* Have a job in which I'm directly responsible for the work done by others.

___ *Change and variety:* Have work responsibilities that frequently change content and setting.

___ *Stability:* Have a work routine and job duties that are largely predictable and not likely to change over a long period of time.

___ *Security:* Be assured of keeping my job and a reasonable financial reward.

___ *Fast pace:* Work in circumstances where there is a high pace of activity, and work must be done rapidly.

___ *Recognition:* Be recognized for the quality of my work in some visible or public way.

___ *Excitement:* Experience a high degree of (or frequent) excitement in the course of my work.

___ *Adventure:* Have work duties that involve frequent risk taking.

___ *Profit, gain:* Have a strong likelihood of accumulating large amounts of money or other material gain.

___ *Independence:* Be able to determine the nature of my work without significant direction from others; not have to do what others tell me to.

___ *Location:* Find a place to live (town, geographical area) that affords me the opportunity to do the things I enjoy most.

___ *Time freedom:* Have work responsibilities that I can work at according to my own schedule; no specific working hours required.

This systematic assessment is a necessary first step in career planning. Otherwise, you're pulling career choices out of thin air and may run the risk of choosing poorly and being dissatisfied. Some students can easily evaluate their strengths and weaknesses. If you're one of those students, you're probably ready to begin exploring career choices.

But if you had difficulty with this section, it may help to talk with a career counselor at your school. Career counselors are trained to help you identify your strengths and order them according to what is most important to you.

—III——III——III—
What Are Your Career Choices?

The federal government lists more than 31,000 career fields. How many can you name? If you're like most college students, your list begins to get sketchy beyond thirty-five or fifty occupations. Most students admit they don't know much about occupations. Few have accurate information about typical on-the-job activities, necessary skills, occupational outlook, salary, methods of entry, or related fields—even for their most likely occupational choice. Obviously, you can't make a good choice if you don't understand what your choices are.

You certainly can't explore 31,000 career fields, either, but you can focus your research on the most appropriate careers for you. Many reference works can help you focus on these careers. Some emphasize the need to analyze your skills. The *Dictionary of Occupational Titles (DOT)*, published by the U.S. Government Bureau of Labor Statistics, is organized by the level of skill with people, with data, and with things that a career field requires of a worker. Other systems emphasize interests.

Dr. John Holland, a psychologist at Johns Hopkins University, has developed a system based on several key factors about individuals that is designed to help you identify career choices. He separates people into six general categories (see Figure 11–5), based on differences in their interests, skills, values, and personality characteristics—in short, their preferred approaches to life. His categories include:*

□ *Realistic:* Characterized by competitive/assertive behavior and by interest in activities that require motor coordination, skill, and physical strength. People oriented toward this role prefer situations involving "action solutions" rather than tasks involving verbal or interpersonal skills. They like to take a concrete approach to problem solving rather than rely on abstract theory. They tend to be interested in scientific or mechanical areas, rather than cultural and aesthetic fields.

□ *Investigative:* Describe themselves as analytical, rational, logical, problem solvers. Value intellectual stimulation and intellectual achievement. Prefer to think rather than to act, to organize and understand rather than to persuade. Usually have strong interests in physical, biological, or social sciences. Not apt to be "people oriented."

□ *Artistic:* Value self-expression and relations with others through artistic expression. They dislike structure, prefer tasks involving personal or physical skills, and are more prone to express emotion than other types

_____

* Adapted and reproduced by special permission from *The Self Directed Search Manual,* by John L. Holland, Ph.D. Copyright 1978. Published by Consulting Psychologists Press, Inc., Palo Alto, CA 94306.

Figure 11–5 *Holland's Hexagon*

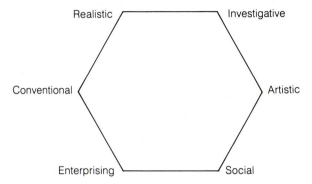

are. They are like investigative people, but are more interested in the cultural-aesthetic than the scientific.

☐ *Social:* Describe themselves as kind, caring, helpful, understanding of people. Value helping and making a contribution. Satisfy their needs in one-to-one or small group interaction using strong verbal skills in teaching, counseling, or advising. Drawn to close interpersonal relationships. Less apt to engage in intellectual or extensive physical activity. Interested in people.

☐ *Enterprising:* Describe themselves as assertive, risk taking, persuasive. Value prestige, power, and status and are more inclined than other types to pursue it. Verbally skilled. Use verbal skills to supervise, lead, direct, and persuade rather than to support or guide. Interested in people and achieving organizational goals.

☐ *Conventional:* Describe themselves as neat, orderly, detailed, persistent. Value order, structure, prestige, and status. Possess high degree of self-control. Not opposed to rules and regulations. Skilled in organizing, planning, and scheduling information. Interested in data and people.

In choosing several categories that are most like you, don't let one or two factors keep you from making a choice. Choose the ones that have the *most* true statements about you.

Holland's system organizes career fields into the same six categories. Career fields are grouped according to what a particular career field requires of a person (skills and personality characteristics most commonly associated with success in those fields) and what rewards particular career fields provide for people (interests and values most commonly associated with satisfaction). As you read the following examples, see how your career interests match the category as described by Holland.

☐ *Investigative:* urban planner, chemical engineer, bacteriologist, cattle-breeding technician, ecologist, flight engineer, genealogist, handwriting analyst, laboratory technician, marine scientist, nuclear medical technologist, obstetrician, quality control technician, sanitation scientist, TV repairer, balloon pilot, computer programmer, robotics engineer, environmentalist, physician, college professor.

- *Artistic:* architect, film editor/director, actor, cartoonist, interior decorator, fashion model, furrier, graphic communications specialist, jewelry designer, journalist, medical illustrator, editor, orchestra leader, public relations specialist, sculptor, telecommunications coordinator, media specialist, librarian, reporter.

- *Social:* nurse, teacher, caterer, social worker, genetic counselor, home economist, job analyst, marriage counselor, parole officer, rehabilitation counselor, school superintendent, theater manager, production expediter, geriatric specialist, insurance claims specialist, minister, travel agent, guidance counselor, convention planner, career specialist.

- *Conventional:* accountant, statistician, census enumerator, data processor, hospital administrator, instrument assembler, insurance administrator, legal secretary, library assistant, office manager, reservation agent, information consultant, underwriter, auditor, personnel specialist, database manager, abstractor/indexer.

- *Realistic:* agricultural engineer, barber, dairy farmer, electrical contractor, ferryboat captain, gem cutter, heavy equipment operator, industrial arts teacher, jeweler, navy officer, health and safety specialist, radio repairer, sheet metal worker, tailor, fitness director, package engineer, electronics technician, computer graphics technician, coach, PE teacher.

- *Enterprising:* banker, city manager, employment interviewer, FBI agent, health administrator, industrial relations director, judge, labor arbitrator, personnel assistant, TV announcer, salary and wage administrator, insurance salesperson, sales engineer, lawyer, sales representative, marketing specialist, promoter.

At first glance, Holland's model may seem to be a simple method for matching people to career fields. But it was never meant for that purpose. Your career choices ultimately will involve a complex assessment of the most important factors about you. To display the relationships between career fields and the potential conflicts people face as they consider them, Holland's model is commonly presented in a hexagonal shape. The closer the types, the closer the relationships among the career fields. The further apart the types, the more conflict between the career fields.

Using Holland's model can help you answer the question of career choice in two ways. First, you can begin to identify many career fields that are consistent with what you know about yourself. Once you've identified potential fields, you can use the career library at your college to get as much information as possible about those fields. When making career decisions, you should research career fields for information about:

- daily activities for specific jobs

- interests and abilities required

- preparation required for entry

- working conditions

- salary and benefits

- employment outlook

Second, you can begin to identify the harmony or conflicts in your career choices. This will help you analyze the reasons for your career decisions and be more confident as you make choices.

The chart in Figure 11-6 can help you determine at a glance which career fields complement your interests, personality, skills, and aptitudes. Review the career research you've done and list the five career fields that are most appealing to you *now*. Indicate with a check if the career field offers interests, satisfaction, personality fit, and use of current skills you want to develop, as well as the opportunity to exercise and develop your aptitudes.

College students often view career choice as a monumental and irreversible decision about their lives. The *choice* haunts some students as they decide on a college major. Others panic about "the choice" as they approach graduation and begin to look for a job. They assume that "the decision" will make all the difference in their lives.

This assumption is false, for in its broadest sense career means life path. A career is the sum of the decisions you make over a lifetime. There is no "right occupation" just waiting to be discovered by you. Rather, there are

Figure 11-6 *Career Interest Chart*

Potential Career Choices	Interests Satisfaction	Personality "Fit"	Skills Usage	Aptitude Usage
1.				
2.				
3.				
4.				
5.				

many career choices you may find fulfilling and satisfying. The question to consider is, "What is the *best* choice for me *now?*"

If you want to make the best choice now, we can help you begin. You've already identified five career fields you would consider as potential career choices. The next step is more complex and involves your consideration of the effect of these choices on your life goals and work values. An exploration of life goals and work values allows you to measure the information about the career field you've chosen against what you need to feel satisfied about your work.

The chart in Figure 11–7 can help you determine whether or not your potential career choices will enable you to fulfill your value needs. List your top five potential career choices from Figure 11–6 in the appropriate column. List your ordered life goals and work values from Figures 11–3 and 11–4. Place a check in the box to the far right of the listed goal or value if you feel that the potential career choice will enable you to satisfy that goal or value.

Your Mapmaking Model

Once you have identified several career options related to your interests, skills, values, and personality characteristics, you are ready to begin developing a map for finding your place in the world of work. Your map will help you select a major, elective courses, campus involvements, summer jobs, and other activities between your freshman year, and entry into your chosen career.

In selecting a major, ask yourself four questions: (1) Am I interested in the subject matter? (2) Do I enjoy reading and learning about the field? (3) Do I have the skills necessary for success? (4) Am I gaining skills, information, and perspectives that will be helpful in my career choices? After choosing a major, begin to learn about other academic opportunities in your department. Talk with your advisor about minors, internships, independent study, study abroad, exchange programs, and other options that broaden your academic experience.

As we said earlier, for some people there is a direct correlation between the major and the career. For others, the choice of a major is based on subject interest, not career. If your major is not directly related to your career choices, plan for entry into your first job through work experience or campus activities. Many students are hired as bank management trainees or investment analysts based on their experience as treasurer of a student union committee rather than a major in finance.

Involvement in campus activities and part-time jobs are important in two ways. First, these experiences serve as the basis of a résumé, which you

Figure 11-7 *Comparing Careers to Goals and Values*

Potential Career Choice	Priority of Life Goals	(✓)	Priority of Work Values	(✓)
1.	1.		1.	
	2.		2.	
	3.		3.	
	4.		4.	
	5.		5.	
2.	1.		1.	
	2.		2.	
	3.		3.	
	4.		4.	
	5.		5.	
3.	1.		1.	
	2.		2.	
	3.		3.	
	4.		4.	
	5.		5.	
4.	1.		1.	
	2.		2.	
	3.		3.	
	4.		4.	
	5.		5.	
5.	1.		1.	
	2.		2.	
	3.		3.	
	4.		4.	
	5.		5.	

will write to get your first job after college. Second, through these experiences you develop confidence in your career choice. It is better to discover that you hate inventory control before you graduate and take a full-time job in the field.

This comparison of information about yourself, career information, and the role of life goals and work values makes career planning an effective decision-making process.

Career planning isn't a quick and easy way to arrive at what you want to do with your life, but we think it can be a most effective means to help you discover the best career choice for you now in the sense that the *now* choice will be appropriate in terms of your personal characteristics and goals and will lay the groundwork for future career choices. Career planning *can* help you find your place in the world of work. Take advantage of it.

Suggested Activities

Throughout this chapter we've suggested things you can do to gather information about yourself and about the world of work. We hope you'll follow up on the exercises suggested; we believe they'll help you clarify the most important issues involved in your choice of career and academic major. After you've worked through the exercises in this chapter, here are a few other activities that may help.

□ *Career exploration:* Once you've selected possible career fields, talk with people working in those fields to get a clear idea of what life is really like as a social worker or accountant or office manager.

□ *Choice of a major:* Talk with faculty members about the skills and areas of expertise you'll develop in studying the disciplines they're teaching.

□ *Skill development:* Get involved in work experiences or campus activities that will allow you to develop skills and areas of expertise useful to your career plans.

Suggested Readings

Bachhuber, Thomas D., and Richard K. Harwood. *Directions: A Guide to Career Planning.* Boston: Houghton Mifflin, 1978.

Bolles, Richard N. *The Three Boxes of Life.* Berkeley, Calif.: Ten Speed, 1985.

_____. *What Color Is Your Parachute?* Berkeley, Calif.: Ten Speed, 1986.

Campbell, David. *If You Don't Know Where You're Going, You'll End Up Someplace Else.* Allen, Tex.: Argus Communications, 1974.

Carney, Clark G., Cindy F. Wells, and Don Streufert, *Career Planning: Skills to Build Your Future.* New York: D. Van Nostrand, 1982.

Figler, Howard. *The Complete Job-Search Handbook.* New York: Holt, Rinehart, and Winston, 1979.

_____. *Path—A Career Workbook for Liberal Arts Students.* Cranston, R.I.: Carroll Press, 1979.

Gale Research, *Directory of Directories.*

_____. *Encyclopedia of Associations.* Detroit, Mich. Published annually.

Garrison, Clifford B., et al. *Finding a Job You Feel Good About.* Allen, Tex.: Argus Communications, 1977.

Harris-Bowlsbey, Joann, James D. Spivack, and Ruth S. Lisansky. *Take Hold of Your Future.* Towson, Md.: American College Testing, 1982.

Jackson, Tom. *The Perfect Resume.* Garden City, N.Y.: Anchor Books, 1981.

_____. *28 Days to a Better Job.* New York: Hawthorn Books, 1977.

McLaughlin, John E., and Stephen K. Merman. *Writing a Job-Winning Resume.* Englewood Cliffs, N.J.: Prentice-Hall, 1980.

Occupational Outlook Handbook, 1986–87 ed. Washington, D.C.: U.S. Department of Labor, 1987.

Paetro, Maxine. *How to Put Your Book Together and Get a Job in Advertising.* New York: Hawthorn Books, 1979.

Pearson, Henry G. *Your Hidden Skills: Clues to Careers and Future Pursuits.* Wayland, Mass.: Mowry Press, 1984.

Powell, Randall C. *Career Planning and Placement Today.* Dubuque, Ia.: Kendall-Hunt Publishing, 1978.

Stair, Lila B. *Careers in Business: Selecting and Planning Your Career Path.* Homewood, Ill.: Irwin, 1980.

UNIT THREE

College as Personal Blossoming

12 Minority Students on Campus: Enhancing Cultural Growth and Understanding

Francine G. McNairy

DEAN OF ACADEMIC SUPPORT SERVICES
ASSOCIATE VICE PRESIDENT FOR ACADEMIC AFFAIRS
WEST CHESTER UNIVERSITY OF PENNSYLVANIA

Dan Romero

ASSOCIATE DIRECTOR
CAREER PLANNING AND PLACEMENT CENTER
UNIVERSITY OF CALIFORNIA AT BERKELEY

When I think about my freshman year at a predominantly white university, these are the things I remember: " 'Negro' students who graduate from your high school tend not to do well at this university; therefore, we encourage you to attend a summer precollege program," said a representative from the university. (I did.) "You'll do well here if you never take a math course," stated my advisor during the freshman orientation program. (I never did take a math course, and I paid for it!) Of the 300 students in Psychology 80, no one would sit next to me!

One day, by accident, I wandered into the commuter cafeteria, and there they were—black people! I was so glad to see them that I think I ran toward them. The group was composed primarily of upperclass students and two graduate students. "Hey, what's your aim in life?" hollered Jack, one of the graduate students, as I approached the group. I opened my mouth to respond, but I don't think anything coherent came out. Can you imagine how I felt when they told me that we were in a university of well over 20,000 students and that maybe, just maybe, there were a total of 50 black undergraduate and graduate students? Later I found out that 15 out of the 50 black students were freshmen!

As the semester progressed, I spent a considerable amount of time in the cafeteria and became better adjusted to the university. That corner in the cafeteria was my home away from home. Those black students were my family and support system. They reprimanded me for cutting class and applauded me for my achievements. There were no black faculty, as far as I knew.

Interaction with white students was fairly minimal. They appeared not to know what to say to me, and vice versa. Communication with white faculty members was a little different. They had the information; therefore, I did talk to them. My grades were not that fantastic, though, and it wasn't until my junior year that I became a serious student.

Now I'm a professional social worker with a Ph.D. degree in communication and at a university where I am the Associate Vice President for Academic Affairs. As you will see, my experiences were somewhat different from Dan's.

As Fran indicated, my freshman year was indeed different. I was born and raised in a southwestern state that claims a rich mixture of Hispanic, Indian, and Euro-American cultures. As I proceeded through high school, however, I found that most of the college-bound students taking "college-track" courses I was enrolled in were white students. When I attended the university, the trend continued. While my home state had almost 40 percent Hispanic citizens in the 1960s, the university enrolled about 12 percent Hispanics. The number of Native Americans, blacks, and Asian-Americans at the university was so small as to render them virtually invisible.

I remember my freshman year as one of feeling out of place. Many weekends during the year I would return home, some seventy miles away, to be with family and high school friends. I felt uncomfortable at the university. Looking back, part of the feeling was due to trying to fit into a predominantly non-Hispanic group in which I could be accepted only to a point. I learned that as a Mexican-American, I was accepted in some groups, but not in all, and that even those groups who did accept me did so conditionally. As more Hispanics enrolled in the university toward my junior and senior years, I also learned that for many of them, I was too "establishment" or too white and was not accepted by some members of Mexican-American ethnic organizations.

From my undergraduate experience I learned that minority students encounter a tremendous pressure in college to choose sides—either to become part of your ethnic group's identity or be acculturated into the establishment. I found that seeking my own identity meant not accepting either extreme; I wanted to create a bicultural identity and realized that I would not be understood by some.

I also remember that I knew little about my Hispanic heritage and culture. Much of what I studied and learned about in high school and college ignored the rich culture and history of my ancestors in the Southwest. I looked Hispanic, and at times I felt uncomfortable and out of place associating with my white peers. Sensing that some of our values were dissimilar, my friends simply attributed the disparity to personal, not cultural, differences. I remember, for example, inviting many of my friends to my home to sample Mom's cooking and to be part of the family. Seldom was that favor returned. At the time I surmised there was something wrong with me, but with time I have learned that others may not value a concept such as "mi casa es tu casa" (my house is your house) or the openness associated with my family.

After becoming the first to graduate from college in a family that can trace its *roots back at least eight generations in America, I have completed almost two decades as a college graduate, faculty member, and university administrator and counselor. Currently, I am exploring issues facing a small cadre of minority professionals who have served in higher education for more than twenty years.*

━ⅠⅠⅠ━ⅠⅠⅠ━ⅠⅠⅠ━

We've written this chapter so that all students might better understand the concerns and problems that minority students face every day at predominantly white colleges or universities. Our chapter represents a synthesis of ideas from minority educators, students, and published research depicting the prolonged struggle that many minorities have waged to gain access to knowledge, education, and credentials. These concerns and problems that minority students experience have a long tradition and history. Their resolution will not occur overnight; however, we hope this chapter will contribute toward their solution.

We further acknowledge that there are a number of minority communities represented on college campuses. In no way do we intend to imply that their cultures are identical; certainly one chapter cannot capture the unique qualities within them all. By design, therefore, we have been selective in examining issues that seem to cut across all racial ethnic minority groups. However, many of the examples are taken from our experiences in universities and reflect concerns particular to black and Hispanic students on the campus. Thus we hope to inform minority students of the realities of higher education as well as to provide insight to others so that they might realize the added burdens minority college students face.

━ⅠⅠⅠ━ⅠⅠⅠ━ⅠⅠⅠ━
The Challenge of Minority Higher Education

Higher education is a challenge to anyone. But if you happen to be a minority student and plan to attend a predominantly white college, you need to be prepared to meet additional demands. Over the years, minority students have struggled for access to knowledge and credentials through education. That only 50 percent of black students who enter college graduate is tragic, especially when black communities throughout the United States are suffering from a severe brain drain of their most talented and trained members ("Half of All," 1981).

More than 72 percent of all black students in higher education in the United States are enrolled in traditionally white colleges (Braddock, 1981).

Nevertheless, the predominantly black institutions, most of which are in the South, have continued to be the major supplier of black graduates of four-year colleges. They award 69 percent of all bachelor's degrees received by blacks (Middleton, 1979).

In terms of graduate rates for Hispanics, separate reporting sources have documented differing rates. The U.S. Commission on Civil Rights (1978) has reported that approximately 33 percent of all Hispanic males who enter college complete a degree, and only 15 percent of all Hispanic females who enter college do so. The National Center for Educational Statistics (1980) reports that four years after enrolling in college, 10 percent of Hispanic men and 12 percent of Hispanic women hold the baccalaureate degree compared to 38 percent of white men and 42 percent of white women. Trends for the 1980s reveal that graduation rates have not fluctuated much over the past decade and that Hispanics continue to be underrepresented at all levels of the higher education pipeline.

Unlike black students who have attended historically black colleges, Hispanic students have never had access to a network of traditional Hispanic colleges in this country. Therefore, Hispanic students have been dispropor-tionately concentrated in community colleges and in a few four-year institu-tions. Nationally, some twenty colleges enroll a quarter of all Hispanic students in the United States. Further, from 1970 to 1984 the number of full-time Hispanic undergraduate students increased only slightly, from 2.1 percent of the total number of undergraduates to 3.5 percent (Olivas, 1986).

Most colleges and universities have, in essence, remained in a steady-state stage of enrollment, with some experiencing a reduction in the number and percentage of Hispanic students. Practically speaking, then, this means that, unless you are enrolled in one of a handful of universities in the United States, specifically one in the Southwestern states, you will probably have little or no contact with Hispanic university students. As we look to the year 2000, it is unfortunate that many college students will have had limited experience with a population that has been described as the fastest growing minority group in the United States.

—lll——lll——lll—

Historical Considerations for Minorities in Education

U.S. history has a distinctive Euro-American flavor fanned from the concept of manifest destiny as the nation expanded from east to west. Clearly, other influences were and are present in our country and make up a history of minority populations that have received little attention in textbooks. These include the influence of the American Indian, who was here prior to the arrival of any outside population, and a rich Hispanic flavor that grew from the Southwest. Hispanics have also infused other regions of the country, including a strong Cuban influence in the Southeast and a Puerto Rican flavor on the East Coast. A third influence was the history of blacks in America. Finally, as Asian populations began to emigrate to America in the mid-nineteenth century, a growing Pacific Rim influence began to move eastward from the West Coast.

In terms of history and education, each minority has experienced great difficulty in finding a place in American university life. As an example, the history of blacks clearly illustrates the neglect that minority groups have experienced in attaining an education.

Prior to 1619, blacks came to America as explorers, servants, and slaves. They were part of the first settlement in what now is known as South Carolina. By 1624, every colony except Georgia had black citizens—free people, artisans, and slaves. The slave trade was extensive throughout the North and South. Contrary to popular notion, blacks continuously fought against slavery, many times petitioning colonial leaders for freedom. Soon after the Revolutionary War, New England abolished slavery (Compton, 1980).

Retention of black students during the slavery years was not a problem, since it was illegal for blacks to be educated in most colonies, particularly in the South. In the 1700s the South Carolina legislature ruled that anyone found educating slaves would be fined 100 pounds. In Georgia, the financial penalty for teaching a slave was 50 percent greater than if one willfully castrated or cut off the limb of a slave (Higginbotham, 1978).

While southern colonies intensified their restrictions, other colonies enacted different legal codes to govern, protect, control, or restrict the education of slaves. In 1704, a catechism school for "Negroes" was established by Elias Neau (Bergman, 1969).

But although the earliest laws of this country prohibited blacks from receiving an education, many blacks managed to learn anyway. John Russwarm, the first black to graduate from college, received a college degree at Bowdoin in 1826 (Bennett, 1962). Because blacks were denied entry to colleges, black colleges were established after 1850, beginning with Lincoln University in Pennsylvania and Wilberforce University of Ohio.

American public education was on the rise in the 1800s, but education for blacks became less available. Fearing that education would make slaves aware of a better world than their own, the Southern state legislatures outlawed education for blacks after 1831 (Compton, 1980). In the North and South, free black children were the victims of segregated schools, while black property owners paid taxes to support schools their children could not attend. In 1896, the U.S. Supreme Court, in *Plessy vs. Ferguson,* declared the doctrine of "separate but equal," stating there was no discrimination as long as the separate facilities were equal. It was the norm, however, for black schools to be less "equal," to have less adequate resources than white schools had. This decision remained unchallenged until 1954, when the Supreme

Court, in *Brown vs. Board of Education,* ruled that racial segregation in public schools was unconstitutional (Bremner, 1970).

The 1960s witnessed measurable improvements for blacks: (1) the economic boycott in Montgomery, Alabama, demonstrated that such an action was an effective method of significantly reducing segregation in the marketplace, (2) the end of segregation in such public facilities as lunch counters, (3) the end of segregation in interstate transportation, (4) the admission of more black students into previously segregated colleges and universities, and (5) the development of the black student movement in higher education (Karenga, 1980). Black leaders included Martin Luther King, Jr., Malcolm X, and Angela Davis. Key organizations supporting civil rights efforts for blacks, such as the Southern Christian Leadership Conference, Congress of Racial Equality, National Association for the Advancement of Colored People, and the Black Panther Party, helped raise the consciousness of black youth and opened the doors for further educational opportunities in higher education.

In the past three decades, American higher education has undergone many changes that have centered on the needs of minority students. During the 1960s, universities were awakened to the needs of previously ignored ethnic groups. The civil rights legislation and an era of social justice and responsibility combined with student activism to reexamine the needs of minority students on campus. Faculty, administrators, and students were challenged to acknowledge the presence of minority students on campus. As a response to increased enrollments of minorities, "special admissions" programs emerged at colleges throughout the country.

For minority students, the 1970s were a period of controlled growth and benign neglect. Their growth remained constant or in some cases posted slight decreases. The university response to meeting the needs of minority students generally was to create and support programs such as educational opportunity programs and special services that functioned on a "separate but equal" philosophy. These programs, for the most part, sought to identify and meet student needs outside existing university support facilities. A controlled number of minority students continued to enroll in universities and found their presence not acknowledged or supported by the mainstream of university faculty, staff, and students.

Unfilled promises and conservative financial cutbacks have characterized the 1980s. Amid tight budgets, universities were reluctant to devote resources to the needs of culturally different students. Many administrators, faculty, staff, and students continued to operate from a "color-blind" philosophy, which assumed that all students had similar needs and that cultural differences did not exist or did not have any impact on adjustment to university life.

As we look to the 1990s, minority students continue to lag in graduation rates from high school; thus, growth will be controlled and sporadic at best. As a minority student, you will quite likely be a small percentage of the campus population, less than 15 percent unless you attend a university in the West, where many schools anticipate attracting more than 50 percent minority students, reflecting the tremendous minority growth rates within that region. Unless there are drastic changes to counterbalance these factors, you are likely to experience a "melting pot" atmosphere. Such an atmosphere decidedly negates the diverse and rich cultural traditions, heritage, and values that exist within each racial and ethnic group. Thus the consequences of the melting pot philosophy are that the academic community is limited in its ability to respect, appreciate, and understand those differences. Subsequently, there is an emphasis on fusing all cultures into one mold rather than nurturing a progressive rainbow.

—|||——|||——|||—
Minority Student, White Campus: The Realities

Since the civil rights movement began, black students and educators have weighed the advantages and disadvantages of receiving a college education at a predominantly white college. The advantages often include access to more academic and multicultural resources and a broad social network leading to employment and/or graduate and professional schools. On the minus side, the high dropout level of black students nullifies the gains. While other minority students have not had the option of attending a college or university based on their own cultural history, their realities are quite the same as those of black students. Such factors as racism, a limited social life, and different expectations by faculty tend to negatively affect students from all minority groups.

Social Life

Sometimes minority students will experience a social climate on the campus that will make them wonder if they really belong. Those situations arise when there are social and cultural programs that do not resemble a particular culture. Participating in campus activities might be difficult if you are the only one in the group, organization, or program with a different cultural background. There may even be times when you feel excluded from campus activities.

Many colleges or universities are located in isolated areas. If the campus is miles away from the nearest urban community, social life for minority students might be restricted; they will need to develop appropriate social resources to meet their own needs.

When many Hispanic students assess advantages and disadvantages in attending college, several factors interact simultaneously. Many, who may be the first of their family to attend a university, associate prestige with a college degree. A second advantage stems from the belief that an education will lead to a better job and financial security. This is particularly valuable because it can provide the income to become independent and/or to assist the family in the future.

On the other hand, many minority students who attend college experience or perceive a loss of family contact and cultural identity. From the families' perspectives, the students may be seen as different. They may not speak the traditional language. Minority students might begin to feel uncomfortable around family and visit less, ultimately moving away from traditional values. Those students who are able to blend a traditional culture value system with new ideas from the university environment frequently experience the stress and anxiety of mixing two often incompatible worlds. Thus attending college becomes a series of pluses and minuses that cause stress on minority students' adjustment to school and strain on family relationships. If the stress and strain become intolerable, the minority student will perform at marginal levels and will probably drop out of the university.

A general perception shared by white college students is that all students may face situations of stress and strains. These conflicts are not unique for minority students, but are experiences all students face. Such statements do have a ring of truth, but act to rob the individual of uniqueness and foster a feeling of false commonality among students. White students need to recognize an important reality: Cultural differences should not be minimized, and attempting to do so will usually be met with passive or active resistance, suspicion, and distrust by many minority students. The reality of being a minority on a white campus is that many minority students will affirm and protect boundaries that set them aside as different and not totally assimilate into the main university culture.

For many Hispanic students with traditional values, the social life of campus is further complicated with family obligations. Many Hispanic freshmen enroll in universities located less than fifty miles from their family home. This poses a particular dilemma in the social and campus life of many traditional Hispanic students who feel strong family responsibilities. One undergraduate Hispanic described weekend commitments and conflicts she faced:

> I live in a predominantly Mexican-American community and have traditional Mexican-American values. My first experience at a university was culture shock. Family ties were very important and suddenly not everyone agreed with my values. Even while I lived in the residence hall, my peers could not understand why I continued to ask permission from my family to spend the weekend on campus,

to go away on retreats, or to buy extra items. For me attending school was done in conjunction with family obligations, while for some friends, attending school allowed maximum independence from the family [Romero et al., 1987].

Faculty Expectations

While the quality of social life has considerable impact on students' adjustment to college, academic performance is still the major criterion for success on campus. College is a challenge for most freshmen. If faculty and freshmen share their expectations of each other and believe they can learn from one another, the adjustment period is easier. But if the faculty member has a set of expectations that does not complement those of a student, conflict will ensue and the student may suffer.

In discussing black students, Jewel Taylor Gibbs identifies the kind of problems they might experience at predominantly white colleges or universities. These problems might also apply to other minorities in similar situations. She expresses concern that black students and white faculty members often have expectations about one another that may be incompatible.

One such expectation by faculty has been that black students will be assimilated into the university community without substantial alteration of academic structures or programs (Gibbs, 1973). Gibbs points out that although some black students are admitted into college as "high risk" students, the academic support services available to help strengthen their basic skills have proved inadequate. Many black students, on the other hand, believe the college will be flexible in responding to their needs. Therefore, when their needs are not immediately addressed, they may become frustrated and, in some instances, hostile. The point is, if your needs aren't recognized, you must take responsibility for identifying those resources on campus that can help you function better, and use them to help you. Such resources include your academic advisor, the financial aid office, academic support center, counseling center, library, your college dean, and other key administrators.

The first faculty expectation is accentuated by the second: Black students are expected to compete academically with white students, who generally have superior high school preparation. Many faculty members don't assess individual student skills. On the other hand, many black students expect college courses to be a continuation of high school work and are often confused by the qualitative and quantitative differences in courses and study assignments (Gibbs, 1973).

Imagine that you're enrolled in Math 121: College Algebra. The range of exposure to math among students in that class can vary from a single basic course to two years of high school math. Some students may have learned basic math concepts, while others have more advanced skills. Yet the instructor establishes a pace and level of performance that might exceed some students' backgrounds, and his or her teaching methods will seldom change to accommodate those with little exposure to math. The instructor will require all to keep up with the assignments and attain the expected performance level. No matter what the course is, you will be expected to keep up, despite your high school preparation.

Therefore, you must recognize your own expectations of college and, simultaneously, the college's expectations of you. If they are compatible, it will be easier for you to meet them. If a difference exists, you must identify that difference and take steps immediately to close the gap.

Face It: Racism Does Exist

Racism on college campuses in the 1990s will likely be similar to that of the 1980s—mostly subtle, with intermittent incidents of overt hostility toward minority students. In general, many minorities will not feel welcome on white campuses and will sense that their comfort zone is challenged. As a minority student, you will likely experience slights and insensitivities where you might be excluded from study networks, not asked questions about class material, and have a restricted range of friendships. You are likely to experience stereotyped comments, subtle harassment, and prejudice from faculty and students.

Most fellow undergraduate students who have not experienced the pain of insensitive treatment will say there is no racism on your campus or feel they cannot be held accountable for past injustices. You will be asked by others to examine your attitudes and behaviors. You will probably be called racist and exclusionary for choosing to associate with students with whom you are comfortable. We encourage you to be aware of these situations. Do not let these types of incidents control you or your productivity. Understand them for what they are. It is equally essential, however, that you become aware of and sensitive to your environment while learning the skills that allow you to survive and prosper under adversity.

One of the most decisive ways to deflect racism is to constantly remind yourself of those aspects of your heritage and your family that contributed toward making you the successful person you are. You must believe you have the confidence and the ability to succeed. This is not as simple as it sounds. Often your degree of self-confidence is measured by how the environment responds to you. When that response is negative or indifferent, you must call upon those reserves stored within yourself. One undergraduate black student described it this way:

Black students always have to prove themselves. Some white students have tried to talk me out of doing things simply because they thought I couldn't succeed. A black student who lacks self-confidence might not know how to react to such advice [Evans, 1986].

All minority students must generate within themselves the confidence to succeed.

—||||—||||—||||—
Admission to College Does Not Guarantee Success

Many minority students reading this book are the first in their families to graduate from high school or enroll in college. Such accomplishments, while indeed outstanding, are not considered as indicators of success when you take college exams. It's easy to become involved in the excitement of registering for courses, meeting new people, having more free time, and not being under the direct influence of parents. However, it is also understandable why many minority students become discouraged when their expectations for success in college are not fulfilled. One Hispanic undergraduate explained his experiences:

Midway into the semester things began to crumble. The grades I earned were discouraging. I fell further behind in my classes. I became increasingly anxious and depressed. I would try to avoid all my troubles by taking long rides and spending time by myself. I stopped going to classes, but I continued going to school so my family would not know what was happening to their first in college. I wanted to explode from the pressure and anxiety I was feeling. My ego was shattered, but even more difficult was having to tell my parents that I had failed [Romero et al., 1987].

You must understand that admission to college does not guarantee success. It is vital to strive to achieve the best grades possible, and it is also essential to view the college experience as a growth experience. Success in this light must also be measured not only by academic indicators of performance but also by how you have stretched and grown in personal knowledge and awareness of your strengths and weaknesses.

Given the history of minorities in higher education, and the social, academic, and psychological realities you face at white colleges, it's imperative that you understand the purpose of higher education and the multidimensions of success and responsibilities.

Why Bother?

The realities for minority students in white colleges might shock you and could cause you to ask, "Why bother?" The answer is simple. Because of the 1954 Supreme Court decision, all minorities now have options they previously lacked. Most of their names will never appear in history books, but their persistence and determination have established the foundation for you to be productive in college. Furthermore, their efforts have served to strengthen our communities.

Throughout this chapter, we have been discussing the realities for minority students who elect to attend predominantly white colleges/universities. These realities are indeed reflective of the larger society in which we live. You might implicitly get the impression that to be a successful student, you might have to give up your culture and totally assimilate.

We are not advocating that you forsake your roots, customs, and traditions. It is imperative, however, that you understand your own culture as well as that of the majority population. Ultimately, you will have more peace of mind when you learn to appreciate the importance of all cultures. Success in higher education and in life is not based on your giving up your identity or denying the contributions of others. Quite frankly, it depends on your developing appropriate survival skills, academic and social, that do not compromise the basic values of your culture. Your importance to your family, your community, higher education, and the world is that you indeed have something to contribute.

How Minority Students Can Thrive at White Colleges

The following recommendations are based on two assumptions:

1. Education is a learning process, not merely a union card for obtaining a job. If you learn how to learn, you can obtain any kind of knowledge you desire on any subject. No one can take away your ability to learn, provided you develop a sound process.

2. Education is an active process. Most students are, for twelve years, passive receptacles of information, yet real education involves your taking an active role in the process. You're not a computer that spits back data that was programmed into it. You're a thinking human being who can receive information, weigh its credibility, determine its applicability and utility, and, ultimately, identify other information that supports or contradicts it.

With these assumptions in mind, we'd like to share two concerns. The first is that education presents a series of dilemmas for young minority students. Glasgow (1981) argues that education offers students three alternatives. The first is to adopt the philosophy of the educational system, thereby rejecting the values, customs, beliefs, and philosophies of their home community. The second is to reject educational systems totally and focus on one's community, since it is known and familiar. The third option is a compromise: to deliberately select the positive aspects from both one's community and the educational system.

The recommendations in this chapter support the third option. Significant philosophies, values, customs, information, and behavior must be identified, learned, and experienced by minority youth. You do not have to give up your identities while attending college. Instead, by learning the fundamental, valuable aspects of education, you may emerge with a stronger identity and self-concept.

The second concern results from the first. Minority students should be aware that, while their acceptance into college is an achievement, it's not the be-all and end-all. While they might have worked hard, many equally capable minorities of the same age may never have achieved as much simply because the doors of opportunity were locked in their faces.

A minority student's enrollment in college should result in a geometric progression for one's community. If two people help two people, and the pattern continues, minority communities eventually will have the skills and technology required to overcome all the barriers to full equality. This does not presuppose that everyone should go to college. It does, however, advocate that minority people should have the opportunity to choose!

Therefore, the recommendations for minority student success at a white college are to establish measurable goals; develop a clear sense of self-awareness; identify and appropriately utilize minority administrators, faculty, and student resources; develop critical thinking skills; and get involved in campus activities.

Establish Measurable Goals

A goal is an objective or end that one strives to obtain. It is measurable if you can assess progress and accomplishment after reaching it. Goals are short range if you plan to achieve them in the immediate future. Long-range goals require considerably more planning and time to accomplish; such goals usually encompass a year, five years, or a lifetime of planning and implementation. Goals provide direction and purpose. They should be realistic, yet challenging. Most important, they should be relevant and meaningful to the goal setter.

You might establish a short-range goal on a daily or weekly basis. Such a pattern helps maintain a feeling of productivity and accomplishment. An example is to schedule study hours on a regular basis to complement the courses you're taking. On that basis, a three-credit course should receive a minimum of three hours' study a week.

Another short-range goal might be to pursue the highest quality of work based on your ability and potential. In some courses, that might mean A's and B's; in others, a C might be your best. While we would like to see you excel in all of your courses, it is more important that you take advantage of every opportunity to earn the best grades possible. For some students, "getting by" is sufficient; they perform at a mediocre level. However, minority students are not descendants of mediocre people. Your heritage, like those of so many other races and nationalities, is rooted in pride, determination, and hard work.

Long-range goals require substantial thought and planning. Without working on short-range goals, however, it's practically impossible to achieve the long-range ones, such as career plans. Consider what you want to do with the next four, ten, or twenty years of your life. If you're a minority student, dare to pursue careers that are untraditional, yet critical to the development of your community.

Develop a Clear Sense of Self-Awareness

Learning is an active process, and you are ultimately responsible for your own education. New information, values, and opinions will pass your way daily. It's important that you learn to evaluate them and apply them to what you already know. Because what you learn becomes a part of you, read as much about your history as you can. History encompasses the political, economic, social, and psychological dynamics of a people. If you have no understanding of your own history, you may have problems comprehending your current situation, not to mention your future.

Expose yourself to minority scholars in literature, psychology, economics, business, political science, the arts, sociology, and the natural sciences, and be prepared to discuss this knowledge in any setting. Much of this information will not be in your college texts, but it will be in your college library, and you'll have to work at finding it.

Utilize Other Minorities on Campus

Your first year in college is critical because, among other things, it establishes a pattern for your future education. Needless to say, comprehensive knowledge of "where to turn" is a requisite for graduation. For minority students, special resources represent the bloodline to success in college: minority faculty and administrators and achievement-oriented minority students. Such persons have a wealth of knowledge and skills that, when shared with you, can facilitate your learning processes. Seek these individuals out.

Minority faculty and administrators have been where you want to go. Besides being experts in their academic fields, they know about financial aid, study habits, the limited social life for minorities, and racism. Whatever you may think, the collective knowledge of minority academicians is too valuable for you to ignore. Learn from them and communicate with them.

Other minority students who are serious about learning, especially upperclass students, can be another helpful source. Since they're a part of your generation, they'll be open and candid with you. Study with, learn from, and emulate those who are serious about their futures.

We certainly don't advocate that minorities segregate themselves from the majority community. White administrators, faculty, and students also have valuable knowledge and resources from which minority students can benefit. But minorities must be resources for one another if the success rate of graduates from white colleges is to improve significantly. As Dr. Ron Karenga so aptly put it:

> We don't need any more street corner philosophers. We don't need any more individualists who contribute in their own way. Individuals had 450 years to get their own way together and it hasn't worked yet. It's about time we had a collective effort and moved on that [Halisi et al., 1967, p. 15].

Develop Critical Thinking Skills

Education is a process, not a fact, so never permit yourself to accept information on face value. Learn to ask questions and to think through information logically. Critical thinking rejects emotional reactions. It involves a rational approach, which includes identifying a problem or situation, generating possible solutions, weighing pros and cons, choosing the most appropriate solution, evaluating the outcome, and living with the consequences.

College exposes students to a variety of theories, statistics, values, and other information. While it's important that you know such things, it's equally important that you learn to examine the credibility and utility of course material or informally shared information. Rote memory might get you through some multiple-choice exams, but it won't help you learn to analyze or apply information. More importantly, your ability to thrive in college and beyond depends heavily on your ability to evaluate information correctly. What you see might not be what you get!

Get Involved in Campus Activities

Pursuing a college degree involves more than attending classes, taking exams, and earning grades. College provides an opportunity to obtain a social or interpersonal degree, as well as an academic one. You'll enroll in classes to obtain grades and, ultimately, the bachelor's degree. But simultaneously, you can develop or strengthen leadership and organizational skills by participating in extracurricular activities that could complement your career interests, political positions, social priorities, and cultural concerns.

By earning this second "degree" you'll gain actual experience in developing policies and programs that have an impact on the college community. Such experiences often supplement skills in fiscal management, budget development, program planning and evaluation, community and political organization, and public speaking. Campus involvement will help keep you knowledgeable of current ideas that affect not only your college but also higher education in general.

Quite frankly, the only way to ensure minority input into curriculum, cultural programs, policy decisions, and other significant factors in the college is for minority students, faculty, and administrators to be involved collectively. Gurin and Epps (1975) found that college experiences contribute considerably to the academic performance of minority college students. They described the "committed achiever" as the most successful type of minority student. The committed achiever has more contact with faculty outside the classroom, belongs to more campus groups, holds more leadership positions on the campus, and participates more often in at least some minority organizations.

For a well-rounded college experience, determine which extracurricular activities and organizations meet your needs and interests. Develop those skills that lend themselves to future employment possibilities. And if you're black, Hispanic, Asian-American, Native American, or of some other minority group, seek those ties that contribute to the collective organization of your community.

These recommendations are designed to help you as you proceed through your freshman year. Naturally, there is no substitute for hard work and commitment, and no miracle cures to push you through your college career. Only perseverance, thoroughness, and discipline will move you toward success. Be assured, however, that if you follow these recommendations, you'll have a more fulfilling academic year.

A final word to minority students reading this chapter: You are already a survivor in that you have enrolled in college. You have the intellect and ability to succeed at this stage of your life. You join other minority students who, as a collective unit, have the potential to change the immobility of the masses of minorities. Take note of your historical past, examine the realities of the present, and prepare yourselves to shape the future. You have the equipment to conquer and surpass the educational opportunities your ancestors obtained for you. We share these words from Clark (1939) with you as you proudly walk forward.

Equipment

Figure it out for yourself, my lad
   You've all that the greatest of men have had,
Two arms, two hands, two legs, two eyes,
   And a brain to use if you would be wise,
With this equipment they all began,
   So start from the top and say, "I Can."
Courage must come from the soul within,
   The man must furnish the will to win,
So figure it out for yourself, my lad,
   You were born with all that the great have had.
With your equipment they all began,
   Get hold of yourself and say: "I Can."

Anonymous

Suggested Activities

1. Discuss the implications of the high dropout rate of minority students from predominantly white colleges.

2. Discuss the critical skills needed to build a stronger minority community, as defined by minorities in such disciplines or professions, as sociology, political science, public administration, business, and education.

3. Examine your reason(s) for attending college. Establish short-range and long-range goals for your college career. Develop an evaluative mechanism to measure your accomplishments.

4. Identify and interview a number of faculty members and administrators of your minority group. Determine their area of expertise and what resources they have that might enable you to thrive in college.

5. Identify minority graduates from your institution who have been successful in their chosen careers.

6. Identify minority upperclass students who are committed achievers, and interview them to determine how they have been successful students.

7. Identify key committees/organizations that have an impact on the minority experience. Become actively involved in at least one of them.

8. Commit yourself to attend a cultural event on your campus, such as a Black History Month lecture or Cinco de Mayo celebration. If you appear to be a minority at an event or feel uncomfortable, explore these feelings and understand these are feelings many minority students experience when they attend nonethnic campus events.

9. Organize a cross-cultural potluck in your organization or residence hall by asking participants to bring a dish based on their ethnic cultural background. Compare and contrast foods and how easy or difficult they were to prepare. Discuss implications for acculturation and assimilation.

10. Organize a workshop to examine if racial conflicts occur on your campus and the rationale for those conflicts.

Suggested Readings

Anaya, Rudolfo A. *The Legend of La Llorona: A Short Novel.* Berkeley, Calif. Tonatiah-Quinto Sol International, 1984.

Aranda, Charles. *Dichos: Proverbs and Sayings from the Spanish.* Santa Fe, N.M.: Sunstone Press, 1977.

Astin, Alexander W. *Minorities in American Higher Education.* San Francisco: Jossey Bass, 1982.

Baldwin, James. *Nobody Knows My Name.* New York: Dell, 1961.

Bulosan, Carlos. *America Is in the Heart.* Seattle: University of Washington Press, 1981.

Camarillo, Albert, ed. *Latinos in the United States: A Historical Bibliography.* Santa Barbara, Calif.: ABC-Clio, 1984.

Carmichael, Stokely, and Charles V. Hamilton. *Black Power—The Policies of Liberation in America.* New York: Vintage Books, 1967.

Chu, Louis. *Eat a Bowl of Tea.* New York: Lyle Stuart, 1961.

Douglass, Frederick. *Narrative of the Life of Frederick Douglass, an American Slave, Written by Himself.* Edited by Benjamin Quarles. Cambridge, Mass.: Harvard University Press, 1960.

DuBois, W. D. Burghardt. *The Souls of Black Folk.* New York: Fawcett, 1961.

Grant, Joanne, ed. *Black Protest—History, Documents, and Analyses 1619 to the Present.* Greenwich, Conn: Fawcett, 1974.

Haley, Alex, and Malcolm X. *The Autobiography of Malcolm X*. New York: Grove Press, 1976.

Higginbotham, A. Leon, Jr. *In the Matter of Color and the American Process—The Colonial Period*. New York: Oxford University Press, 1978.

Hobson, Geary, ed. *The Remembered Earth*. Albuquerque, N.M.: Red Earth Press, 1979.

Lincoln, Kenneth. *Native American Renaissance*. Berkeley: University of California Press, 1983.

Martinez, Joe L., and Richard H. Mendoza. *Chicano Psychology*. New York: Academic Press, 1984.

Mura, Yama Milton. *All I Asking for Is My Body*. San Francisco: Supa Press, 1979.

Robeson, Paul. *Paul Robeson Speaks: Writings, Speeches, Interviews, 1919–1974*. Edited by Philip Foner. New York: Brunner-Mazel, 1978.

Silko, Leslie M. *Ceremony*. New York: Viking/Penguin, 1975.

Soto, Gary. *Living Up the Street*. San Francisco: Strawberry Hill Press, 1985.

Woodson, Carter G. *African Background Outlines: Or, Handbook for the Study of the Negro*. New York: Negro University Press, 1936. Reprint. Greenwood, 1968.

Wright, Richard. *Native Son*. New York: Harper & Row, 1940.

References

Bennett, L., Jr. *Before the Mayflower: A History of the Negro in America, 1619–1962*. Chicago: Johnson Publishing, 1962.

Bergman, P. M. *The Chronological History of the Negro in America*. New York: Harper & Row, 1969.

Braddock, Jamills Henry II. "Desegregation and Black Student Attrition." *Urban Education 15*, no. 4 (January 1981): 403–418.

Bremner, R. H., ed. *Children and Youth in America: A Documentary History. Vol 1*. Cambridge, Mass.: Harvard University Press, 1970.

Clark, Glenn. "One of Dr. Carver's Favorite Poems," in *The Man Who Talks with the Flowers: The Life Story of Dr. George Washington Carver*. St. Paul, Minn.: Macalister Park, 1939.

Compton, Beulah Roberts. *Introduction of Social Welfare and Social Work.* Homewood, Ill: Dorsey, 1980.

Evans, Gaynelle. "Black Students Who Attend White Colleges Face Contradictions in Their Campus Life." *Chronicle of Higher Education,* April 30, 1986, pp. 29–30.

Gibbs, Jewel Taylor. "Black Students/White University: Different Expectations." *Personnel and Guidance Journal* 51 (March 1973): 463–469.

Glasgow, Douglas G. *The Black Underclass—Poverty, Unemployment, and Entrapment of Ghetto Youth.* New York: Vintage Books, 1981.

Gurin, Patricia, and Edgar Epps. *Black Consciousness, Identity and Achievement.* New York: Wiley, 1975. p. 366.

"Half of All Black College Students Never Graduate." *Gary Crusader,* December 26, 1981, pp. 1-2.

Halisi, Clyde, and James Mtume, eds. *The Quotable Karenga.* Los Angeles: US Organization, 1967.

Higginbotham, A. Leon, Jr. *In the Matter of Color—Race and the American Legal Process—the Colonial Period.* New York: Oxford University Press, 1978.

Karenga, M. R. "Black History from Civil Rights to Human Rights," *The Black Collegian 10,* no. 4, (February/March 1980): 10–16.

Middleton, Lorenzo. "Enrollment of Blacks Doubled Since 1970," *Chronicle of Higher Education* 17 (January 29, 1979): 2.

National Center for Educational Statistics. *The Condition of Education for Hispanic Americans.* Washington, D.C.: U.S. Government Printing Office, 1980.

Olivas, M. A. *Latino College Students.* New York: Teachers College, Columbia University, 1986.

Romero, D., S. Castillo, R. Velasquez, E. Dominguez, and T. Rodriquez. "The Hispanic Freshman Experience: Conceptualizing and Researching the Development of Mexican American Students." Paper presented at the National Conference on the Freshman Year Experience, Irvine, Calif. January 1987.

U.S. Commission on Civil Rights. *Social Indicators of Equity for Minorities and Women.* Washington, D.C.: U.S. Government Printing Office, 1978.

13 Developing a Personal System of Values

Richard L. Morrill

PRESIDENT
UNIVERSITY OF RICHMOND

For the past twenty years or more I have had a special interest in the topic of values. My doctoral dissertation involved a comparison of the philosophy of values of two contemporary theorists, one an American and one a Frenchman. Both as a college teacher and in my work as the president of a university, I have continued my studies and reflection, including writing a book on the topic several years ago.

I suppose that some of my interest in the field comes from my own experience as a college student, especially during my first two years. I had been brought up in a conservative home in which standards of personal behavior were tightly enforced. When I went off to college, however, I confronted ways of living that contradicted the ways I had been reared. As I met people who both thought and acted differently with regard to everything from alcohol to personal relationships, it was time to think through the basis for my own positions. Undoubtedly, some of my continuing interest in the topic of values dates to these early personal challenges.

As president of a university, I find that the issue of values continues to be a central one in the experience of most freshmen. For many students the challenges are indistinct and tend to pass quickly, but for others a lengthy and sometimes troubling process of adjustment is set in motion. Experience has taught me that, whatever else, a clear understanding of values and how they function is a crucial first step in making the best ultimate decisions in the values realm. I hope that this brief chapter will contribute toward that end of a better understanding of values.

American society has always shown a particular concern about values. Some would explain this by America's strong religious heritage, while others would relate it to our culture's dominant focus on the rights and happiness of the individual. Whatever the reasons, over the past decade our society has been especially concerned about the uncertain state of American ethics and values. Scandals on Wall Street, sharp divisions over controversial issues such as abortion, deception by TV evangelists, and a preoccupation with material success among many young people are just several of the ways in which our society has recently experienced ethical disorder and a confusion about values.

—|||——|||——|||—

What Are Values?

Discussions about values often generate more heat than light because the very word *values* means so many different things to different people. For some, values refer to the specific positions that a person might hold on controversial moral questions, for example, that capital punishment is right or wrong under various circumstances. To others, values refer more properly to those things most important to a person, such as a good job, a lovely home, nice clothes, a fancy car, and family ties. Another approach to values portrays them more as ideals or goals and uses such abstract nouns as truth, justice, love, peace, success, tolerance, and equality to refer to them. Given this jumble of meanings, let's pause to get our bearings on how best to understand the term values.

When it comes to understanding values in the context of college education, many thinkers would propose that we can best do so by comparing them with other aspects of our ordinary human experience. We use many terms to identify different forms of human thought and behavior: attitudes, feelings, beliefs, ideas, concepts, and, of course, values. When we apply one of these words to ourselves or to other people, we are usually describing some facet of our experience as human beings, often in ways that help us to define our own individuality or the nature of a group or institution. As we talk about the beliefs, feelings, ideas, and attitudes that we hold, we are typically exploring those characteristics that make us who we are and set us apart from other people. In this list of personal characteristics and forms of experience, we often find that our values occupy an important place.

One of the things that many recent thinkers have noticed is that values seem to have a quite different place in our lives than do ideas or feelings. Above all, our values apparently commit us to taking action, to doing something, while the other forms of experience do not necessarily do so. When we truly hold a value, in other words, we act on it. On the other hand, it seems to be perfectly consistent to have ideas, beliefs, attitudes, and feelings that do not lead to any specific action. They may, of course, involve some action but not necessarily. For instance, no contradiction is involved in feeling sad about something but not doing anything about it. We might be watching a television program showing people who are starving in Africa that gives us a feeling of sympathy or regret, but we may never take any action whatsoever based on that feeling. Or perhaps we have the attitude that honesty is the best policy and express that position verbally in many different ways, while at the same time finding ourselves distorting the truth under any number of convenient circumstances.

We can conclude from these cases that attitudes, feelings, beliefs, ideas, and many other forms of experience and behavior do not qualify as genuine values unless they meet some additional tests. As we are trying to learn ever more about who we are, and as the college experience pushes us steadily in the direction of self-knowledge, the ability to find our true values becomes an extremely important consideration. In finding our values we discover our deeper selves, we come face to face with our identities as unique persons and as responsible agents for our own lives. If our values lead us to do something about them, then our feelings of sympathy may be a genuine value for us to the extent that they motivate us to take an action—for instance, if our feelings of sympathy for starving people cause us to raise funds to help those suffering. Action can take many different forms and should not be thought of only as some form of actual physical motion. Action may be thinking and talking continually about a problem, trying to interest others in it, reading about it, or sending letters to officials regarding it. The basic point is that when we truly hold a value it leads us to make some impact upon our world.

As we test for the values in our lives, we also look for other characteristics of them. We consider, for example, whether we have accepted our alleged value by choice, whether it is something for which we accept personal responsibility and individual ownership. Many forms of our behavior are the result of things that others have taught us, especially our parents. Many things we have learned from our parents and others close to us will come to count fully as our values, but there is an essential process through which you must fully appropriate those things or beliefs for yourself. You must personally accept or reject something before it can become a value.

Freshmen in college commonly find themselves arguing for political or religious positions, for example, by defending their ideas on the basis that they have always been taught such and such by their parents. A position on politics or religion of this sort may well be a belief but, according to our definition, would not count as a value. Any belief or behavior that is primarily a result of what someone else expects of us without our own active and free choice of it is not a true value for us, whatever else it might be.

Finally, many commentators have noted that our values involve us in a positive relationship with any given line of conduct or behavior. This means that we tend to strongly affirm or prize our values. To one degree or another we become attracted to our values and affected by them. For instance, we might find that our values lead us to take a public stand because we are ready to defend anything that is related to them. We are proud of our values and the choices to which they lead. We also find ourselves ready to sacrifice for them and to establish our priorities around them. Our values have a genuine allure and draw forth our loyalties and commitment. Because they hold sway over us, our values can also be a source of judgment when we fail to fully realize them in our daily lives. If truth is one of our values, we know that it can be a stern judge when we fail to live up to its requirements. There is, in other words, a real aura of pressure or "oughtness" surrounding the values that we have chosen for ourselves. In sum, values are those standards of choice that guide individuals and groups toward satisfaction, fulfillment, and meaning. They are present in our lives as those often hidden authorities in the name of which we make our choices and set our course in life.

—▪▪▪——▪▪▪——▪▪▪—

Discovering Our Values

By the time we start college, most of us have at least a fair sense of what our values are. Yet one of your key tasks during college is to be able to become more conscious and articulate about the values that define your own approach to life. Students typically find the college years to be a time for locating and testing their values by tracing their full implications through comparison with those of other people, by analyzing, and by giving voice to them.

Finding our values is both a simple and a complex task. The place to begin is not with some complex theories about ourselves, but with the actual choices that we make in response to life's demands and opportunities. Although the process of discovering values involves many stages and levels of analysis in a task that is never complete for any human being, surely the place to begin is with the actual life that we are living. In this process no one is neutral for no one can escape choices based on values. Everyone has values, although they are held with varying degrees of clarity and commitment.

As one general exercise in discovering our values let's consider some of the reasons that you have decided to attend college and this particular college. Why are you here? Many students will say that they chose a certain college where they are enrolled because of its academic reputation. Is this true for you and, if so, what do you mean by reputation? Are you interested in the prestige that comes from enrolling in the college? As a value, prestige may signify an interest in high achievement and in meeting demanding standards. Obviously, a value such as prestige can run in many other directions; one important test would be to see whether the weight of the value for you is more at the level of name recognition and "the right label" or whether it represents a commitment to genuine academic distinction. The process of finding values that stand behind our choices is a never-ending one that involves a continuing exploration of our choices and their implications.

Many students say that they have chosen a college because it offers the best opportunity for a good job in the future. Is this true for you? The choice to seek education in terms of its employment benefits suggests any number of possible values. Does this mean that economic security is one of your top values, or does it suggest that you are defining personal success in terms of obtaining wealth? Once again, the point is to examine your actual choice and to move behind or beyond that immediate choice and ask for its implications. How much are you willing to sacrifice to achieve the goals connected with the value? Does the achievement you are seeking bring fulfillment on a short- or long-term basis? How will your obligations to your family and the society at large relate to the particular value at hand? Under situations of conflict, what comes first?

As this extended example makes clear, we can put a whole series of questions to ourselves to gain a fuller understanding of the values to which we are committed. We may often begin with some of the tangible and obvious expressions of our choices—such as scholarships received, campus attractiveness, family influence, and reputation, in the case of college—and go from those immediate factors to the deeper reasons that stand behind them. The place to begin is with the concrete forms of our lives and to move to the values that underlie and orient our decisions. We are constantly testing ourselves in this process of self-analysis to see whether our choices are motivated by genuine values that involve a consistent pattern of action, of affirmation, and of free choices.

If the test of valuing is met, then we begin to explore the full implications of the value we are committed to. How did we become committed to this value in the first place? How does it relate to other values, since a conflict in values is an ordinary and unavoidable part of our lives? How far are we willing to go in service to this value? What sacrifices do we accept in its name? How do the values we have chosen provide us with a meaning for our future? We are never finished with the effort to give an ever sharper and clearer account of exactly what our values mean and of the implications they have for our lives and those around us.

Through various techniques such as values clarification, you can use simple tests, checklists, and other exercises to get a fuller sense of what your values are. In one exercise developed by Milton Rokeach in *The Nature of Human Values,* people are asked to rank two different series of values. The first list of eighteen values are intrinsic values that represent the end or purpose of life. The second list of eighteen are more instrumental in nature—they represent ways of behaving that may be necessary to reach a good life. Take some time to carefully rank the values on these two lists from number 1 to 18.

INTRINSIC VALUES

___ A Comfortable Life (a prosperous life)

___ Equality (brotherhood, equal opportunity for all)

___ An Exciting Life (a stimulating, active life)

___ Family Security (taking care of loved ones)

___ Freedom (independence, free choice)

___ Happiness (contentedness)

___ Inner Harmony (freedom from inner conflict)

___ Mature Love (sexual and spiritual intimacy)

___ National Security (protection from attack)

___ Pleasure (an enjoyable, leisurely life)

___ Salvation (deliverance from sin, eternal life)

___ Self-Respect (self-esteem)

___ A Sense of Accomplishment (making a lasting contribution)

___ Social Recognition (respect, admiration)

___ True Friendship (close companionship)

___ Wisdom (a mature understanding of life)

___ A World at Peace (freedom from war and conflict)

___ A World of Beauty (beauty of nature and the arts)

INSTRUMENTAL VALUES

___ Ambitious (hard-working, aspiring)

___ Broad-minded (open-minded)

___ Capable (competent, effective)

___ Cheerful (lighthearted, joyful)

___ Clean (neat, tidy)

___ Courageous (standing up for your beliefs)

___ Energetic (active, untiring)

___ Forgiving (willing to pardon others)

___ Helpful (working for the welfare of others)

___ Honest (sincere, truthful)

___ Imaginative (daring, creative)

___ Independent (self-reliant, self-sufficient)

___ Intellectual (intelligent, reflective)

___ Logical (consistent, rational)

___ Loving (affectionate, tender)

___ Obedient (dutiful, respectful)

___ Polite (courteous, well-mannered)

___ Self-Controlled (restrained, self-disciplined)

Other chapters in this book can provide you with a sense of your values as they come into play with reference to specific contexts such as choosing a major or selecting a career. Various exercises can be helpful ice breakers in starting your analysis of values, but ultimately the process of values awareness should become like second nature and be practiced continually.

College and Personal Values

Almost all students find that the college years involve a significant challenge to their existing personal and moral values. The challenge typically comes through friendships and relationships with new people whose backgrounds, ideas, goals, and desires run counter to your own prior experience. This clash with diversity can be unsettling; it may initiate a process of challenge and change in your own values that can be both exciting and threatening.

The encounter with diversity takes many forms, ranging from different habits of studying and sleeping that create conflicts with a roommate to deep philosophical differences over the purposes of life. Many freshmen find some of their most startling challenges in the diverse personal moralities that surround them. Some students have been taught in home or church that the use of alcohol, for example, is wrong and that the abuse of alcohol is deeply sinful. Students with a conservative philosophy on drinking alcohol may find that friends whom they respect and care about use alcohol in many ways that make them uncomfortable.

How do you deal with the circumstances in which you may not approve of some aspects of a friend's way of life? Do you try to change his behavior, make judgments against him, or withdraw from the relationship? Part of the problem is often that the friend demonstrates countless good qualities and values that make the suspect conduct itself seem less significant. In the process your own values may begin to change as a new kind of relativism begins to develop: "I don't choose to do that, but I'm not going to make any judgments against those who do." Much the same pattern of response often develops with reference to sexual involvements. People with one set of standards find themselves friends with others whose behavior is very different than their own. The challenge to a perceived set of moral values can then be severe and result in a lot of personal turmoil.

Outside a detailed knowledge of a concrete set of circumstances, we cannot know which response to a challenge to values is most fitting. Tolerance for others is a central value in our society and a value that often grows through the college experience. On the other hand, it is easy to think of cases in which tolerance can become indulgence of another's destructive tendencies. It is one thing to accept another's liberal but responsible use of alcohol at a party, but quite another to fail to challenge a drunk who plans to drive the car you're about to enter. Sexual intimacy in an enduring relationship is one thing and a series of abusive, one-night stands is quite another. They do not deserve the same response, and a failure to challenge destructive conduct is no sign of friendship.

Are there better and worse ways to deal with these challenges to personal and to moral values? The beginning of an answer, and only the beginning, resides in an awareness of the nature of values themselves. As we saw earlier, true values must be freely chosen by the person and cannot be accepted simply on the authority of another person. After all, the purpose of values is to give meaning to our lives through the choices that we must make. To try to make sense out of the complex circumstances of our own lives by using someone else's values makes little sense and ultimately simply will not work. Thus, in a time of challenge, we must try to find those values that are appropriate to the situation and that offer the prospect of giving that situation purpose and meaning for ourselves. If we tried to apply the values of our friends or parents in a new situation without making them truly our own, the result could produce much unhappiness and failure.

Many people make the mistake of fleeing from the challenge of diversity, of failing to confront the meaning of different moralities. The problem with this strategy is that at some time in their lives, often within a year or two, these people find themselves unable to cope with the next set of challenges to which they are subject. They do not grow as persons because they do not own their values or live out of them. Although only a first step, we must work through challenges to our own moral values by finding answers that truly make sense to us in providing the basis for moving ahead with our own lives. Often our received values prove to be adequate for the diverse experiences at hand, but even the acceptance of traditional answers requires that we make sense of them for ourselves.

College and Intellectual Values

In addition to the values that regulate our personal and moral choices there are political, economic, social, religious, and intellectual values. As we involve ourselves in the search for truth and knowledge, a whole set of intellectual values comes into play. These values serve as the standards and authorities guiding our conduct in academic pursuits. Intellectual values such as clarity, accuracy, rigor, and excellence circulate around the fundamental value of truth. One of the most striking transitions that occurs during the college years has to do with the way in which a student's understanding of the nature of truth changes.

Many students enter college with the assumption that the purpose of education is to have an unquestioned authority pour truth into the student as an open receptacle. Some students assume that there is a single right answer to every problem and that the teacher or the textbook as authorities will be the source of truth.

Most students soon find, however, that this black-and-white concept of truth is not shared by most college professors. A whole set of intellectual values undergirding most professors' assumptions about truth represent an initial shock to many students. Professors tend to see truth in a much more contextual, flexible, and variable way. It is not that the professor is cynical about the possibility of truth, but rather that the scholar's role is understood as involving a continual, open-ended search for truth. The professor's interest is in asking for as many valid interpretations of the information as can be found, and this search can both confuse and threaten you if you assume that there is but a single, authoritative answer. College teachers ask continually for the reasons that a position is held, for the best arguments for a given point of view, for the assumptions on which a given position is based, and for the evidence that confirms or counts against any given claim.

In all, just as with personal and moral values, college-level education involves the assumption that, as a student, you will become a maker of your own meaning, on your own, with the ultimate responsibility for judgments of truth and error resting in your hands. The whole system of a university's intellectual values—openness, freedom of inquiry, tolerance, rigor, and excellence—is based on this approach and there is no escaping it.

Assessment of Values

We have stressed that the essential first step in developing a values system is for you to become your own maker of meaning whether in the sphere of personal, moral, or intellectual values. But it is only a first step because you must be aware not only of making meaning but also of making a meaning that can lead to a coherent and fulfilling life. As crucial as it is to develop your own values, it is equally important that you find the right values. Little is accomplished if a person develops a genuine system of values that leads to conduct that is egocentric, dishonest, cruel, and irresponsible. It is not enough to own your values; you must think about owning the right values.

The question of the "right" values cannot be given any simple answers. Yet clearly all of us who have accepted life in a democratic society and membership in an academic community such as a college or university are committed to a wide range of significant values. To participate in democratic institutions is to be committed to such values as respect for others, tolerance, equality, liberty, and fairness. Similarly, those who are members of an academic community are usually passionate in the defense of academic freedom, the open search for truth, honesty, and collegiality, civility, and tolerance for dissenting views. In all these fundamental ways there is a substance of values without which we would not be what we are.

Although our participation in a democratic society and in academic communities has settled many of the deepest questions of the nature of the right values, many issues relating to values are open for continuing and legitimate discussion and disagreement. One of the most promising dimensions of an education that effectively addresses values is to give the educated person a process for coming to terms with value choices. The process is similar to the ways in which a good education teaches us to think. That is, an education in values can teach us how to value while leaving to our own independence the actual choices that we will need to make. In teaching us how to value as well as how to think, a good education will help us to be concerned about a series of overarching questions relating to values.

Through a good education you will become sensitive, for example, to whether or not your values are consistent with each other. Where we find cases of unjustified inconsistency we will know that a contradiction between values can be just as harmful and foolish as a contradiction between ideas. We will also discover that our process for assessing values will make us particularly sensitive to the points at which our values are too limited in scope and fail to provide us with a comprehensive outlook on life. We will learn that our values may work very well within the small circle of our family but tend to produce conflict with individuals with a different background. This will press us to reach for common ground, to try to find those areas of agreement where we can overcome conflict. The pressure always to move outward, to enlarge our circle of association, to move ever more toward the universal sphere of the human family beyond all divisions, beyond all racism, beyond all sexism, is a direction in which we seem always to have to go to find our true and best selves.

So it goes with many other tests by which we can measure the depth, the richness, and the adequacy of our values. We know that many of our choices fail to meet the test that time itself provides, and that partying away precious hours the night before a crucial exam simply fails to meet the test of relative worth. Life teaches us that transient satisfactions and pleasures leave us with little if they rob us of opportunities and accomplishments that may stay with us for a lifetime.

And so it goes. Our life itself is continually giving us tests as to which values will create coherent, consistent, and enduring results that will produce the greatest integrity and the greatest fulfillment of our potential. Just as we can be educated with regard to ways of thinking so we can be educated with regard to our valuing and our choices. This too is what college is all about, and the opportunity for both personal and intellectual growth is yours. May you seize it and reach your best possibilities by finding and affirming the truest values.

Suggested Activities

1. Do a values survey of a group of your friends (one at a time or in a small group) using the lists of intrinsic and instrumental values included in the article. When you have enough responses, at least twenty, do an analysis of the patterns and frequencies of the answers.

2. Share your analysis of the responses with those who participated in the survey. Discuss with the participants the reasons that they ranked the values as they did.

3. Encourage the respondents to assess or test their reasons with reference to others' responses and the criteria of choice discussed in the article—that is, consistency, coherence, comprehensiveness, authenticity.

4. Ask the participants to do the values ranking exercise a second time and compare the results with the first set of rankings. Try to develop a set of hypotheses about what changes, if any, were the result of the process of the discussion and the assessment of values.

14

Relationships: Communicating with Yourself and Others

Robert A. Friday

ASSISTANT PROFESSOR OF COMMUNICATION
DESIGNER/TRAINER, NEW STUDENT SEMINAR
DUQUESNE UNIVERSITY

When I speak with my students about relationships I look inside myself for the feelings and desires that have evolved from my childhood through my college days in the late 1960s until now. I go back in time to remember the constant questions of who to be with and what to do with them, as I passed through the era of sex, drugs, and rock 'n' roll.

Looking back, I now realize that when I entered college, I entered a new world of relationships. I still remember my roommates, and I hope to visit with them again someday. When I dated, there were times that my heart, filled with emotion, led me away from serious study and into the depths of a relationship I knew would last a lifetime. The joy, excitement, and exhilaration of those moments is now balanced in my memory with the tragic sense of loss, emptiness, and rejection that I felt when we found ourselves mismatched or called to pursue different directions in life. Then friends consoled me with the cliché of having been better to have loved and lost than never to have loved at all.

I know now that I never lost in the giving and receiving in any relationship even though the bond did not last a lifetime. I still have all of the feelings I ever felt and remember fondly those who led me to dizzy heights and those who brought me back to stability. And I am growing every day with a new understanding of why I feel what I feel. The relationships that I have with my wife, children, parents, students, friends, neighbors, and colleagues are stronger and fuller because of the relationships I had in college.

Even though I am now a professor of communication, a designer and trainer of a New Student Seminar program, an international corporate and educational consultant, a farmer, a husband, a father, and a son, I am still a freshman deep inside—looking at the world of relationships in total wonder—awestruck at how we attract, involve ourselves, and change forever the directions of the lives we touch.

—ııı—ııı—ııı—

In this chapter I want to show how communication is the basic substance of the relationships that we all experience in life. In the following pages I will define and discuss three levels of relationships and the kinds of communication that will lead you to discover the joy of understanding yourself and connecting with others: (1) *intrapersonal communication,* the path to and the relationship we have with ourselves; (2) *interpersonal communication,* the messages we send from ourselves and receive from others close to us; and (3) *ethical communication,* the impact that our communication has on others. As you proceed, be aware that the rules for communicating with yourself, others, and the larger social environment are all basically the same. In short, love, hate, honesty, deception, respect, and disrespect bring about the same results regardless of whether you are communicating with yourself, your roommate, an intimate partner, a classmate, business associates, or the entire American electorate—as Senators Gary Hart and Joe Biden found out in their 1987 bids for the presidency.

—ııı—ııı—ııı—

Intrapersonal Communication

You are not ready to develop deep and lasting relationships with others until you have such a relationship with yourself. A good relationship with yourself is the product of hard work. It seems strange that we have to work at getting to know ourselves, since we are with ourselves all the time. But just as fish will be the last to discover water, we are the last to discover the difference between how we see the world and what the world is really like. Intrapersonal communication—communication with yourself—requires time spent alone, usually doing something that helps you introspect, or look into yourself. As a freshman, I spent a few hours several times a week jogging or exercising. Those hours always left me physically and mentally refreshed because I was giving myself the time to sort through my own feelings and interpersonal problems.

Getting to Know You

As a freshman, you are entering a world of newfound knowledge. Some ideas will be exciting and others objectionable. Why do you receive some ideas positively and others negatively? Developing objective and honest communication with yourself is a necessary stage in becoming an educated person. As you explore your origins and compare your family, background, and values with others, you will improve your understanding of why you think what you think, why you say what you say, and why you do what you do.

If you approach a situation with a fixed attitude, you may think you are actually seeing the situation, when you may only be seeing your attitude toward that situation. How many times have you seen the sun set? The attitude, or "lens," built into our language tells us that we are seeing the sun set when actually, the earth is rotating.

To develop rewarding relationships, you must know yourself. You must know if you are honest, trustworthy, reliable, desireable, fair, cooperative, helpful . . . the list goes on. Such traits can be understood only through reflection on your experience in social relationships. For example, if you take on a small responsibility, such as making plans to meet a friend at a particular time and place and then fail to show, your friend and others may feel that you are unreliable. People who are considered unreliable are less likely to be given responsibility. In this way your personal quality—unreliability—could directly affect your relationship with others and, ultimately, your career. Should you find yourself making commitments that you fail to keep, you may be saying "yes" to things you don't really want to do. Sometimes we say yes to please others. Learning to say no can actually boost your personal credibility.

The process of intrapersonal communication is the act of a person reflecting on his or her personal and often private values, desires, needs, and dreams and comparing them to the feedback from those who know us well. Until we listen to others' observations of us, and honestly take into account that some of what they say may be valid, we may be hiding in our own dream. As we weed through the perceptions of ourselves and others, we come to know our strengths and weaknesses. We come to grips with what we like about ourselves and what we would like to change in ourselves.

I recall one of my students who wanted to be a great rock star. Yet her vocal or musical talent was never expressed. She focused on the rock star role, ignoring the caring interpersonal skills and sensitivity that were her nature and the organizational capacity that she was developing. Actually, she had a very low opinion of herself. She did not see her daily actions as a very successful student because those actions did not lead her any closer to the goal of becoming a rock star. She saw herself as a failure, even though she was a loving and successful person to those around her. Until she began to set aside the fiction—in fact, take off the Walkman cassette player—and listen to the feedback from those who knew her from her actions, she was unable to have realistic and rewarding relationships with herself, others, and her work.

—▪▪▪—▪▪▪—▪▪▪—
Interpersonal Communication and Intimacy

Your earliest relationships are reciprocal. While it may appear as if a baby is helpless, such is not the case. From a Darwinian perspective, children survive because they are so cute, loving, and fulfilling to most of the adults who have them. Thus, your first relationship follows the rule of all relationships—*you have to give to get.*

Building any relationship starts with revealing yourself. Poker players keep their cards hidden and try to overpower or bluff their opponents. Healthy relationships cannot be based on strategies that beat or bluff the other person. Healthy relationships are love relationships that come from the center of each person, as Erich Fromm so clearly expressed in his timeless statement in *The Art of Loving:*

> Love is possible only if two persons communicate with each other from the center of their existence, hence if each one of them experiences himself [or herself] from the center of his [or her] existence. Only in this "central experience" is human reality, only here is aliveness, only here is the basis for love. Love, experienced thus, is a constant challenge; it is not a resting place, but a moving, growing, working together; even whether there is harmony or conflict, joy or sadness, is secondary to the fundamental fact that two people experience themselves from the essence of their existence, that they are one with each other by being one with themselves, rather than by fleeing from themselves. There is only one proof for the presence of love: the depth of the relationship, and the aliveness and strength in each person concerned; this is the fruit by which love is recognized [1956, p. 103].

The idealized, romanticized relationship is not generally pictured with the conflict and sadness mentioned by Fromm. But in reality, "fighting is inevitable between true intimates. Quarreling and making up are the hallmarks of true intimacy. However earnestly a mature person tries to live in harmony with a partner, he will have to fight for his very notions of harmony" (Bach and Wyden, 1969, p. 11). Fair fighting is a form of revealing yourself. The fair fighter avoids blaming the other person and concentrates on expressing how they feel and what they need. When intimates assert themselves to each other in this fashion, they come to know their partner's feelings and move toward accommodation.

Other times, especially after a couple experiences a moment of great intimacy, a fight may break out over nothing at all. Studies of married couples reveal that fights sometimes meet emotional and psychological needs. After intimacy, distance often has to be established so that one person does not engulf the other (Bach and Wyden, 1969). Learn to identify and clarify with your roommate or partner the reason for the conflict and then discuss it together.

If you or your partner is establishing territory, that's okay. No one is being rejected. Give each other the space to express individuality. If issues of differences come up—as they should—be sure you are both talking about the same thing: Define the issue. If one considers the issue to be serious, set aside a time to discuss it. The moment you come home from work or school is not a good time to fight about an important issue. The quiet of the evening is a more productive time for most people to wrestle with their differences.

Communicating with Roommates

Living with a roommate has a great impact on the lives of most resident freshmen. If you have not previously shared a room over a long period of time, your roommate will probably have a greater impact on your sense of private space and territory. You may not ever have thought that some "stranger" might open your closet and consider your clothes as his or her own. Yet your roommate may have spent his or her entire life sharing in this fashion, all the while assuming that everybody acts this way. Nobody is to blame for the negative feelings that arise when situations like this occur. (If the roommate situation is new to you, read "Your College Residence" in Robert Friday, *Create Your College Success* [Belmont, Calif.: Wadsworth, 1988]. It has detailed instructions for preparing yourself for and proceeding through roommate negotiation.)

Roommates are usually total strangers who physically share our most private space. To move from strangers to friends, roommates must invest a great amount of time defining how they feel about everything from the temperature of the room to having guests in for visits. Roommates must know what is personal and what can be shared, study and sleep habits, music and noise preferences, attitudes about drugs and sex, and, above all, confidentiality. If you have a roommate, take time to get to know him or her. You may not ever become close friends and hang around together, but you are living together and are destined to learn much from the experience.

Sometimes roommates need to fight over issues like neatness or behavior. Pretending that everything is all right, when you are actually furious that your roommate has left a mess in the room will destroy your relationship in the long run. Your resentment will surface in other ways while he or she will assume that everything is just fine. To avoid such conflict, you should come to an agreement as to how the room should be managed. When deviations from the agreement occur, discussion should promptly follow. Put a "do not disturb" sign on the door and proceed to explain how you feel about the situation. Be calm and polite. Give each other every opportunity to reflect, explore, and talk. Such conversations are rarely easy at first, but the experience will prepare you for a lifetime of positive communication with friends and intimates.

Eight Elements of Constructive Interpersonal Communication

Successful interpersonal communication usually contains the eight elements that follow. (Stinnett, and Walters, 1977, discuss elements 2 through 7.) Examine them carefully. Devise a plan for incorporating these elements or guidelines into your communication with friends, roommates, and dating partners. Once you incorporate these guidelines into your interpersonal communication style, you will find a new richness in the human growth that occurs when people come together.

1. *Revealing yourself.* Know who you are and express this honestly to others. If you explain to the other person what you like and don't like, you are establishing rules of behavior for your relationship. If you like to drink now and then when you are on a date, that may not bother someone who does not prefer alcohol as long as you do not get drunk. On the other hand, if you have preferences such as premarital sex that require the participation of your partner, you should find a way to indicate this aspect of yourself. Many people believe that taking off their clothes in front of another person is a most intimate and private form of communication. If your date reveals that sexual relations should be reserved for marriage, he or she is establishing a rule of behavior. If you do not agree but wish to develop a relationship with your date, have a discussion to bring out both points of view on the issue of sex in relationships. Perhaps you will decide that you like him or her enough to postpone sex until later. If, on the other hand, you did not discuss and reveal, but simply tried sexual advances, you could be communicating your disrespect for your date.

When you have always had control over your private space and possessions, sharing a room or a home can be difficult at first. I can still remember when my wife moved into the house I had lived in for five years prior to our marriage. As her possessions marched in the door and "displaced my world," I experienced a noticeable amount of confusion and frustration. We knew that she was moving in, but neither of us thought to discuss how her presence would affect "my space."

Some preferences are negotiable and others are not. Explore your preferences openly and together.

2. *Mutual respect.* The ideal person may exist in your mind, but he or she may be very hard to find on campus. Chances are the person sitting beside you in class or those you live with in the dorm or at home do not fit all of your criteria for an ideal partner. You cannot change someone into your ideal. Trying to change someone is usually a hopeless task because it begins with your disrespect—your nonacceptance of him or her.

Roommates, friends, and partners should explore beliefs and values together without making judgments. If you begin by trying to understand why your roommate tends to be neat or sloppy, you might arrive at some mutual accommodation. People who respect each other usually try to accommodate the needs of one another. Most people like to work out a harmonious agreement if they are given the chance. For example, maybe you can agree that both of you will clean the room every Saturday morning and try to keep it clean during the week. If you approach your roommates with disrespect, however, calling them "neat freaks" or "slobs," you will be provoking hostility instead of agreement.

If you find yourself on a date with someone who is experimenting with drugs, you are perfectly within your rights to tell that person that you disapprove and do not want to participate. If your date respects you, he or she will not use drugs while spending time with you. If you both have a good time on a drug-free date and wish to pursue the relationship, the drug user may choose to change behavior out of respect for the partner. Such a change would be occurring in response to respect for the other.

3. *A common frame of reference.* A shared background of experience, ideas, and attitudes can be very important in the development of a deep understanding and appreciation of one another. One of the most difficult experiences for freshmen occurs when a dating partner from high school does not go to college. College accelerates your growth on both the intellectual and emotional levels. The love felt for the high school sweetheart becomes both distant and near, confused and clear, as the freshman's worldview expands and the loved one left behind remains much the same. For a while the old shared background, experiences, and emotions span the growing distance. As new experiences go unshared, the pain of the loss of the bond evolves into many other feelings.

Sometimes guilt, fear of rejection, or denial of the effects of distance are felt or expressed. The resolution to this dilemma is never easy, and exploring your feelings with counselors and friends is important. Feedback will help you keep the issues clear in your mind. Honest discussions with your friend back home are also important.

Having friends in common and appreciating the same cultural or social events increase feelings of belonging. The lack of a common frame of reference can cause individuals to feel alienated or alone in the presence of each other. People from different cultural, racial, or economic backgrounds often have difficulty communicating and developing relationships. One of my black students spoke recently about the differences that separated her from her white roommate. Rap music and rock 'n' roll became just one example of the contrast in their majority/minority cultural backgrounds. Neither wanted to give up her music for the other. Each had a different set of friends. While they were good roommates for a year, they never became friends—mostly because of the distance between their frames of reference.

4. *Active listening.* Paying attention to direct verbal messages is only the first level of listening. Most communication that occurs between two people is of a nonverbal nature. Try saying, "Hey, glad to see you," while looking away. Ask them which message you communicated. Chances are they will wonder if you are really glad to see them.

Facial expression, tone of voice, posture, and sense of physical, psychological, or emotional distance (amount of sharing) are all aspects of active listening. If you are not listening, you are not in communication. You are not in a relationship with the person who is trying to communicate if you do not attend to all of his or her signals.

5. *Checking the meaning of communication.* "This is my understanding of what you mean by_____." "I wanted to clarify your meaning in my mind because I think it is important that we understand each other." This is how you use active listening to practice revealing yourself, express mutual respect, and explore and extend your common frame of reference. So complicated are human signals that it may take a decade of communicating with someone before the need to check communication is reduced.

Most of us are rather sloppy with our language on the interpersonal level. There is a difference between "you make me angry when you leave your clothes lying around the room" and "I get angry when you don't clean up our room and help keep it the way I expect my room to look—especially when I am having a friend over." The first statement implies that the less-than-tidy roommate is responsible for, and the cause of, the other roommate's anger. The second statement communicates that the roommate feels anger because the untidy roommate does not live up to his or her expectations. If these two roommates are good communicators, they will resolve that the anger is not justified if the expectation is not communicated in advance. Roommates should negotiate a contract to clarify the expectations that each has about the way the shared space should be managed.

6. *Empathy.* When you put yourself in the place of the other person and do your best to feel what he or she is feeling, you can understand the emotional state of the other person and meet his or her needs. Don't confuse empathy with sympathy. Whereas *sympathy* is an expression that you share similar feelings, *empathy* is an actual projection of your personality into the personality of another. In empathy we walk a mile in a friend's shoes. We place ourselves in his or her situation and try to see the world as he or she sees it. In empathy you take the time to sit with a friend and explore who said or did what, why they said or did it, and what the work or action means. Empathy includes meaningful exploration and concludes with advice: "If I were in this situation I would. . . ."

7. *Acknowledging the legitimacy of another's feelings.* Feelings are not always logical. Each of us experiences physiological cycles. Our reactions to temperature and seasonal changes are so individual that one natural phenomenon can leave one person energized and another depressed. Though the mental and emotional states of others may defy our logic, we must acknowledge the legitimacy of those feelings.

Few people forthrightly state their feelings unless they have known each other a long time and have a history of good communication. In the early stages of relationships, most people let out little signals to see if the other will pick them up and respond. We tend to test to see if our friend cares before we open up. Indicate that you sense the other wants to talk. Ask what he or she is thinking or feeling, and you will open up that deeper level of interpersonal communication.

In our culture, women talk more about feelings whereas men tend to keep feelings locked up inside. In the early years of dating, men often do not recognize feelings as a legitimate topic of conversation. True intimacy can develop only when both partners learn to talk about the things that are important to the other.

Rather than sending out test signals or just jumping into a topic, you might ask your partner or friend if he or she has ever discussed "X" feelings or situation. If a response is slow in coming, you might discuss this subject in your past and then ask for feedback. This approach will give both a better chance to understand where the other is coming from. It is important to share past experiences to build a common frame of reference.

8. *The acceptance of conflict.* Most people prefer to avoid conflict. We have somehow developed the notion that conflict equals rejection. Nothing is further from the truth. Most often conflict between friends or partners indicates that one sees a problem in the relationship and wishes to correct it for the benefit of both. "Marital conflicts . . . may enhance stability because they may lead to *change,* and change, by removing the sources of conflict, may make the situation rewarding enough for the partners to want to remain in it" (Scanzoni, 1970, p. 75). Remember, the best part of intimate communication is often the recognition of differences, arguing, resolving, and making up. When an argument concludes with an increase in appreciation for each other, you can be sure that you are building a positive intimate relationship.

When you want to raise an issue with a friend, partner, or roommate, be sure that you set the scene properly. Don't try to get into an issue while you are racing to class or when your roommate or friend is working on a term paper that is due the next morning. Try something like: "I have been thinking about the way we have been _____" or "I would like to discuss how I feel when you _____. Can we take a walk tomorrow after class and discuss our feelings on this?" The other person now knows the issue is going to be discussed and probably has a good idea of the role he or she has played in the situation. You have given the other person time to get ready. In doing this, you avoid springing a topic, which often produces tension and defensiveness. Remember, the objective is to arrive at a *mutual agreement*—not to beat the opponent.

Ethical Communication

Some people go through stages in which they want to get but not give. If you find yourself saying to the object of your love, "I need you and can't live without you," you are probably stuck in a dependent situation. You should reevaluate yourself and your needs and find ways to give in order to get what you need.

Good Idea, Wrong Reason

I talked with a young woman who, after four years of hard study and career exploration, suddenly announced that she was going to marry her boyfriend and have children. I congratulated her but pointed out that this was a rather surprising change in direction and asked whether her sudden desire to become a wife and mother was related to her fear of leaving school and starting a career search. She agreed that the two feelings were probably related but that she did want to get married and have a family some day. We discussed right and wrong reasons for getting married. If she was avoiding the fear of failure by electing the security of marriage, wasn't she placing a large burden on her boyfriend? Could he *make* her happy?

She talked things over with her boyfriend and discovered that they shared some of the same anxieties. This is quite natural. Most people feel a little nervous when facing so much uncertainty. Now they are growing in their relationship by facing their fears together; because they know each other well, they can help one another. Remember that a relationship is a bridge that both people must be able to cross to each other. After a while, being needed makes one responsible for continuous giving—often without getting.

Fear of Rejection

A much more unhealthy or even ethically questionable communication occurs when individuals use others to get what they want. These relationships are often built on the one-sided communication of poker players. Many who communicate in this fashion are actually afraid of being rejected.

Ironically, in the drive to be accepted, such a person negates the preceding elements of intimate interpersonal communication. Such unsuccessful interpersonal communication is usually characterized by:

- Pretending to reveal yourself but actually making up or selecting aspects that you think the other person will like.

- Giving lip-service respect to the other person, which is often just empty flattery.

- Attempting to take on the frame of reference of the other person—only to appear awkward and out of place.

- Spending more energy on what you have to say rather than listening to the other person.

- Failing to check the meaning of what has been said because you do not really want any differences clarified—often out of fear of rejection.

- Failing to empathize with the other person's feelings and often holding back the expression of your own true feelings.

- Denying the legitimacy of the other person's feelings. "You can't be serious" is the kind of expression often used to attempt to cause the other person to question the legitimacy of his or her own feelings.

- Avoiding conflict because you are unwilling to lay your true feelings on the line.

Many people feel unsure of themselves during a time of growth and change. Most freshmen feel some anxiety about whether they will make friends, be liked, or be loved and accepted. I have heard countless stories of students who have lied or deceived others, apparently in the hope of being accepted as a friend. Such occurrences seem to be most common in the freshman year when anxiety over the fear of rejection combines with other personal crises such as shifting identity and loss of contact with family and friends.

I have heard of students making up brothers and sisters because their roommate came from a large family. One student had to confess that she did not like ballet after her initial false enthusiasm. Her boyfriend had gone to considerable expense to surprise her with season tickets to the Pittsburgh Ballet Theater. The irony was that after breaking up over this miscommunication, they kept running into each other at basketball and hockey games. He didn't think women were interested in sports. She never mentioned that her goal as a communication major was to become a sports commentator!

If you find yourself communicating deceptions in order to fit in, it's time for some honest intrapersonal communication. Write a letter to yourself exploring your development in your early years among your family and friends. Emphasize all of the times that people have loved and accepted you. Tell yourself what you do well, why you like to do it, and how good you feel doing it. Get out a calendar and block out some time that you can dedicate to doing what you like to do, and do it. Finally, look over all of the possible clubs, organizations, and activities that you can get involved in on or near your campus, and join one. You will most likely find that if you develop an honest communication with yourself and begin an activity that you enjoy, you will find yourself making friends with those who share your interest.

Unethical Relationships

The way you treat others is really a statement about yourself. If you willingly let someone think that he or she is loved just so you can seduce him or her into a sexual act, you are degrading that person from the level of a human being to the level of a plaything. In such acts you, too, become an object because you must hold back in the deception game rather than communicate your humanity. Whether the prize so deceptively sought is sexual pleasure, social status, information, money, or something else, the result is the same and is expressed in an African proverb: What goes around comes around. Eventually the deceit becomes known because few can live a lie for a lifetime or because subsequent events force both parties to show their true colors. Since the rule "you have to give to get" still stands, the givers of the world advance in the getting and the deceivers, or poker players, lose.

Sexually Transmitted Diseases

Ethics and morals are guidelines that have been handed down for thousands of years because they work. That is, people who followed certain codes survived and prospered while those who took other paths perished. In the past thirty years Americans have moved away from the traditional values that promoted virginity and sexual abstinence before marriage. Such guidelines once served to keep a person emotionally and psychologically clear from entanglements, less likely to be compelled to marry because of pregnancy or die from abortion, and free from sexually transmitted disease.

With the discovery of penicillin and the invention of birth control devices, many began to ignore these ethical and moral guidelines. I am not saying that going beyond the traditional guidelines makes you a bad person. But ignoring the reality of today's sexually transmitted diseases can cost you your life and the lives of those you love. We have every reason to believe that, until a cure can be found, AIDS will continue to spread like wildfire in populations that condone having several or multiple sexual partners. This has been the case in Uganda, where over half of the population will die from AIDS before the turn of the century. In expressing the biological reality, one of my students said, "When you sleep with someone, you are sleeping with everyone he or she has slept with for the past six years."

The introduction of AIDS into our society should compel you to reconsider the life-threatening consequences of unsafe sexual activity. The tragedy too often is that an act of love is now becoming an act of death. You don't want to die from AIDS, and you don't want to be responsible for giving it to someone else. Having sex without the proper use of a condom is dangerous. Ignoring the issue because you are embarrassed to talk about it is like pretending it is safe to swim in shark-infested waters. If the cure does not come soon, and there is no reason to expect it will, those who survive will be the ones who talk about sex and practice it safely. The sexual freedom of the 1960s and 1970s is dying a painful death while a new openness is being born. Be a part of the openness. Many excellent videos and pamphlets are being produced on the subject of sexually transmitted diseases. See them, read them, and discuss them. If you are going to have sex, explore the subject with your partner, and arrive at an agreement that protects you both. (See Chapter 17 for additional information.)

Relationships with Friends and Colleagues: Networking

Whether in love, academia, or business, sharing and giving relationships are the keys to advancement, to being loved, to getting new and refined ideas or increased profit. In academic advisement, selection of a major, career development, or job hunting, your network is your biggest asset. In communication we talk about networking as the quintessential art of communicators. Networking is the art of building a web of relationships by beginning with those close to you and developing relationships with those close to others through referral and interview. The most successful networkers are kind, open, friendly, giving, and *respectful* of others' needs and wishes. Phrases like "I am glad to meet you," "How may I help (or serve) you?," and "Thank you very much for_____" are often spoken sincerely by successful people practicing the art of networking. All of the elements of successful communication between intimates can be applied in a more formal way to successful communication between colleagues and others in your network.

Your relationships with roommates, neighbors, and good friends are the first level of your network. We have all heard the old saying that "It's who you know not what you know that counts." Actually, it's how you know other people and how they know you that counts. If you are known to other people as an honest, caring person, your reputation will precede you, and your path to success will be paved by your friends.

Suggested Activity

1. Review the eight elements of constructive interpersonal communication in this chapter. In brainstorming a class discussion, give examples of how these eight elements would be applied in the following situations:

   a. Your roommate has had visitors in your room several nights a week for the past few weeks. You are having difficulty studying with the noise and confusion, and you feel that you should not have to leave your space to find the quiet that you require.

   b. You are going on a date with someone you find attractive. You want to go some place where you can get to know him or her and have a good time. Your biggest fear is that you won't be able to think of anything to say. Where should you go and what should you talk about?

   c. You have not been sexually active, but your dating partner of two years was before you met. You both have been discussing marriage. You are thinking about sexually transmitted diseases and you want to be sure that your partner does not have a disease, yet you don't want to bring up the subject and get a negative reaction from your partner.

References and Suggested Readings

Bach, George R., and Peter Wyden. *The Intimate Enemy.* New York: William Morrow, 1969.

Fromm, Erich. *The Art of Loving.* New York: Harper & Row, 1956.

Laslett, Barbara. "The Family as a Public and Private Institution: An Historical Perspective." In *Intimacy, Family and Society,* edited by Arlene Skolnick and Jerome H. Skolnick. Boston: Little, Brown, 1974.

Perlman, Helen Harris. *Relationship: The Heart of Helping People*. Chicago: University of Chicago Press, 1979.

Rogers, Carl. "Communication: Its Blocking and Facilitation." In *Language, Meaning, and Maturity,* edited by S. I. Hayakawa. New York: Harper & Row, 1954.

Rosenfeld, Jeffery P., ed. *Relationships: The Marriage and Family Reader*. Glenview, Ill.: Scott, Foresman, 1982.

Scanzoni, John. *Sexual Bargaining: Power Politics in the American Marriage*. Englewood Cliffs, N.J.: Prentice-Hall, 1970.

Stinnet, Nick, and James Walters. *Relationships in Marriage & Family*. New York: Macmillan, 1977.

Developing Leadership and Life Skills Through Involvement in Campus Activities

Dennis A. Pruitt

VICE PRESIDENT FOR STUDENT AFFAIRS
DEAN OF STUDENTS
UNIVERSITY OF SOUTH CAROLINA

It seems like only yesterday that I entered college as a shy, naive freshman, publicly cocky but privately semiconfident. In those days, being a freshman was a truly humiliating experience. All freshmen were given beanies, which we had to wear our first semester. Colleges and universities had a rigid class system, and as freshmen we were considered to be the lowest common denominator of all the classes. As freshmen, we had no privileges and were constantly taunted by upperclassmen. How times have changed!

I left home to attend college. In my own mind, I felt as though I suffered through every conceivable trauma known to the freshman college student. But those experiences helped me to realize something important about college. I went to college hoping, at best, to survive, to get a college education against all the odds. My parents, my high school counselor, my older sister, and my classmates had warned me that I'd be lucky if I made it past the first week. Luckily, I became involved in athletics, student government, and other areas of campus life. It brought to my attention, as I hope in this chapter to do for you, that college is not a time to survive, but rather a time to thrive. If you use the entire campus as a living-learning laboratory, you will grow, learn, and develop as a person far beyond your wildest expectations.

I am currently the Vice President for Student Affairs and Dean of Students at the University of South Carolina. Our most important goal in Student Affairs is to create a challenging and supportive campus environment that provides students with an enriched education. But this is only half the formula that ensures that learning will occur. As a student, you must become actively involved in your education by engaging in a variety of learning opportunities. Only then can you receive the maximum benefit from your collegiate experience.

—III——III——III—

The Holistic Approach to Education: Mind, Body, and Soul

The importance of using the entire campus as a learning lab can best be understood by reviewing the various reasons students come to college. You may be seeking to increase your earning power, to gain training for a good job, or simply to enjoy social activities. Many students have always assumed they'd go to college because their parents didn't have an opportunity to get a college education when they were young. Others feel that in today's society you just "have to have a college diploma."

All these reasons for attending college are good ones, but why are you *really* in college? Believe it or not, I discovered the real reasons students attend college while attending a rock concert. During intermission, the famous rock star had granted the customary interviews, and a reporter asked what characteristics were needed to be successful in the entertainment industry. The star replied candidly and without hesitation: "First, as I was growing up I found out everything I could about the music and entertainment industry. Second, I developed skills so I could use the knowledge I acquired. As a result, I can play over twenty musical instruments. I have written dozens of songs. In other words, I can *apply the knowledge* I have acquired in a productive manner. Third, and most importantly, I'm one heck of a nice guy! Everyone, everywhere likes me!"

If you think about what this famous entertainer said, those are more than likely the real reasons you're attending college. You are there to pursue knowledge you don't have, to develop skills in applying the knowledge you acquire in a way that benefits you and society, and you're also there to learn how to get along with others. No one would argue that many of these needs are fulfilled by the experiences you have in the classroom. But you can enrich your knowledge and skill level as well as accelerate personality development if you take the risk to become involved in campus life as either a participant or a leader.

In college, you'll meet people of different races and religions, from various economic and social strata, even from many different countries. You'll also find an infinite number of differing, sometimes conflicting, philosophies about almost anything and everything: politics, economics, religion, and social problems. Many of the people you meet will be quite different from you and your previous friends. If students can increase contact, acquire knowledge, and gradually learn to tolerate, accept, and appreciate students who differ from themselves, they will succeed in achieving one of the major goals of attending college. This sort of informal learning can occur in the classroom, on the athletic field, in the residence hall, or in a student organization meeting.

—III——III——III—
An Historical Look at Campus Activities

Campus activities were not always an important part of the student's educational experience. Historically, many educators felt that moral, social, physical, and spiritual development should not interfere with the pursuit of knowledge. In the 1800s, campus activities were started by students themselves as a means of expanding (and in some cases, escaping) the rigorous, and often dry, curriculum of that era.

The classes in those days were taught with virtually little class discussion. Professors taught as if they were the repository of all knowledge. As a result, students decided they wanted to discuss topics (such as politics, philosophy, or the issues of the day) in a setting where free discussions could take place. (Free discussion usually did not take place inside the classroom because the professor was the only expert.) Debating teams were one of the first known cocurricular activities, followed by athletic events (intramurals) and academic clubs. Students organized themselves, as they still do today, by common interest or cause. Since those times, many educators have acknowledged that a university or college has a responsibility to develop a student not only intellectually, but culturally, ethically, physically, spiritually, and socially as well. Today, on virtually every college campus, a variety of campus activities are available for student participation and leadership. Let's review the major types of activities on most campuses.

- *Intramurals* are sports competitions between clubs, teams, or individuals within the campus. At most colleges, competition exists for major sports such as football, basketball, softball, and swimming. In intramurals, unlike intercollegiate competition, every student can participate. Intramural programs and events are often structured by competition level so all can enjoy the experience.

- *Club sports* revolve around a specific athletic interest, such as a club for bodybuilding, bowling, fencing, karate, sailing, or windsurfing.

- *Outdoor recreation* usually includes camping, hiking, rappelling, whitewater rafting, and similar activities.

- *Intercollegiate athletics* may be open to nonscholarship participants, who are commonly referred to as walk-ons. Many institutions have a closed athletic system in which only scholarship athletes participate, but you can be a loyal "fan in the stands," a cheerleader, or a member of the marching band or spirit club.

- ☐ *Honor societies* (some are secret membership organizations) represent some of the oldest groups on campus. Among hundreds of local and national honorary societies, some of the better known include Mortar Board (senior honor and leadership society), Omicron Delta Kappa (collegiate leadership society), and Golden Key National Honor Society (to promote scholastic achievement and excellence).

- ☐ *Professional and academic organizations* generally represent each of the academic disciplines on your campus. Among others, you might find on your campuses the American Chemical Society, the American Society of Mechanical Engineers, the Black Law Student Association, Graduate Women in Business, and the Medical Student Association.

- ☐ *Greek letter organizations* (which usually have national affiliations) are both service and social organizations. Students will recognize these sororities and fraternities as the "Greeks" on campus.

- ☐ *Social and special interest organizations* can encompass virtually any and all student interests, including the Association of Afro-American Students, the Athenian Literary and Debating Society, the Chess Club, the Gay Students Association, and the Italian Club.

- ☐ *Political organizations* on many college campuses exist only in national and/or local election years. Examples of political organizations are the Rainbow Coalition, the Young Republicans, and the Young Democrats.

- ☐ *Service organizations* espouse the true meaning of altruism by serving others. Such organizations include: Alpha Phi Omega, Bacchus, Circle K, and the Student Alumni Association.

- ☐ *International associations* provide a support group for foreign students and assist in representing their needs to your institution. Such organizations include the Chinese Student Association, the Association of Iranian Students, and the International Committee Against Imperialism and Oppression.

- ☐ *Military organizations* generally work to create an interest in the military, and include the Blue and Gold Society (Navy), the Arnold Air Society (Air Force), and the Company (Army).

- ☐ *Student media organizations* are generally popular and active on college campuses. They include the student newspaper, magazine, yearbook, radio station, and cable television station.

- ☐ *Religious organizations* are among the most active and most supportive organizations on campus. Most campuses have traditional and untraditional organizations, which include the Baptist Student Union,

Hillel (Jewish), Muslim Student Association, Campus Crusade for Christ, the Way Campus Outreach, and the Presbyterian Student Center.

☐ *Student unions* generally have a group of committees responsible for bringing major entertainment to campus, including dances, concerts, art exhibits, lectures, and videotape and travel programs.

☐ *Residence hall and student government associations* enable students to participate in the governance of the institution. Often each residence hall, or academic major, will have a representative on the student senate. Check with your campus activities office and with your residence hall advisors to learn about these opportunities.

☐ *Musical organizations* are plentiful and in most cases you need not be a music major to participate. They include a marching band, concert band, concert chorus, and performing vocal or instrumental groups of all kinds such as a jazz band.

While you may not have all these clubs or organizations on your campus (and the exact names and purposes may differ), a wide range of similar clubs exists on your campus. Why does virtually every college and university in America support so many clubs and organizations? (At the University of South Carolina we have almost 300 groups.) Because we know these clubs can provide tremendous learning opportunities for all students.

Furthermore, most colleges have student activities or student life offices that will assist you and your friends in establishing a new organization. If you're interested, simply meet with the advisor in the appropriate office on your campus. You'll be surprised how easy it is to get an organization started, and what wonderful learning can occur as you plan it.

━ⅲ━ⅲ━ⅲ━
Benefits of Participation and Leadership in Campus Activities

All of these activities offer exceptional opportunities for both participation and leadership. Each student learns and benefits from his or her experiences in campus activities in various ways, depending on the frequency and level of involvement in the activity. A student who only goes to one or two meetings of a service organization benefits less than the student who attends all meetings, actively participates in group projects, and eventually becomes club president.

However, all students who participate in or lead student organizations are exposed to a variety of useful skills, including (but not limited to) motivational techniques, conflict resolution, communication, validation techniques such as praise and criticism, facilitating an effective meeting, accepting and delegating responsibility, committee management, decision making, problem-solving methods, project management, planning and organizing, and volunteer recruitment techniques. This is an impressive list of workplace skills, but an even more impressive list of benefits exists for your personal development.

Students who participate in and lead student organizations have the opportunity and the resources to develop many skills. For instance, time management becomes more essential to the student who has assumed extra responsibilities. Students learn to cope with financial management, interpersonal communications skills, power (your own as well as the power of others), and success and failure through participation in organizations.

Furthermore, as an involved student, you'll find that you learn to be more resilient, overcome shyness, and handle stress. Involved students generally exhibit a high degree of self-esteem. They are keenly aware of their personal strengths and limitations. Involved students and student leaders are a unique breed; they are more likely to be dependable, active, persistent, responsible, and much more achievement oriented than students who don't assume leadership positions. Active students almost always tend to be more popular, too—another good reason to be involved in the student organization of your choice.

—III—III—III—

The Big Payoff

The biggest payoff for being an active, involved student is that you'll learn the tools of program management: how to organize an activity, program, or project. Program management has four components, but each involves a complex process. First, you must select the activity for the participants or audience. Second, the event or activity must be properly promoted. Third, you must produce the activity—actually have the dance or concert. Finally, you must evaluate the event to determine its success.

Program management—the selection, promotion, production, and evaluation of an activity—appears on the surface to be a simple process, but many experts spend years developing proper program management skills. Involved students and student leaders can get a head start on their fellow students (who will be joining them in the search for jobs) because they are actually developing and practicing techniques for program management, day in and day out, while in college. What a payoff!

Another payoff is learning to take risks within the comforts of a protective environment. Colleges and universities set up rules and procedures to protect students from excessive risk, but in many clubs you'll have an advisor who will encourage you to push yourself to the limits by accepting new challenges. The mentor relationship you establish with your advisor, and the freedom to operate with your peers within the protective climate of the university can foster creativity. In a society where creativity is stifled, you'll find that yours is rewarded and that your ability to generate ideas and solutions increases. Learning to take risks and to use creative approaches to resolve problems are other good justifications for spending your out-of-class time as a leader.

—III——III——III—
The Formula for Involvement

If there were a formula for getting involved in campus activities, I would gladly provide it. But because there is no formula, the process for involvement becomes more adventurous. Some hints may help you. First, get involved in the club or organization *early* in your college career. Once involved, stay involved! Accept responsibilities for even minor assignments such as hanging posters, sitting at a voting booth, or arranging the cleanup committee (we call it "dirt work") for a major activity. Work up to the major task assignments when you feel comfortable with your leadership skills. As you do these tasks, learn all you can about program management and working with people. Try leadership techniques you've seen others use. Don't be afraid to take risks and don't ever be afraid to fail. Never hesitate to ask for the advice of those who are older, wiser, and more experienced than you. Often, such insights can prevent an embarrassing program flop.

Basically you must want to be involved and only you can determine how to do it. But remember, you don't have to be the president, or even the vice president, to have a satisfactory experience.

I'll never be able to adequately express how valuable my participation and leadership experiences were to me. But I'd like to close with this thought: Your college years will be among the best of your life. The thousands of experiences you have in college will provide you with positive experiences and memories for many years to come. My challenge to you is this: Give something back to your college and to your organization. Do something for them by being an involved student or leader, so that you'll leave a legacy just as one was left to you. It's a great adventure. Go make some memories!

Suggested Activities

1. Visit your student union.

2. Visit your campus activities office and schedule an appointment with an advisor there to discuss opportunities on your campus.

3. Review your student handbook to better appreciate the wide range of programs, activities, and organizations available for your involvement.

4. Contact your volunteer action center, either on campus or in your community, to discover involvement opportunities.

5. Discuss with your friends, roommates, or classmates the possibility of joining, together, an established club or organization.

6. Discuss with your friends, roommates, or classmates the formation of a new student organization providing activities in your areas of common interest.

7. Seek out students who are currently highly involved in a student organization. Ask them why they are involved, how they got involved, and what benefits they are receiving.

8. Try to arrange an internship with an active administrative office on campus such as the development office, alumni, admissions, or president's office.

9. Enroll in a class that focuses on community services, leadership training, or organizational management (a public administration course, an ROTC course, a business course).

10. Write a term paper for one of your classes about involvement and leadership—its dues and rewards.

11. Read a biography about one of the great educational, political, religious, or philanthropic leaders.

Suggested Readings

Jennings, Eugene E. *An Anatomy of Leadership—Princes, Heroes, and Supermen.* New York: Wiley, 1978.

Lassey, W. R., and R. R. Fernandez, eds. *Leadership and Social Change.* La Jolla, Calif.: University Associates, 1976.

Lawson, J. D., Leslie Griffin, and Franklyn Donant. *Leadership Is Everybody's Business.* San Luis Obispo, Calif.: Impact Publishers, 1976.

Lawson, L. G., J. Lawson, and R. A. Donant. *Lead On! The Complete Handbook for Group Leaders.* San Luis Obispo, Calif.: Impact Publishers, 1982.

O'Connell, Brian. *Effective Leadership in Voluntary Organizations.* Chicago: Follett Publishing, 1976.

Rudolph, Frederick. *The American College and University*. New York: Random House, 1982.

Student Leadership Development Series. One article per issue in *Programming Magazine,* published by National Association of Campus Activities, Box 11489, Columbia, S.C.

University Associates. *The Annual Handbooks for Group Facilitators,* 1972–1983. San Diego, Calif.: University Associates.

Wilson, Marlene. *The Effective Management of Volunteer Programs*. Boulder, Colo.: Volunteer Management Association, 1978.

16 Living at Home, on Campus, and with Friends

Richard D. Wertz

VICE PRESIDENT FOR BUSINESS AFFAIRS
UNIVERSITY OF SOUTH CAROLINA

I've always enjoyed my association with colleges and universities, both as a student and as an administrator. In fact, my positive undergraduate and graduate experience had much to do with my returning to the academic world.

I grew up in a small university town in Pennsylvania and lived there until I finished high school. I had planned to attend Penn State early in my high school career, even though it had an enrollment twice the size of my hometown. I was somewhat concerned about its size, but I wanted very much to go to school there. I lived in a residence hall during my freshman year, and this turned out to be a highly supportive environment for me. Good friendships and pleasant experiences contributed to the easy adjustment I made to college life.

Subsequently, I lived in a fraternity at Penn State that housed sixty-two men. This differed from the residence hall in that fraternity members were responsible for managing themselves, paying the house bills, and taking care of matters on their own. At the fraternity there were plenty of people to talk to and many opportunities for relaxing after studies were over.

In graduate school, I lived in an apartment off campus with two other students. Apartment living was very different from life in the dorm and the fraternity house. My apartment mates and I had to do everything on our own, from buying groceries to cooking and cleaning. And, of course, we needed to practice self-discipline, since no one was there to make sure we studied!

The three different living experiences I had in college, along with the many other positive experiences from those days, led me to choose college administration as my lifelong career. As I look back, I realize how important it was for me—and how important it is in general—to find the proper residence environment in college. My aim in writing this chapter has been to make you aware of that, too.

—|||——|||——|||—

After you have decided to attend a particular college or university, the next most important consideration is where to live. Many options are available, but your choices can generally be narrowed down to three. You may decide to live (1) on campus, (2) at home, or (3) with friends. At least two of these categories offer a wide range of options that I'll be discussing in more detail.

The college experience centers around the academic work your professors require of you. You attend college to learn and to develop intellectually, but an equally important aspect of college is your total development: academic activities; interaction with faculty, staff, and other students; time outside the classroom; and the total living experience on or off campus.

A great deal has been written about the "total development of the student." Colleges and universities have always recognized the importance of academic work and a formal education. During this century, higher education has directed more attention to the development of the student as a total person. The process of individual development has reached new levels as those of us in the university setting realize more fully the necessity of enhancing student development.

One of the best descriptions of student development was written by Arthur Chickering, who has studied the development of students for years. Chickering (1969) says there are seven steps, or what he likes to call "vectors," that young people confront as they go through college:

1. *Achieving competence.* This includes intellectual, social, and interpersonal competence as well as physical and manual skills.

2. *Managing emotions,* in particular those involved in aggression and sex.

3. *Becoming autonomous.*

4. *Establishing identity.*

5. *Forming interpersonal relationships.*

6. *Clarifying purposes* that include vocational and recreational interests, vocational plans and aspirations, and general life-style considerations.

7. *Developing integrity,* which is concerned with a valid set of beliefs that serve as a guide for behavior.

These stages will be a major part of the collegiate living situation. Whether on or off campus, alone or with friends, with parents or relatives, your living situation will change dramatically from what you were used to previously. Let's consider these various kinds of living arrangements and what you may expect from each.

The economic outlook is creating a phenomenon in the United States that seriously threatens the ability of many to pay for college. Financial aid cutoffs have caused some middle-class families to become ineligible for assistance, and this development has created college admissions problems for some students. Caught between affluent families who can afford to pay high tuition rates and the less affluent parents who qualify for aid, the number of middle-class students continues to dwindle. Even if middle-class families can manage to pay high tuitions, where will these students live? And can those who must live at home afford a car to travel back and forth from class?

We have already begun to think of financing a college education much as we think of financing a home or car. It's a long-term process to bring together the resources to pay thousands of dollars in tuition annually for four years.

Living on Campus

For many students, going to college means living away from home, making new friends, getting settled in a new environment. Living on campus can be an exciting and interesting experience.

Dormitories, or residence halls, are a product of the European influence on higher education. Cambridge and Oxford Universities in England were seen as models of what higher education should be like in America. Residence halls were constructed in American colleges in an attempt to involve students in the academic life of the college and to allow them to meet with, learn from, and live with faculty members.

This ideal situation occurred at some universities, but met with difficulty at many other colleges, where the residence halls were convenient places for students to live, but served no real educational purpose as had originally been intended.

The strong interest in fraternity and sorority houses grew out of this concept and answered a need for students who wanted both a place to live and membership in an organization.

For approximately twenty years, American higher education has taken a renewed interest in residence halls. Because students spend many hours each day in the residence hall, colleges and universities began taking a closer look at what other activities they could provide for students in these halls.

As a result, institutions began providing such activities as informal talks with faculty members invited over for coffee or evening get-togethers; a "free university," which allows practically anyone with an interest or ability in some topic to present that topic; floor or hall intramural athletic contests; social interaction among the residents on the floor, in the hall, or with other halls; seminars by faculty or staff on campus or by personnel in business and industry off campus; international cooking nights; guest speakers from on or off campus discussing current topics; and other activities suggested by the residents themselves.

If you've chosen to live in a residence hall, take advantage of the time you spend there. Participate in activities that may be new to you or that you know nothing about. You may be surprised to find a new area that interests you or for which you have some real talent. This setting offers a chance for you to excel at no risk. There are no grades or stressful expectations. Go ahead and try something new. You may actually learn something and have a good time doing it!

What can you expect if you plan to live on campus? Several options or choices are available, and you'll need to consider each of them.

First of all, living on campus calls for a different sense of responsibility and behavior. You may be used to parents who expect you home by a certain hour or ask you to check in with them by phone. In the residence hall, your counselor or hall director may be around to supervise, but generally no one is keeping tabs on you or demanding that you be in at certain hours.

And in most cases you'll be sharing your room with at least one other person. This calls for an adjustment to the living patterns of others and demands that you show consideration toward them. In most residence halls, a number of people live in a hall, although many residences now feature apartment-style living. This situation means another adjustment—living with many individuals in the same building and sharing bathrooms, lounges, and study areas.

Living on campus presents you with a great opportunity to associate with other college students and to grow and learn together. A strong feeling of friendship and togetherness develops as students share their college experiences.

Living in a residence hall is also a time to learn and study together. It's a time to expand your thoughts about what life has to offer. You'll probably engage in many late-night "rap sessions" on limitless topics. Students living on campus have the opportunity to explore new frontiers of thinking and thoughts about themselves, their lives, and their immediate world. Close friendships often develop and a sense of belonging prevails. The development of lifelong friendships is not unusual among those who first meet in a residence hall.

In a residence hall, as in any other living environment, you must learn to budget your time. For the most part, it's your responsibility to keep up with assigned academic work and to stay current with classes. Looking after personal belongings and keeping your room in order is also entirely your responsibility, as are keeping track of room keys, student identification cards, meal cards, and other valuables.

In most cases, an undergraduate or graduate advisor will be assigned to your hall. In some cases a full-time college employee will be in charge of your residence hall. You may seek out a residence hall staff member for many kinds of assistance. The staff member will probably be close to your age and trained to deal with many kinds of situations—and is usually available to students around the clock, day and night. Feel free to contact him or her when you need help or just want to talk.

Theme Halls

To help make residence halls worthwhile educational and learning experiences for students, "theme halls" have been established recently. Allowing students to explore or expand areas of interest, such theme residences may be language houses (such as Spanish or German), honors halls, creative arts halls, or architecture halls, for example. Special interest halls or houses may have a relationship to a college major, a hobby, or an outside interest, and they enable students with common interests or talents to live, learn, and pursue those interests together.

On many campuses, these theme halls are available during your freshman year, and most campuses allow you to continue the arrangement as you progress toward graduation. As an incoming student, you thus get a chance to match your campus residence to your personal interests.

Coeducational Living

Not long ago, all residence halls offered by colleges and universities were strictly single sex. That is, men and only men lived in men's halls and women and only women lived in women's halls.

This option is still available. However, another option on most campuses is coeducational living, where the students on the floor above or in the next room may be of the opposite sex.

This development has led to a great deal of publicity in the media, and the public has often criticized colleges and universities for having coed dorms. But the coeducation option has now been widely accepted in most sections of the country.

For the most part, coeducational living allows women and men students to get to know each other as individuals and, consequently, a healthy respect develops for the opposite sex. Instead of the wild, unsupervised partying many people expected, men and women students have learned to live together like brothers and sisters; friendships blossom and people are allowed to develop as individuals in an environment that reflects the real world.

Students in coeducational residences tend to attend events, participate in activities, or generally travel in groups more than as single couples in dating relationships. Formal dating certainly occurs and always will; however, the group phenomenon is an interesting aspect of male/female relationships in college, and it allows women and men to do things together without a sense of obligation or commitment.

Peer Pressure in Residence Halls

Just as coeducational living has been a fairly recent development, so has the elimination of curfew or restricted hours. In the past, students (especially women, unfair as that was) were required to be in their residence halls at a certain time each night. For violating these curfew rules, students were "campused" or restricted to their residence halls for a certain period, suspended from college, or expelled permanently.

At most colleges and universities today, no curfew hours exist. You're responsible for your own behavior. With this freedom comes a great deal of pressure from your friends to experiment. Such pressure may force you to decide about your own behavior with regard to drinking, drugs, or sex. You need to be prepared for such peer pressure and think about how to handle it. Peer pressure may have existed in high school, but in college the stakes may be higher and the consequences may be greater.

College will force you to make decisions about a number of things regarding your personal life. And living with a group of students twenty-four hours a day in a residence hall necessitates more decisions. Remember that you are your own person. You don't need to be pressured into anything, and you don't have to do something you'd rather not because a friend or a group of friends is pressuring you. Ideally, college will add to your feeling of independence and to a clearer establishment of yourself as a person. You'll be learning to work through your own decisions and problems more and more as you grow through college.

Friends who pressure you into things, as you already know, may turn out not to be friends after all. Friends who stick by you, offer advice and assistance, but do not pressure you may be your best friends. Remember: You become like the people you associate with, so choose your friends carefully!

Going Home Again

After living in the residence halls for a period of time, you'll probably adjust to group living, learn to become independent, "go it" on your own, and develop as a person. As a result, returning to home and family may bring with it the feeling of change. When you return home, many things may be different, and such changes may alter your relationship with your parents and relatives. In a residence hall, you may be achieving full adult status and independence, and this is a natural and healthy experience. Going home again, however, changes all that. You leave home as a teenager moving into adulthood, and each time you return, you're more of an adult.

Be aware of this change and understand the effect it may have on those at home. Your evolving status as an independent adult will be natural and should progress, but this shift may be difficult for your family to accept. Tact and diplomacy certainly will be called for, and your patience may be tried when parents, relatives, or friends treat you as a schoolboy or schoolgirl. Remember that their intentions are for the most part good, and be tolerant if they're slow in accepting you into the adult fold.

So why choose a residence hall? For the friendships that will develop. For the maturity and growth that will help you gradually establish your own identity. For the experience you will surely gain by living with others in a new setting. For the opportunity to take part in different activities, programs, projects, and learning experiences. And for the exciting prospect of getting to know yourself as a person through the new people and experiences you'll encounter and the opportunity to be taking care of yourself. One more reason: Students living in residence halls tend to stay in college longer than those who don't! Extensive research indicates that students living on campus do earn higher grade-point averages, have a higher rate of staying in college, and adjust to college better.

Living at Home

The pattern of life in high school is far more regimented and structured than what you will experience in college. High school starts at the same time each day and follows a fixed daily schedule. The day even ends at the same time for most high school students. This is rarely the case in college. Each day may call for a different schedule. Although classes may be in sequence, they usually don't meet every day. There will be days when classes start early or run late, and there will be time between classes. You won't always be able to have lunch at the same time each day because of class schedules.

Given such realities, a student living at home will have many adjustments to make. Your schedule will dictate leaving or returning home at times completely different from high school, and the rest of the family will have to adjust to this new situation. As these changes occur, patience—yours and your family's—will certainly help.

Resolving Issues

Try to work out in advance any situations that may lead to potential conflict with the family. Although you may have enjoyed a great deal of freedom while living at home in high school, your parents probably felt they still exercised some supervision. As you develop as an adult, you'll expect less supervision, and living with parents under these circumstances can strain the student/parent relationship! Discuss with your parents—the sooner the better—how living at home while attending college will necessitate a different pattern of living for you.

Just as your coming and going from the house will surely change from your high school days, so will your study habits. Reading and writing requirements may often dictate "all nighters" or at least some late-night study sessions. Younger brothers or sisters may need to be kept quiet so you can get ready for the big exam the next day. The demands of academic work may take you away from traditional family outings and further strain the family relationship.

You can reduce or eliminate some of this stress and strain by reaching an early understanding. Sometimes, though, the conflict may not be resolved while you're living at home. In any event, life needs to go on for your family while you live at home. Therefore, both you and other family members will need to make sacrifices.

Since you'll probably have college friends who also live at home, discuss your areas of concern with your fellow commuters to see how they may have worked things out or what they may be doing in situations you're concerned about. You should also become friends with students who live in residence halls, to become acquainted with their life-styles. Spending time with students in the residence halls is a good opportunity for the student living at home to experience what it's like to live away from home. Although economic circumstances may require you to live at home, remember that, at some point, we all leave home.

Living at Home with Spouse/Children

If you're living at home as a husband or wife, a different sort of adjustment is required—especially if one spouse is a student and one isn't. Budgeting time for study will be extremely important, and you'll have to allow enough time for academic work while either working or doing household chores. The parent attending college will need to work out a schedule to cope with both college and children's demands, and both parents must come to an agreement about priorities.

For married students, budgeting time is crucial if you're to succeed in college, and the strain of college will be heightened when children are involved. Making a schedule that takes into account both of these responsibilities and sticking to the schedule should be an early priority.

Holding Down a Job

If you must work while in college, the way in which you budget time is important because work hours mean fewer study hours. There are, of course, only so many hours available for other activities, and you'll need to weigh one against the other carefully so that neither academic work nor leisure time suffer. As in marriage and child rearing, the demands of a job mean complying strictly to a tight schedule to allow you time for study and other activities. Generally, a student carrying a full-time course load should be working no more than twenty hours weekly. If you must work more hours, consider taking fewer courses.

Living with Friends

The student living in the residence halls will be making an adjustment both to living with others as well as to not living at home. Living with friends also requires an adjustment. You'll have many things to consider and work out; discuss these considerations with your intended roommates ahead of time.

Living with friends probably means living in an apartment. Unlike living at home, where the family may take care of meals, laundry, housekeeping, and other tasks, living with friends requires that all parties share in household chores.

In choosing your apartment, remember that where you live influences your study habits and living patterns. A place far away from campus presents transportation problems, and commute time subtracts from study time. A noisy place makes studying difficult.

When you've found the right accommodation, review the lease carefully. Thoroughly understand the length of the lease, deposits, subletting, responsibility for repairs, and rent due dates before you sign a lease.

What about choosing the right roommate? Living with your friends can be pleasant or result in frustrating situations. Be sure the persons you want to live with as roommates are compatible with you. This decision is as important as choosing the right accommodation.

Budget Planning

Life away from home in off-campus quarters with friends will be challenging. Setting up housekeeping requires that you develop a number of skills. First of all, financing the venture will require adherence to some sort of budget. You'll need to set aside funds for rent, food, utilities, and telephone service—plus everything from toilet paper to curtains.

It's more than a good idea to work out in advance a budget that everyone can live with. If a group living arrangement is to succeed at all, everyone involved must contribute his or her share, and those shares will have to cover all expenses involved. What you may take for granted in a residence hall or at home will have to be provided for when living with friends. And someone in the group will have to make certain that routine bills are paid. (See Chapter 21 for pointers on money management.)

Cooperation in sticking to the budget is paramount. As expenses vary, you'll need to adjust your budget. Sometimes unknown expenses—an illness or accident, for example—will occur and should be taken into consideration when preparing the budget. You may discover the groceries you bought and hoped would last two weeks are gone in five days. Or the utility bill may be twice what you budgeted for, even though you tried to conserve energy this month.

Sharing Housekeeping Duties

If your group is cooking for themselves, someone will need to grocery shop regularly. If you all prepare meals separately—meal times and tastes may vary—you'll need to be considerate of each other's food. You'll also need to take turns cleaning the living areas or assigning regular specific duties to specific persons. How the kitchen is cleaned and the condition it's left in will require cooperation and agreement from all parties. The same is true for cleaning bathrooms and general upkeep.

Living with friends off campus is the most independent life-style of them all. No parents or relatives or residence hall staff will be around in this situation. You'll be responsible for your own actions. Demands on your time generally will be greater because of housekeeping chores. You need to budget time adequately to include study and relaxation in your schedule.

Finally, living together with friends will require consideration of others' belongings and possessions as well as their rights and privacy. Without parents or hall staff around, you'll have to work out disagreements among yourselves. Being on your own really means just that when you live with friends off campus. It can be a worthwhile and fulfilling experience when handled properly, as well as a great deal of fun. And working things out in advance can contribute substantially to the success of living off campus with friends.

Living Options: Making the Choice

Your first year at college in any of these living alternatives will be an adjustment, just as college itself is an adjustment. Living on campus, at home with parents, or off campus with friends are options available to you, and you may experience them all during your college years, because each year offers you an opportunity to rethink your living arrangements. If you live in a residence hall during your freshman year, for example, you may join a sorority or fraternity as a sophomore and live there until graduation. The student living with parents may decide to move on campus or into an apartment.

The point is that change is possible and that alternatives are available. Some students choose to live in a different setting each year, while others are more comfortable staying with one situation. There's no ideal solution to choosing a residence, other than to say that the best arrangement is what's best for you. Seek a setting that allows you to study, make friends and socialize, and to get the most out of college.

Most assuredly, financial circumstances and other considerations will play a part in this decision. But choosing the right living arrangement will play a major part in your success throughout college.

Suggested Activities

1. Compile a list of questions to be settled with roommates as you think about what it would be like to live with friends off campus. Visualize what you might need for an apartment, what living there would be like, and how you would keep it orderly.

2. If you live off campus, interview several students living in residence halls and compare the pros and cons of dorm life to those of off-campus living or living with parents.

3. Arrange a debate in class with students living on campus, off campus, and at home, arguing the pros and cons of each situation. Discuss what you learn from this experience.

References and Suggested Readings

Chickering, A. S. *Education and Identity*. San Francisco: Jossey-Bass, 1969.

DeCoster, D. A., and P. Mable, eds. *Student Development and Education in College Residence Halls,* Washington, D.C.: American Personnel and Guidance Association, 1974.

Feldman, K., and T. M. Newcomb. *The Impact of College on Students*. San Francisco: Jossey-Bass, 1970.

Sanford, N. *The American College*. New York: Wiley, 1962.

17 Developing a Healthy Life-Style

Linda Morphis

HEALTH NURSE SPECIALIST
GYN/OB NURSE PRACTITIONER
STUDENT HEALTH CENTER
UNIVERSITY OF SOUTH CAROLINA

After working for many years in big-city hospitals, I became increasingly aware that many of the illnesses and deaths I saw were related to the way people lived and that the majority of problems were preventable. This awareness led me to a greater awareness of my own health, and I began trying to improve it. I changed my eating habits and gradually committed myself to regular exercise. One of the high points in my life was completing a 26.2-mile marathon several years ago. The natural outgrowth of this experience has been a desire to help others become well and to support them in developing the skills necessary to live a healthier life. My goal is to reach people before they become sick.

I feel that we're all capable of positive change and that our potential for self-discovery and growth is virtually unlimited. What follows is designed to help you become aware of this potential, too. By developing a healthy life-style, your body can become strong and your spirits can soar. It's an exhilarating prospect!

—||||—||||—||||—

David Carlson awoke with a start and looked at his clock. Darn! Overslept again! He vaguely remembered hearing the alarm ringing harshly in the quiet dorm room and realized he must have turned it off and gone back to sleep. "I've got to stop doing this," he mumbled irritably to himself. Staying up late studying, not sleeping well when he did fall asleep, and feeling as if he could hardly drag himself out of bed the next morning had become a typical, unpleasant routine for David.

He hurriedly dressed and headed for the elevator, stopping only long enough to buy a Coke and a candy bar. The annoying thought of the ten extra pounds that had mysteriously appeared on his body since coming to school entered David's mind, but he pushed it aside. "I need all the energy I can get this morning," he thought as he left the vending machines.

A clear, crisp autumn morning greeted David as he walked across campus, but he was too intent on getting to class to notice. If he hadn't already taken all the cuts allowed in his English 101 class, he would definitely not be out yet. It was a morning he would rather forget. He felt rotten—not being able to sleep, lacking energy, feeling sluggish and fat—yet he didn't understand what was going on or, even worse, what to do about it.

David's story is a familiar one. If you identified with it, you're not alone. Unfortunately, too many college students accept feeling tired and sluggish as "normal." However, the good news is that it doesn't have to be that way. You can affect your health in a very positive way. You don't have to wake up each morning feeling tired and irritable. You can feel good every day. You can have abundant energy and a real zest for life. The things you do daily can have an important impact on your general well-being in the long run, as well as in the short run, while you're in college. Getting the proper exercise and choosing wholesome, nutritious foods can help you feel better and work better each day.

Before you set up roadblocks—such as I don't have time to exercise; running is boring; I can't eat properly between classes; the campus snack bar serves nothing but junk food—pay attention to some positive thoughts that have to do with taking better care of yourself. After all, you're an important person, and you deserve special treatment.

Many people who have gotten into the habit of running three times a week or more actually claim they are more productive after exercising than before. "I spend about ninety minutes stretching, running, showering, and dressing," says one professor. "By the time I get back to work, I feel recharged, and my mind actually seems to function better and more sharply and clearly than before. I amaze myself with the amount of work I can accomplish in one such afternoon."

Or listen to a university student who found she *could* eat properly, even in the university cafeteria. "I don't starve myself ever," she says. "I choose salads from the salad bar, broiled rather than fried foods; I take advantage of all the fresh cooked vegetables they serve (sometimes I just load up on vegetables and skip the meat), and look for chicken or turkey or fish instead of beef."

These are not "health food nuts" or "exercise freaks" speaking, but rather typical individuals who realize that the habits they acquire at this point in their lives are likely to help—or haunt—them for years to come.

What's your defense against growing into a lumpy, listless body? Or your excuse for not trying to grow out of one? The proper combination of diet and exercise *now* can provide many of the right answers. The message is clear: Americans may literally be digging their graves with their teeth. The leading causes of death in our country—heart disease, cancer, stroke, and diabetes—are linked to the way we eat, either indirectly through obesity or directly through the types of food we put into our bodies. Millions of Americans are malnourished, not in the traditional sense, but in the form of overconsumption of highly processed "junk foods" that are loaded with sugar, salt, and fat.

Sugars found in their natural state (in fruits, vegetables, grains) are digested slowly and enter the bloodstream gradually, while refined sugar is rapidly absorbed. Some scientists believe this influx of high sugar levels in the blood creates imbalances in our system and may be related to the onset of diabetes or mood swings such as depression. Research also indicates that high salt intake contributes to elevated blood pressure, and strong evidence links to heart disease the intake of foods high in saturated fat.

The average college student consumes approximately 126 pounds of sugar per year and two to five times more salt than is necessary for the body to function, and as much as 40 percent of daily calorie intake comes from fat.

There's no question that it's difficult to counteract these unhealthy eating habits. In our society, with processed convenience foods so readily available, you need awareness and extra effort to choose foods that are wholesome and as unprocessed as possible. Becoming nutritionally aware includes realizing that the foods you eat actually do become you! It's a biological fact that cells in the body are developed and replaced as food is broken down and utilized. By eating well, you are treating your body with care and respect; you're arming yourself with basic tools that are physically essential for achieving your potential.

Your Nutritional Assessment

To help assess your nutritional habits, try the following self-scoring test.* You must recognize what habits you already have before beginning to make changes.

---

* Prepared by Dr. Roger G. Sargent, Professor, College of Health, University of South Carolina. Used with permission.

Circle point score if applicable to your diet.

PART I

POINTS

1. I have one to two cups of milk or milk products (yogurt, cottage cheese, and so on) per day. 1
2. I use low-fat or skim milk and/or milk products. 1
3. I eat ice cream or ice milk no more than two times a week. 1
4. I use solid, soft, whipped or liquid margarine in place of butter. 1

TOTAL POINTS EARNED: _____

PART II

5. I do not eat meat, fish, poultry, or eggs more than once a day. 1
6. I do not eat red meats (beef or pork) more than three times a week. 1
7. I remove or ask that fat be trimmed from meat before cooking (also circle point if do not eat meat). 1
8. I have no more than one to three fresh eggs per week, either in other foods or separately. 1
9. I have meatless days and have such meat substitutes as legumes (beans, peas, and so on) and nuts. 1
10. I usually broil, boil, bake, or roast meat, fish, or poultry (also circle point if do not eat these foods). 1

TOTAL POINTS EARNED: ___3___

PART III

11. I have one serving of citrus fruit (such as oranges) each day. 1
12. I have at least two servings of dark green or deep yellow vegetables each day. 1
13. I eat fresh fruits and vegetables when I can get them. 1
14. I cook vegetables without fat (if I use margarine, it is added after cooking). 1
15. I usually eat fresh fruit rather than pastries. 1

TOTAL POINTS EARNED: ___3___

PART IV   POINTS
16. I eat whole grain breads and cereals.   1
17. Cereals that I prefer are usually high bran or
    high fiber.   1
18. Cereals that I buy are low in the amount of
    sugar added.   1
19. I prefer brown rice to common white enriched
    rice.   1
20. I usually have four servings of whole grain prod-
    ucts (cereals, breads, brown rice, and so on) per
    day.   1

                    TOTAL POINTS EARNED: 4

PART V
21. I am within five to ten pounds of my ideal
    weight.   1
22. I drink no more than 1½ ounces of alcohol per
    day.   1
23. I do not add salt to food after preparation and
    prefer foods salted lightly or not at all.   1
24. I usually avoid foods high in refined sugar and
    do not use sugar in coffee or tea.   1
25. I normally eat breakfast and it usually consists of
    at least bread or cereal and fruit or fruit juice.   1

                    TOTAL POINTS EARNED: 5

For your nutritional rating, place points earned in appropriate box:

	EXCELLENT	GOOD	FAIR	POOR	YOUR SCORE
Part I	4	3	2	1	_____
Part II	5–6	4	3	2	_____
Part III	5	4	3	2	_____
Part IV	5	4	3	2	_____
Part V	5	4	3	2	_____

                         TOTAL POINTS EARNED: _____

Excellent   23–25
Good   19–22
Fair   14–18
Poor   9–14

    If you scored less than "good" in your overall rating or on any part of the
test, chances are you have room for improvement in the way you eat. A good
way to begin is by choosing fewer processed foods.

▬III▬III▬III▬
Whole vs. Processed Foods

How do you tell the difference between whole, natural foods and refined, processed ones? A simple way to tell is by asking yourself how close the food is to the state in which it came from nature. The greater the number of additions, subtractions, or modifications, the less natural it is. The changes usually involve the addition of salt, sugar or other sweeteners and fats or oils and the removal of fiber. Other changes might include a loss of vitamins and minerals, a reduction in flavor and taste, and the addition of preservatives, artificial coloring agents, and other chemicals.

When sugar and fats are added and the fiber removed, one obvious result is unwanted and unnecessary calories. The potato is a perfect example of what happens when processing takes place. The most natural way to prepare a potato is to bake it in the skin. This will give you about 125 calories, plus fiber and vitamins, including a good amount of vitamin C. With a pat of low-fat margarine, the total number of calories is still only around 200.

Now, if you eat a serving of french fries instead of a baked potato, you get around 400 calories, a big decrease in vitamin C, and very little, if any, fiber.

Let's go further and say that instead of the fries, you eat potato chips. This means you will very likely eat a large amount before you feel satisfied, and you'll be getting around 500 calories, a whopping amount of salt, almost no vitamin C, and no fiber.

So, when you really think about the food you give your body, it makes sense to choose wholesome, natural foods rather than processed foods laced with chemicals and preservatives.

▬III▬III▬III▬
How to Eat Better

To further help individuals in their efforts to eat healthier, the U.S. Senate Select Committee on Nutrition and Human Needs has established dietary goals for Americans. The following list describes those goals:

1. *Increase complex carbohydrate consumption:* Of the foods you eat each day, the greatest number of calories (50 to 60 percent) should come from fruits, vegetables, and whole grains. These foods are classified as complex carbohydrates (refined sugars are not included).

2. *Reduce intake of fat and foods high in fat:* This can mean cutting down the amount of red meat eaten (and that includes hamburgers), substituting

more poultry and fish, and having meatless days several times a week. Fat is more concentrated in calories (1 gram of fat has nine calories, while 1 gram of carbohydrate or 1 gram of protein has four calories); therefore, foods that are high in fat content automatically have twice as many calories as low-fat foods.

3. *Reduce cholesterol intake to about 300 milligrams/day:* Go easy on meats (especially fatty red meats and pork), shellfish (shrimp, lobster), and eggs. Substitute skim or low-fat milk for whole milk. One egg has almost 300 mg of cholesterol, and it may be wise to have no more than three eggs per week.

4. *Decrease consumption of sugar and foods high in sugar:* Limiting the intake of processed foods will go far toward reducing the amount of refined sugar in your diet. Approximately 80 percent of the sugar we eat is "hidden sugar." This means sugar has been added to the product and we may not be aware of it. Get into the label-reading habit. Ingredients are listed according to their percentage within the product. For instance, if sugar is first in the list of ingredients, that means the product has more sugar than anything else and should, therefore, be avoided.

5. *Reduce salt consumption by half or more:* Again, limiting processed foods, salty snack items (chips, salted nuts), and most of the "fast foods" so readily available will go far in reducing salt intake. Experiment with other seasonings and spices (such as lemon, pepper, oregano), rather than using salt. Read labels. Look for the words *soda* and *sodium,* and the symbol "Na" on the labels (*sodium* bicarbonate, mono*sodium* glutamate, *sodium* benzoate, and so on).

But what if you live on campus and usually eat in the cafeteria or nearby places? With the foods they serve, it can be hard to eat sensibly. The following healthful hints are offered to those of you in this predicament:

- Keep fresh fruit available in your room for between-meal snacks.
- Nuts and dried fruits (raisins, figs, dates) are also healthy snacks, but keep in mind their high calorie content.
- Drink fruit juice, skim milk, or water with meals rather than soda.
- Choose fresh fruits over pastries for dessert.
- Choose baked or broiled meats over fried, and select fish or poultry rather than red meats (beef and pork).
- Seek out restaurants that have salad bars.

In our fast-paced, overprocessed, convenience food-oriented society, eating well can definitely be a challenge. It may take effort in the beginning, but once you establish a sound pattern, choosing healthy foods becomes automatic.

Experiment, have fun, be creative—make an unbelievably good sandwich using whole grain bread, tofu and tahini spread, sprouts, and tomato rather than a hotdog. (Your first adventure will be to discover what tofu, tahini, and sprouts are!) Have a luscious drink made with vanilla yogurt and fresh strawberries, rather than the chemical-laced, nonmilk "shakes" available at fast-food places.

Remember, eating whole, nutritious foods *can* make a positive difference in the way you feel. The choice is yours. Make it a wise one.

Eating Disorders: Anorexia and Bulimia

In an effort to attain the "ideal" body, many people are unfortunately caught in the trap of abnormal eating behaviors. Anorexia and bulimia are two conditions involving complex emotional, psychological, and physical factors. While young women are more commonly affected, young men are certainly not immune to the disorders.

Anorexia is frequently described as "self-starvation" and this is actually what happens. Those with anorexia typically begin a diet to lose weight and the process becomes totally out of control with severe restriction of calories and excessive, strenuous exercise. Issues concerning self-esteem and achievement, control of events, parental expectations, and sexuality are frequently involved. Without treatment, anorexia can lead to death as the body becomes more and more depleted of its normal reserves.

Bulimia is characterized by binge eating of huge quantities of food followed by self-induced vomiting and excessive use of laxatives. Those with bulimia will usually stay at an average or slightly above-average weight, despite their behavior. Embarrassment, guilt, unwillingness to discuss the problem, and fear of discovery are feelings that accompany bulimia; bulimics are aware that this eating pattern is abnormal, while anorexics may be skin and bones and still see themselves as fat.

Although bulimia is not as life threatening as anorexia, it is a serious problem and numerous medical complications do occur. Bulimia can significantly interfere with one's day-to-day activities and the enjoyment of life.

Individuals with anorexia and/or bulimia (they can occur together) can be helped. If you or one of your friends has eating behaviors similar to the ones described, or if you are worried that your eating habits are not normal, contact counseling services at your school, the Student Health Center, or a local mental health clinic. Know that you are not alone. As we learn more about these disorders, more caring and supportive individuals are being trained to help. Support groups are available in many areas; you do not have to fight the battle alone.

—|||—|||—|||—

Let's Get Physical

We all want enough energy to do the things we like and need to do to be successful in college. Do you often feel a drop in your energy level in the early afternoon? Do you engage in some kind of vigorous exercise for twenty to thirty minutes at least three times a week (running, swimming, or brisk walking)?

Most of you who answered yes to the first question probably answered no to the second one. As odd as it may seem, you usually get more energy back from exercise than you put into it. It's as if energy invested in exercise yields an energy profit. A few minutes of exercise (instead of a candy bar) may give you the extra energy you need. At the same time, by choosing exercise instead of a snack, you avoid the extra calories, and therefore the extra body weight, that you don't need.

The following are some basic questions frequently asked by students who want to begin a regular exercise program.

How Do I Get Started?

The essential ingredients of a good beginning are (1) take it easy and (2) have fun. Many people who don't continue to exercise after starting overexert themselves in the beginning. It's as if the motivation they've finally generated to overcome their lazy ways takes them too far, too fast, and they burn out. Maybe they've heard the phrase "No pain, no gain," and they believe that unless you suffer, exercise does no good. Muscle aches and twinges of joint pain are normal occurrences when you start. They should disappear in less than a week.

One way to know if you're overexerting while jogging or running is to take the "talking test." During exercise you should be able to carry on a conversation with someone exercising with you.

What If I Don't Have the Time to Exercise?

The less time you feel you have for exercise, the more exercise can help you! When you invest a small amount of time and energy into exercise, you make a profit. You get back more energy than you put in and you can use this energy to accomplish what you need to accomplish. The increased level of energy and alertness can help you be more efficient, and this saves time.

What's the Best Exercise?

The best exercise is one you do consistently. For most of us, that means it should be relatively inexpensive, convenient, and enjoyable (or at least not painful). It also should be steady, sustained, and vigorous activity.

The ideal exercise conditions the muscles and cardiovascular system and makes you physically fit, but is not overly strenuous. Your *target exercise zone* is between 60 and 80 percent of your maximum oxygen intake. Exercise below 60 and above 80 percent simply doesn't offer enough benefits for the effort expended. Your target exercise zone is approximately the same as 70 to 85 percent of your maximum heart rate. To compute your target heart rate (the heart rate you need to reach for the best conditioning benefits), simply subtract your age in years from 220. Your target heart rate zone is 70 to 85 percent of this number. For example, if you are 20 years old, your target is 140 to 170 beats per minute.

A good exercise session begins with five to ten minutes of stretching and warm-up. Usually, twenty to thirty minutes of exercise in the target heart rate zone provides excellent benefits to the cardiovascular system. After exercising, there should be a five to ten minute cool-down period of less effort before you stop exercising.

Constant and rhythmic activities such as walking, jogging or running, swimming, aerobic dancing, racquetball, cycling, and cross-country skiing are best.

How Do I Know If I'm in the Target Zone?

To find out whether your heart rate is in the target zone, you simply count your pulse. To do this place your thumb on your chin and feel the carotid artery on the side of your neck. It's important to count your pulse as soon as you stop exercising because your heart rate slows down quickly. Count your heart beats for 10 seconds and multiply by 6.

You can stop exercising briefly to check your pulse to make sure your heart rate is in the target zone. If your rate is below 70 percent of maximum, you need to exercise more strenuously. If your heart rate is above 85 percent of maximum, you need to slow down. Soon you'll know whether you're in the target zone simply by physical sensations of heart rate and breathlessness, without continuously checking your pulse rate.

What Are the Benefits of Exercise?

Exercise can make you feel fantastic! More specifically, regular target zone exercise can stimulate the following physiological changes:

1. Reduce resting heart rate

2. Reduce blood pressure

3. Increase heart size and cardiac work capacity

4. Increase heart-pumping efficiency

5. Increase oxygen-carrying ability of the blood

6. Increase respiratory efficiency

7. Reduce body weight and percent body fat

8. Suppress appetite

9. Burn up stored fat tissue

10. Prevent adult-onset diabetes

Many people don't realize that exercise also has important psychological benefits. Exercise promotes a feeling of well-being; it has a tranquilizing and muscle-relaxing effect, prevents depression, promotes feelings of self-control, self-confidence, and improved body image, and encourages sound sleep.

Regular vigorous activity may just be the overlooked answer to many physical and emotional problems. The first step is the hardest. After that, the rewards of being a physically fit and active person greatly outweigh the initial effort.

—Ⅲ—Ⅲ—Ⅲ—

Sexuality

Becoming clear on sexual issues is an important part of a healthy life-style, and that involves self-image. A primary part of your self-image is your maleness or femaleness, with sexual behavior the physical expression of that part of your identity. Expressing yourself sexually with another can be either positive and enriching or destructive to yourself and to others. Only through awareness, understanding, and responsible sexual behavior can you establish your sexual self-confidence and experience the joy of sex. Sex does not *establish* who you are—it *expresses* who you are.

Read that again. Sex does not *establish* who you are. While sex itself is perfectly natural, bragging about it is usually in poor taste. All too often, college freshmen find themselves listening to all sorts of fanciful stories about the sexual experiences of other college students. It may seem as if everyone in college were a walking encyclopedia of sex! But while talk about sex certainly has become more open in recent years, the act of sex remains a private matter between just two individuals and, while it can be a joyous experience, it's not a prerequisite for success and happiness in life.

Peer pressure can transform sex from expression into obsession, and that can take most or all of the pleasure out of it. No book can tell you what your choices should be, and you shouldn't listen to your friends just because their ideas seem right for them. Sexual feeings and desires are natural aspects of being human, and engaging in sexual intercourse is a personal moral decision. Before you determine the degree of intimacy appropriate in a relationship, you should examine your values and clarify your feelings. Ultimately, nobody else can determine those values for you.

Discrimination in how you express yourself sexually can ward off the guilt, worry, and remorse that too often limit the beauty of sharing oneself sexually with another individual. Sexual expression, therefore, can be part of an enduring and intimate relationship and requires all of the characteristics we have described before: self-knowledge, courage, communication, trust, forgiveness, and fun.

For more information about sex, find out whether your college or university offers a course in human sexuality, and take it. You may also want to visit your campus counseling center or peer advisement center. Like everything else in life, sex can be more rewarding if you do your homework before you take the final.

Sexual Responsibility: Birth Control

Although responsibility is the common thread running through all aspects of a healthy relationship, sexual intimacy makes special demands for responsible behavior. Unwanted pregnancies and sexually transmitted diseases are potential consequences of sexual activity that you must deal with in a mature and responsible manner. Although most birth control methods were developed for use by women, both partners should share the responsibility for preventing unwanted pregnancy. Resources for further information on contraceptive methods are available on most college campuses. It's important to understand the mechanics, benefits, and risks of all types of birth control methods, so that you'll select a method that best suits your needs and sexual behavior pattern. Here is a brief summary of current contraceptive methods. Contact your health center on campus for more detailed information.

Oral contraceptive ("the pill"). Oral contraceptives, which must be prescribed, are tablets that contain hormonal substances. Those that contain only synthetic progesterone ("mini pills") do not specifically prevent ovulation and are not sufficiently contraceptive to be recommended for that particular purpose. Pills that contain estrogen and progestogen ("combination pills") prevent ovulation and are the most effective nonpermanent pregnancy preventive presently available. Certain restrictions to their usage exist, but by and large they are safe for 85 percent of the total female population and 95 percent of those of college age.

Surgical sterilization. With surgical sterilization, a woman's fallopian tubes are cut, tied, blocked, or removed to prevent the egg from reaching the uterus ("tubal ligation"). For a man, a portion of the vas deferens is removed to prevent sperm from traveling from the testes to the prostate ("vasectomy"). A physician must perform these operations, which have no known side effects and are intended to be permanent; such procedures are seldom recommended until after a couple has had children or are absolutely certain they don't want any. Obviously, it's seldom the technique of choice for university students.

Intrauterine device (IUD). An intrauterine device, or IUD, is a small plastic or plastic and metal device that sometimes also contains synthetic hormones; it is inserted into the uterine cavity. It probably prevents pregnancy by physically disturbing the uterine lining, but is much less effective when the user has had no children. It carries the chance of unrecognized expulsion as well as a markedly increased risk of deep pelvic infection with secondary infertility. These problems have caused most manufacturers to stop making IUDs, and the majority of practitioners no longer recommend them.

Barrier techniques. With barrier techniques, we come to a place for male participation. In fact, to achieve maximum effectiveness, the male must participate! Additionally, here for the first time we have a pregnancy-prevention technique that also provides some degree of protection against the spread of sexually transmitted infections, especially when the male partner gets into the act. There are four major types of barrier contraceptives. We will mention each separately, but it's only when both partners accept mutual responsibility and each uses a barrier simultaneously that maximum protection is attained. This level of effectiveness still falls somewhat short of that provided by oral contraceptives, but consistent use leads to a reasonably close approximation, especially when combining two methods (condom and spermicide).

1. *Condom (Prophylactic, Rubber):* A condom, a sheath of latex or animal membrane, may be purchased without a prescription and is placed over the erect penis before vaginal entry. Its purpose is to prevent semen from escaping, but it must be applied with a little "slack" at the end to prevent rupture upon ejaculation, and careful removal of the penis from the

vagina is essential to prevent spillage. Starting intercourse before applying a condom decreases its effectiveness to the level of withdrawal.

2. *Spermicidal Chemicals:* Spermicides include foams, creams, gels, and suppositories that don't require a prescription for purchase. They are inserted into the vagina shortly before intercourse in order to kill sperm as well as block their entry via the cervix into the upper reproductive tract.

3. *Vaginal Sponge:* The vaginal sponge is the newest (and most expensive) of the nonprescription barriers. It has the advantage that you insert it one time in order to get twenty-four-hour dispersal of a spermicide. The polyurethane foam is also shaped to fit closely to the cervix.

4. *Diaphragm and Cervical Cap:* Both the diaphragm and cervical cap must be fit individually by a practitioner who will supply the unit or provide a prescription for it. Although they are classified together, these should not be confused with one another. The diaphragm has been around for years and has a well-defined record of effectiveness, whereas the cervical cap is not yet universally available and must be considered experimental. The diaphragm requires the accompanying use of a spermicidal cream or gel to achieve adequate protection. Regular inspection for even the smallest of holes and replacement at reasonable intervals are essential. Moreover, an intervening pregnancy or a weight gain or loss of fifteen to twenty pounds warrants a reevaluation because of a possible size change.

Withdrawal (coitus interruptus). As the name implies, withdrawal is accomplished by the male withdrawing from the vagina before ejaculation. Unfortunately, occasional "leakage" of semen may occur without either participant being aware of it, and at other times the emotions of the moment overwhelm one's best intentions. Either event will result in the presence of sperm in the vagina; hence, this method is not reliable.

Rhythm. The theory of the rhythm technique is that certainty of the time of ovulation (release of an egg) allows a couple to avoid intercourse when conception is most likely. In reality, the practice is much more difficult and requires more stability and knowledge than most young people have had the opportunity to obtain.

Douching. Douching involves washing the semen out of the vagina immediately after intercourse and provides the poorest results of any method mentioned. No self-respecting sperm will wait around long enough for this sort of nonsense.

After-the-fact medication ("morning-after pill"). There are various types of high dosage female hormones that many practitioners recommend for use shortly after unprotected intercourse (a maximum of 72 hours). They prevent implantation of an egg by altering the uterine lining tissue. At present these are not recommended by the Food and Drug Administration and require carefully controlled use.

Sexual Responsibility: Sexually Transmitted Infections

The newer term for venereal disease (VD) is sexually transmitted infection (STI) or sexually transmitted disease (STD). No matter what we call them, the meaning is the same—infections that are almost always spread by sexual intercourse. Whenever and wherever sexual activity increases, so does the incidence of STIs.

The best possible protection against STIs is, of course, not being sexually active. Otherwise, knowing your partner and limiting the number of partners should both be priority precautions. If you have decided to become sexually intimate with an individual, decide beforehand to be verbally intimate with that person. This means establishing a relationship that can include clear, open dialogue concerning STIs. You might say something like this: "Look, I feel like we're headed for a sexual relationship and I have some concerns about sexually transmitted infections. I do care for you, and I also care for myself. I need to know if you've been treated for or have any infection—anything I need to know about. You can ask the same of me."

A further important precaution is the use of barrier contraception. As previously mentioned, in addition to providing contraception, these methods offer protection against STIs. Even if you or your partner is already using the pill, use condoms and a spermicide. Evidence shows that spermicides that contain nonoxynol-9 kill some STI microorganisms, and condoms protect against a variety of STIs, including AIDS.

Often, negative attitudes about condoms are related to beliefs that condom use is unsatisfying, uncomfortable, and unnatural; to feelings of embarrassment; and to the idea that condoms can interfere with sexual sensation. Discuss the use of condoms and spermicides with your partner. Be assertive—your well-being is reason enough to insist they be used.

It is sometimes easier to have thought of possible responses before bringing up the subject of condoms. The following suggestions may be helpful in overcoming a partner's objections:*

IF THE PARTNER SAYS:	YOU CAN SAY:
"This is an insult! You seem to think I'm some sort of disease-ridden slut or gigolo."	"I didn't say or imply that. I care about us both and about our relationship. In my opinion, it's best to use a condom."

---

* Used with permission from Alan Grieco, "Cutting the Risks of STDs," *Medical Aspects of Human Sexuality*, March 1987. © Hospital Publications, Inc.

"None of my other boyfriends uses a condom. A real man is not afraid."	"Please don't compare me to them. A real man cares about the woman he dates, himself, and their relationship."
"You didn't make Jerry use a condom when you went out with him."	"It bothers me that you and Jerry talk about me that way. If you believe everything Jerry says, that's your problem."
"I love you! Would I give you an infection?"	"Not intentionally, of course not. But many people don't know they're infected. I feel this is best for both of us at this time."
"Just this once."	"Once is all it takes."
"I don't have a condom with me."	"I do." or "This time, we can satisfy each other without intercourse."
"You carry a condom around with you?! You were planning to seduce me!"	"I always carry one with me because I care about myself. I made sure I had one with me tonight because I care about us both."
"I won't have sex with you if you're going to use a condom."	"Let's put it off then, until we have a chance to work out our differences."

A brief discussion of the major STIs follows. Remember that campus or local health clinics are readily available and are excellent resources for further information and/or treatment. All STIs require medical attention, and all partners must be treated.

Chlamydial infection or NGU. Chlamydial infection or NGU (Nongonococcal urethritis) is a potentially serious and very prevalent disease. It has become more common than gonorrhea. The symptoms may include a puslike discharge from the tip of the penis or from the vagina and a tingling sensation upon urinating, but frequently—especially in women—there are no obvious symptoms. Some men may have such a slight discharge that they will hardly notice it. Treatment is with an antibiotic. Symptoms, if they appear, usually do so about one to three weeks after contact with the infected partner. Pelvic inflammatory disease (PID), a consequence of untreated chlamydial infections in women, is a leading cause of infertility.

Gonorrhea. This bacterial infection usually causes symptoms two to ten days after infection. Men may notice a white discharge from the penis, as well as pain when urinating. Women frequently will not have any symptoms. Examination and culture of the infected area can verify if you have a gonococcal infection. An untreated infection can lead to pelvic inflammatory disease, sterility, arthritis, and problems in newborns of an infected mother. Treatment is with an antibiotic.

Genital herpes. This is a disease caused by a virus (Herpes Simplex Virus II or HSV II), and there is presently no known cure. The disease causes painful, fluid-filled blisters that form on the genitals. These will rupture and eventually heal without scars. The disease recurs in most people infected with herpes, most often during times of physical or emotional stress. Treatment can prolong time between outbreaks and soothe the symptoms; it will not make the disease go away. Even so, if you suspect you may have genital herpes, seek medical assistance because several other diseases may cause similar sores on the genitals. You must avoid sexual contact when sores are present. Herpes is thought to be associated with an increased risk of cervical cancer in women and can have serious effects on an infant delivered through the infected vagina. Symptoms of herpes usually appear two to twenty days after you have come into contact with the infection. You can also get genital herpes from a very similar virus (Herpes Simplex Virus I or HSV I), which causes cold sores or fever blisters in the mouth. Oral-genital sex and kissing should always be avoided if mouth sores are present.

Genital warts. Genital warts (condyloma) first appear as small pink or red cauliflowerlike growths on the vaginal lips, penis shaft, urinary opening, and rectum. They are usually painless, but some people may have itching, burning, or slight bleeding from these areas. In some cases, warts may extend into the vagina up to the cervix. These warts may become so large in pregnant women as to make a vaginal delivery impossible. In males, they may spread up to the urethra and cause blockage. Genital warts may also increase a woman's risk of developing cervical cancer. The average incubation period of condyloma is one to three months, but may extend to several years before symptoms develop. Removal methods include acids, blistering agents, laser treatments, freezing compounds, and even surgical excision. Treatment depends on the size and location of the wart.

AIDS. AIDS stands for the Acquired (not inherited) Immune Deficiency (a breakdown of the body's defense system, producing susceptibility to certain diseases) Syndrome (a spectrum of disorders and symptoms). People with AIDS suffer from unusual, life-threatening infections and/or rare forms of cancer. Information on AIDS changes almost daily as we learn more about the syndrome. To date, we know that AIDS is caused by a retrovirus, called Human T-Lymphotropic Virus Type III (HTLV-III) or Human Immunodeficiency Virus (HIV). This virus is extremely fragile and does not survive outside body cells. It is present in the body fluids (notably in blood, semen, and saliva) of people who have been infected; these people may or may not have symptoms. Although it is certainly transmitted by blood and semen, there is no evidence that AIDS is transmitted by saliva because the virus is present in very small amounts. While anyone can get AIDS, these high-risk groups have been identified: 70 to 75 percent of people with AIDS have been homosexual or bisexual men; 17 percent have been intravenous (IV) drug abusers. A significant percentage of the homosexual/bisexual group also have used IV drugs. Others at high risk have included hemophiliacs (who receive products made from the blood of many donors) and blood transfusion recipients. The availability of the antibody test for HIV is having a significant impact in reducing the number of cases transmitted by blood or blood derivatives.

It is important to understand that AIDS is not a disease striking only homosexual or bisexual men or drug abusers. People who don't belong to any of the established risk groups, women as well as men, have contracted AIDS; most have been sexual partners of those in one of the risk groups. AIDS can be transmitted sexually between men and women; some female prostitutes carry the virus, since they have multiple sexual partners and commonly are intravenous drug abusers. AIDS may also be transmitted from mother to infant before or at birth.

All people with a positive blood test for the antibody to the AIDS virus must regard themselves as carriers of the virus; whether or not they have symptoms, they are contagious and can transmit the infection to others. Although previously stated, it is worth repeating—condoms and spermicides are effective barriers against the transmission of the AIDS virus.

At this time, there is no cure, effective treatment, or vaccine for AIDS and none likely in the foreseeable future. It's a killer—educate and protect yourself!

One of the most exciting challenges of being in college is the freedom to create your own personal life-style. It's a new experience and a new beginning. As a college student, you have more power and responsibility than ever before, and using your power to help yourself become healthier offers many rewards.

Your health, both physical and emotional, has a great deal to do with your success as a student, and personal habits, the things you do on a day-to-day basis, have everything to do with being, and staying, healthy.

By choosing a life-style that includes nutritious foods, vigorous physical activity, and quality relationships, you take a giant step toward health, well-being, and success.

You can be vigorously alive, feel great, and be alert and prepared. You can have sufficient energy not only for meeting the daily demands of classroom assignments but also for the fun, social events, and personal relationships that enhance college life. Now is the time for establishing patterns that can positively affect the quality, and very likely the quantity, of your life.

Suggested Activities

1. Keep a record of everything you eat or drink for one week. Make a note of how you felt, where you were, what activities you were doing, and how hungry you were. At the end of the week, review your diary and look for patterns: Are you eating a lot between meals? Are you eating foods high in refined sugar and fat? Are you eating when you aren't very hungry? Are you eating for recreation (when you're bored or anxious or when you watch TV, for example)?

2. With several of your classmates, identify campus or community resources that can assist you in the following areas: nutrition and weight control, exercise and physical fitness (including aerobics classes, jogging groups or clubs), and wellness or health promotion. Report your findings to the class.

3. Organize a Fun-Run for everyone enrolled in the freshman seminar classes at your college.

4. Plan a nonmeat potluck meal. Have each student bring a dish to share with the class.

5. Interview a representative of your local public health department or campus health center and report on the incidence of STIs in your area.

6. Invite someone from a local family planning clinic to speak to your class on sexuality and contraception. Hand in questions on 3 × 5 cards for that person to answer. (Cards enable students to remain anonymous.)

Suggested Readings

Boston Women's Health Collective. *The New Our Bodies, Our Selves*. New York: Simon & Schuster, 1984.

Brody, Jane. *Good Food Book: Living the High Carbohydrate Way*. New York: W. W. Norton, 1985.

Cooper, Kenneth H. *The Aerobic Program for Total Well-Being*. New York: M. Evans & Co, 1982.

Davis M., M. McKay, E. R. Eshelman. *The Relaxation and Stress Reduction Workbook*. Oakland, Calif.: New Harbinger Publications, 1982.

Farquhar, John W. *The American Way of Life Need Not Be Hazardous to Your Health*. New York: W. W. Norton, 1978.

Mullen, Kathleen D., Robert S. Gold, Philip A. Belcastro, Robert J. McDermott, *Connections for Health*. Dubuque, Iowa: William C. Brown, 1986.

18 Smashed, High, or Smart? Alcohol, Drugs, and You

Reid H. Montgomery, Jr.

ASSISTANT PROFESSOR OF CRIMINAL JUSTICE
UNIVERSITY OF SOUTH CAROLINA

Michael Shaver

DIRECTOR, CAMPUS ALCOHOL PROJECT
UNIVERSITY OF SOUTH CAROLINA

As a college freshman I attended a large state university and joined a fraternity. I noticed at many parties that some frat brothers used alcohol to gain attention. It seemed evident, however, that attention given a heavy drinker at a party did not translate into respect and positions of leadership in the fraternity. Real leaders did not need the short-term attention that drinking seemed to provide.

After receiving my undergraduate degree in psychology, I volunteered for the United States Army. At that time, graduate school was no ticket out of military service. During one party held by my unit after a long military exercise, I drank several mixed drinks and was sick as a dog all night long. This unpleasant experience was enough to show me that overindulgence was not worth the price in sickness to be paid.

My next interaction with alcohol and drugs was as a federal probation officer at the U.S. District Court in Washington, D.C. It never failed to amaze me that young men or women would risk damage to their future careers by purchasing drugs to obtain a temporary high. A $100 drug purchase, for example, from an undercover federal drug agent, could result in arrest with a fine and a period of federal probation as a penalty. Only later did these first-time offenders realize the true cost in terms of lost job opportunities because of their arrest records.

Each semester as I begin my criminal justice classes, I try to drive home the point that students should be selfish and not let drugs or alcohol ruin their careers and lives. Just because a friend is drinking or using drugs does not mean that you have to follow that example. Friendship does not mean you have to take risks with your own future.

Mike also claims he had problems handling his newfound responsibilities in his freshman year. After graduation, he began to work in alcohol- and drug-abuse programs, counseling with individuals and families suffering such problems. Time and time again he found that whatever was making an individual unhappy seemed most easily dealt with by getting drunk or high. Many of these people had poor skills in dealing with others, and many were not able to hold jobs.

Both of us feel that prevention is a far better solution than treatment. Working with students to help them understand their responsibilities with respect to alcohol and drugs has been a rewarding, if challenging, experience for each of us.

— ||| — ||| — ||| —

As you've read elsewhere in this book, college forces you to begin making many new decisions on your own, perhaps for the first time in your life. While some of these decisions may result in mistakes that you promise "won't happen again," the decision to drink alcoholic beverages and the decision to experiment with illegal drugs may have such far-reaching and potentially devastating consequences that they merit a special chapter.

Let's be clear about one thing before you read further: we will not attempt to preach to you about the vices of booze and drugs. That's not our purpose, and besides, we realize how ineffective such a stance would be. People drink; that's a fact of life. How they drink and how they value drinking is something else. The situation for young people is more complex today with new laws making it illegal for anyone under the age of 21 to purchase alcoholic beverages in most states.

As for drugs, nothing has changed regarding their legality. They simply are not legal. More importantly, drugs such as marijuana, cocaine, heroin, and crack have devastated the lives of many young people in recent years.

This chapter contains facts, not preachments. You have a right to know the good side and the bad side. Then you have a responsibility to make a decision that is best for you, not one that is made on the basis of what appears to be best for others.

— ||| — ||| — ||| —
The Good News About Alcohol

Medical researchers are finding that moderate drinkers live longer and healthier lives than alcoholics or abstainers. Moderation is the key word. Most experts would say no more than two drinks a day is a good guide. The American Heart Association recognizes that "there's current evidence that moderate alcohol consumption is linked to reduced heart disease. However, there is not sufficient evidence to recommend use of alcohol with the hope of preventing heart attacks."

Researchers at Stanford University found that alcohol increases a person's level of apolipoprotein A-1 (a protein attached to HDL molecules that helps to clear cholesterol out of the bloodstream). Additionally, a Boston-area hospital found that limited use of alcohol served with cheese increased the walking activity of elderly patients.

—lll—lll—lll—

And Some Not So Good News

Regardless of these potential benefits of moderate drinking, alcohol must be used with care. Heavy drinking can elevate blood pressure, destroy the liver, and damage the brain. Pregnant women must watch their drinking because of the possibility of fetal alcohol syndrome (a combination of physical defects, mental retardation, and growth impairment in the fetus).

Each individual is the ultimate expert on how much alcohol he or she can handle. Unfortunately, children of alcoholics have a greater danger (four to five times more) of becoming alcoholics. The way alcohol affects you can also be influenced by simple factors such as whether your stomach is full or empty of food. Eating high-protein foods such as meats or cheeses, especially before drinking or while drinking, will slow down the absorption rate of alcohol into your bloodstream.

How much and how fast a person drinks are also critical. Remember that a 4-ounce glass of wine, a 12-ounce can of beer, or 1.2 ounces of 80-proof whiskey have about the same amount of alcohol and will have about the same effect on you. As a general rule, the body needs one hour to burn up half an ounce of alcohol. Therefore, you are better off if you sip a drink slowly and have not more than one an hour. Gulping drinks, however, will produce immediate intoxication. As a matter of fact, 20 percent of the alcohol in an average drink is absorbed immediately through the stomach wall linings and is in your system in only a matter of seconds.

Your weight also affects how alcohol will affect you. For example, the same amount of alcohol has a greater effect on a 120-pound person than it does on a 180-pound person. Alcohol is quickly distributed uniformly within the circulatory system. Thus, the heavier person will have smaller concentrations of alcohol throughout his bloodstream and body than will a lighter individual.

Your blood alcohol level (BAL) indicates whether you are intoxicated or not. A reading of 0.10 percent translates as legally drunk in most states. A male student who encourages his girlfriend to keep up with his drinking is not being fair, because women generally have less body water to dilute alcohol; thus their BALs rise faster. Furthermore, older drinkers also have less body water with which to dilute alcohol. The same amount of alcohol produces higher BALs in older drinkers as well as in many women.

—|||——|||——|||—
Responsible Drinking

Responsible drinking, in essence, is the use of alcohol in ways that harm neither the individual nor society. People who drink responsibly realize that, while alcoholic beverages can help them relax and enjoy certain events more completely, too much drinking can turn enjoyment into sullenness, irritability, and general alienation from other people. In simpler terms, moderate drinking can put you at ease. Gulping drinks simply to become drunk can turn a potentially enjoyable event into a nightmare for the drinker as well as for those who might come into contact with him or her.

What are some strategies you can follow to drink responsibly? One simple rule is to eat heartily before drinking. Milk is very good for coating your stomach and slowing the absorption rate of alcohol. A good personal policy is to set a limit on how many drinks you are going to have and then stick to it. Don't let another person's desire to drink as much as possible be your guide for the evening. Other strategies are to dilute your drinks with juice or water and to drink slowly.

Always respect a person's decision not to drink. Drinking is an individual decision that should not be subject to peer pressure. If you are hosting an end-of-semester party, for example, act in a responsible manner to serve as a model for your guests. And don't make alcohol the primary focus of the party. If it becomes the primary focus, ask yourself why you're holding the party in the first place. Is it just to get drunk and make a fool of yourself? If so, was it really as much fun as you thought it would be?

—|||——|||——|||—
Drinking and the Law

Equally important to consider when you begin making decisions about your own drinking habits are the legal consequences of overindulgence. An arrest and conviction for driving under the influence (DUI) can have an enormous impact on your life. When you are stopped for DUI, most police officers will present you with a DUI traffic citation, which comes with an automatic fine, as much as $200 or higher in some states. You are also likely to spend the night in the local drunk tank. Furthermore, your car will be towed for a fee of around $50. A local magistrate may also have the option of putting you in jail for up to thirty days. If that occurs you may lose your job, multiplying the high cost of overindulgence.

A student who spends thirty days in jail will have a difficult time passing courses and explaining his arrest record to future employers. Even if you don't go to jail, the cost of your arrest increases. Many states require the offender to successfully complete an Alcohol and Drug Safety Action Program before reinstating a driving license. The offender must pay about $250 to participate in the program.

A bigger expense for a DUI offender, however, is an increase in insurance premiums. Insurance companies use a special formula to determine rate increases for drivers who violate traffic laws. Penalty points are assessed according to the seriousness of each individual violation. A driver with a first-offense DUI conviction will be assessed 15 penalty points, which at $20 per point will add $300 for one year of liability insurance, as well as an additional $300 for collision insurance. The total increase during the driver's suspension period and the ensuing three-year probation comes to about $2,100. For a DUI arrest involving an accident, this figure jumps to approximately $2,800. These costs are in addition to any premiums the driver might already be paying.

If a driver contests the DUI charges brought against him in court, he will probably incur the cost of hiring an attorney. This can range from $500 to $1,000. Winning will waive fines and maintain the individual's current insurance rates. Losing, however, can add substantial legal fees to all of the previously mentioned costs.

But the biggest price paid by a drunken driver might be a person's life. As many people die from alcohol each year as did in the entire Vietnam war. The majority of states have raised the drinking age to 21. A bartender or store owner convicted of selling beer, wine, or distilled spirits to anyone under 21 years of age, in most states, will be fined $100 to $200 and/or jailed for thirty to sixty days.

Many students might think they can get around the new drinking age laws by obtaining a fake identification card. States have taken action to increase the penalty for presenting false or improper identification in order to obtain alcoholic beverages. The penalty in South Carolina, for example, is a fine of $50 to $100 or as many as thirty days in jail.

Individuals who enjoy drinking a beer in their cars will find this an expensive habit in some states. The fine for an open container of beer, wine, or any alcoholic beverage in a car is generally $100 or thirty days in jail. If you are arrested and fingerprinted, your files are sent to the FBI in Washington, D.C. If you later apply for a federal job or want to serve in the military, your background will be checked through the FBI. Increasing your chances of future success is another reason you should be careful with the use of alcohol or drugs.

Myths About Drinking

As a college student, you should also be aware of some of the false myths related to sobering up. Alcohol that has accumulated in the bloodstream has to be burned up, or oxidized, by the liver. That bodily function occurs at a constant rate of about three-fourths to one ounce of alcohol per hour. Coffee merely turns a sleepy drunk into a more wide-awake drunk.

Oxygen and exercise have negligible effects in helping the liver do its work any faster. A cold shower doesn't help either. The only thing that will sober individuals up once they have gotten drunk is time.

Here are some other myths associated with drinking behavior:

- *Alcohol is a stimulant.* In truth, alcohol acts as a depressant on the central nervous system.

- *People are friendly when they're drunk.* Maybe. But they also tend to be more hostile, more dangerous, more criminal, more homicidal, and more suicidal. Half of all murders and one-third of all suicides are alcohol related.

- *People get drunk or sick from switching drinks.* What usually causes an adverse reaction to alcohol is drinking too much.

- *It's rude to refuse a drink.* Nonsense. What's rude is trying to push a drink on someone who doesn't want it or shouldn't have it.

- *"What a man! Still on his feet after a whole fifth."* When we stop thinking it's manly to drink too much, we have begun to grow up. It's no more manly to overdrink than it is to overeat.

- *Alcoholism is just a state of mind.* It's more than that. It is a real illness, and scientific evidence indicates that physiological dependence is involved.

- *Most alcoholics are skid row bums.* Only 3 to 5 percent are in this category. Most alcoholic people (about 70 percent) are married, employed, "regular" people like you and me.

- *It's only beer.* Sure. Just like it's only bourbon, or vodka, or gin. One beer or one glass of wine is about equal to one average highball. You get just as drunk on beer or wine as on "hard" liquor.

When One Drink Is Not Enough

Alcohol is the third leading health problem in the United States, behind heart attacks and cancer, with an estimated 10 million problem drinkers.

One study points out that half of all car accidents are alcohol related (23,000 deaths a year). One special report reveals that 200,000 college students are arrested annually for drunk driving. One-half of all campus arrests are alcohol related. Additionally, the majority of campus and fraternity property damage is a result of the influence of alcohol.

Early Warnings of Alcoholism

You should become aware of alcoholism's early warning signs. One sign is the need to drink in the morning to start the day. Drinking alone from a desire to escape reality or boredom or loneliness is another. Watch also for drinking to relieve hangovers, thereby perpetuating a vicious circle: the more you drink, the worse you feel, and the more you drink.

A sign that friends can notice is the drinker's marked personality change after taking one or more drinks. Alcoholics also try to rationalize their drinking behavior with such comments as "I just need one more to relax" or "How about one for the road?"

Blackouts (alcohol induced amnesia) are a serious sign of a drinking problem. A drinker in trouble is one who must gulp drinks for the effect that rapid drinking produces. Absenteeism from work (or classes) or impaired job performance because of drinking are other warning signs.

The person who requires medical or hospital attention as a result of alcohol use is certainly headed down the road to ruin. Once drinking has passed a certain point, alcoholism becomes a disease. That happens when the drinking cannot be stopped by a mere resolution on the part of the drinker. If you need to get help for yourself or for a friend who has developed a drinking problem, contact the university counseling center.

Alcoholics Anonymous (AA) is the best program for helping alcoholics stay sober. AA helps individuals face their lives as alcoholics, accept their disease, and keep in touch with it so that they do not lapse into wishful thinking that they can drink again. Most alcoholics have some difficulties getting started on a sober life; AA offers guidance, support, and discipline.

Trends in Drug Use

When Len Bias, a University of Maryland basketball player who had just been drafted to play with the Boston Celtics, died from a drug overdose, his death received national attention and caused many to take a hard look at the problems of drugs. Americans are currently spending $50 billion a year to buy the deadly white powder called cocaine. More than 22 million people have tried it; 12 million use it at least once a year.

Cocaine is a drug extracted from the leaves of the coca plant, which grows in South America. It is usually sniffed or snorted into the nose, although some users inject it or smoke a form of the drug called freebase.

The dangers of cocaine use vary, depending on how the drug is taken, the dose, and the individual. Regular users report feelings of restlessness, irritability, anxiety, and sleeplessness. People who use high doses of cocaine over a long period of time may become paranoid or experience what is called a "cocaine psychosis," which may include hallucinations of touch, sight, taste, or smell.

Overdose deaths can occur when the drug is injected, smoked, or even snorted. Death is a result of multiple seizures followed by respiratory and cardiac arrest. This, in the view of some medical experts, is what happened to Len Bias.

Marijuana (grass, pot, weed) is the common name for a crude drug made from the plant *Cannabis sativa*. The main mind-altering (psychoactive) ingredient in marijuana is tetrahydrocannabinol (THC). A marijuana "joint" (cigarette) is made from the dried flowers and leaves of the plant. The amount of THC in the marijuana determines how strong its effects will be.

A common adverse reaction to marijuana is the "acute panic anxiety" reaction. People describe this reaction as an extreme fear of losing control, which causes panic. The symptoms usually disappear in a few hours. In research studies, students had reduced skills in math, verbal exercises, and reading comprehension after using marijuana. Furthermore, students did not remember what they had learned while they were "high."

Long-term regular users of marijuana may become psychologically dependent. The drug may become the most important aspect of their lives. Daily marijuana use among college students, however, fell significantly between 1980 and 1985, from 7.2 percent to 3.1 percent based on one survey of 1,100 college students.

This same study revealed that college students generally drink less daily than their age group taken as a whole. Many college fraternity groups today are carefully monitoring drinking behavior at parties because of increasing lawsuits. The parents of one college student were awarded $250,000 several years after their son passed out and died after a fraternity party. The court said the fraternity was responsible for the death.

Controlling Illegal Drugs

In a recent speech, President Reagan stated, "we're getting tough on drugs, and we mean business." He ordered the executive branch to set up mandatory tests for federal workers in sensitive jobs. The courts seem to be following the nation's concern about drugs and sentencing drug offenders to long terms of confinement. For example, in August 1986 a federal court in

Greenville, South Carolina, sentenced one man to 104 years in prison and a fine of $4.5 million. He was convicted of running a cocaine ring out of his auto cleanup shop.

Arrests for drug crimes rose 15 percent last year to 811,400. However, law enforcement officers still catch only a small fraction of the violators. The amount of cocaine smuggled into the United States is expected to be 150 tons this year—twice the 1985 level. The average sentence for federal drug offenses has jumped 20 percent since 1980, to over five years.

Furthermore, one study found that about 80 percent of those behind bars say they have taken drugs, twice the ratio in the general population. Other reports indicate that one-third of inmates in federal prisons are serving time for drug related violations. Prison rolls have gone over the 500,000 mark, in large part because of state and federal laws requiring imprisonment for narcotics sales involving as little as $10.

A recent poll by the Roper Organization of 1,003 Americans listed "fighting the drug problem" as the number one issue of pressing importance to those polled. A headline in *USA Today* on September 5, 1986, read "Gate Wide Open for Flood Of Cocaine." The article related that 18,000 flights were made by drug traffickers last year into the United States but only 210 planes were spotted and only 64 were caught.

Another report states that "Americans now consume 60 percent of the world's production of illegal drugs. An estimated 20 million are regular users of marijuana, 4 million to 8 million more are cocaine abusers, and 500,000 are heroin addicts."

The National Institute on Drug Abuse estimates that 30 percent of all college students will use cocaine at least once before they graduate and up to 80 percent of all Americans will try an illicit drug by their mid-20s. The institute found that heroin, the leading illegal killer drug, was responsible for at least 1,263 deaths in 1986.

The Meaning of Addiction. What does it mean to be addicted? Some experts believe addiction is just another way of saying drug dependence. One study reports that a chemically dependent drug user is one who meets some of the following criteria: increasing frequency of drug use, increasing amount of use, increased tolerance levels, withdrawal symptoms if drug use stops, and tendency toward continued use despite negative effects on physical condition, social skills, or work behavior.

Drug dependence can include physical as well as psychological dependence. Physical dependence, as defined by experts at Rutgers University Center of Alcohol Studies, is the altered biological chemical state produced by repeated administration of the drug; continued administration of the drug is necessary to prevent a withdrawal symptom.

Psychological dependence occurs when individuals think that the effects of a drug are necessary for their well-being. Many drug experts believe the seven most dangerous drugs are cocaine, crack, phencyclidine (PCP), heroin, fentanyl, meperidine, and MDMA (hallucinogenic amphetamines).

In the Final Analysis, It's Up to You

We trust we have been steadfast to our promise to provide facts instead of preachments. These *are* the facts. We hope you will debate, discuss, and argue them with your fellow students, your professors, and other friends. If you need help, talk to friends and fellow students about your problem. Better yet, counsult hall advisors and residence directors. Caring professors, academic advisors, counseling centers, and chaplains' offices are other nearby help centers for those who may be in doubt about the effect of alcohol and/or drugs in their lives.

If you are, as the adage goes, true to your own self and not swayed by the pressures of society, you're already in a better position to say no when your personal value system tells you that to do otherwise could be a tragic mistake.

Suggested Activities

1. If you owned your own company, would you hire someone who had an arrest record for marijuana use? Defend your answer.

2. What should the federal government do to reduce the drug problem?

3. Is the legal drinking age of 21 fair? Discuss.

4. How would you handle someone who was drunk and insisted on driving home?

5. Should employers have the right to test their employees for drug use?

6. If you were dean of students at a university, what would be your policy with regard to student alcohol use?

7. From the suggestions in this chapter regarding the regulation of alcohol and drugs, choose one and debate the issue with a friend. Consider both sides, even though you may doubt the validity of the other side.

EXERCISE   Alcohol: Facts vs. Myths

Take this brief quiz. Then, check the correct answers against yours and discuss the reactions to the answers and other information in this section with other members of your class. How misinformed were you and they about drinking? How has the information in this section changed your views about drinking?

1. People do things when they are drunk that they would never do when sober. True or False?

2. About what percentage of adults in America drink alcoholic beverages?
   a. 95 percent   b. 70 percent   c. 50 percent   d. 33 percent

3. Alcohol is a stimulant. True or False?

4. Fifteen percent of all people killed in drunk driving accidents are in their teens. True or False?

5. How many alcoholics are estimated to be in the United States?
   a. 500,000   b. 5–6 million   c. 9–10 million   d. 15 million

6. Most people can judge when they are too drunk to drive. True or False?

7. In most states, the blood alcohol level at which you are legally drunk is:
   a. 0.05   b. 0.10   c. 0.12   d. 0.15

8. Americans spend as much on alcohol as they do on education. True or False?

9. Best estimates indicate that _____ percent of all highway fatalities are alcohol related.
   a. 10 percent   b. 25 percent   c. 50 percent   d. 65 percent

10. Black coffee, walking, or cold showers will sober up a drunk faster. True or False?

11. A large person will sober up more quickly than a small person. True or False?

12. Alcohol is an aphrodisiac. True or False?

13. Which has the greatest amount of alcohol in it?
    a. one drink mixed with 80-proof liquor   b. one 4-ounce glass of 12 percent wine   c. one 12-ounce beer   d. all have the same

14. A person may overdose on alcohol just as with other drugs. True or False?

15. Certain behaviors can serve as warnings to tell a person that he or she may have a drinking problem. How many can you name?

Answers

1. True. Inhibitions are lowered by drinking, giving us "permission" to do things we might be too shy or smart to do when sober.

2. b. 70 percent.

3. False. Many feel it's a stimulant because it lowers inhibitions, and because it relaxes or loosens us up. In reality, alcohol is a depressant.

4. False. The figure is approximately 60 percent.

5. c. 9–10 million. These are alcoholics, not just heavy drinkers.

6. False. Most people are horrible judges of this. As the brain is more affected by drinking, we are less able to judge our level of debilitation.

7. b. 0.10. You can, however, be arrested and charged with DUI with a blood alcohol level as low as 0.05 if the officer determines that you cannot function responsibly.

8. False. They spend about twice as much on drinking.

9. c. 50 percent. This is approximately 25,000 people per year.

10. False. All you get is a wide-awake drunk. The body processes 1 to 1¼ ounces of alcohol out of your body per hour. Time is the only thing that will sober you up.

11. False. We all sober up at the same rate. A large person may need to drink more than a small one to get to the same level of intoxication, however.

12. False. It lowers inhibitions and makes us more willing to take risks and do things we might not otherwise do, but it also lowers sensitivity and at legally drunk levels can impair sexual performance, especially among males.

13. d. All have the same amount of real alcohol in them, 1 to 1½ ounces.

14. True. When you pass out (not black out), the body is going to sleep so that no more alcohol can be put into it.

15. Here are twelve signals to watch out for:
    1. Drinking when there is a good reason not to, or getting drunk when there is good reason not to.
    2. Having accidents or injuring yourself because of drinking.
    3. Missing classes or appointments because of drinking.
    4. Getting into fights because of drinking.
    5. Being asked to leave a bar or party because of drinking.
    6. Blackouts: When you can't remember what happened when you were drinking, even though you continued to function during that time.
    7. Getting into trouble with the law because of drinking.
    8. Needing a drink to "get you going" in the morning.
    9. Using money for drinking that should have been used for something else.

10. Having shaky hands the next morning.
11. Being told by a doctor that drinking is affecting your health.
12. Feeling the effects of drinking in class or on the job.

Suggested Readings

"America on Drugs." *U.S. News and World Report,* July 28, 1986, p. 52.

Berne, Eric. *Games Alcoholics Play.* New York: Ballantine Books, 1971.

Lingemen, Richard. *Drugs from A to Z.* New York: McGraw-Hill, 1969.

Milan, James R., and Katherine Ketcham. *Under the Influence.* New York: Bantam Books, 1985.

Outerbridge, David. *The Hangover Handbook.* New York: Harmony Books, 1981.

Towers, Richard L. *Student Drug and Alcohol Abuse.* Washington, D.C.: National Education Association, 1987.

19 Stress Management

Kevin King

COUNSELING PSYCHOLOGIST
COUNSELING AND HUMAN DEVELOPMENT CENTER
UNIVERSITY OF SOUTH CAROLINA

I became interested in stress management training when I was in graduate school. At that time, I was put in charge of a large speech desensitization program designed to help people overcome speech anxiety. What no one knew then was that I myself suffered from speech anxiety. Actually, almost everyone does at some point. It's perfectly normal.

I was lucky, though. Being in charge of the speech desensitization program was like taking a crash course in learning how to manage anxiety. I came away from it with a great interest in developing my own stress management skills still further. And I wanted to be able to teach others how they could manage stress more effectively for themselves. In this chapter I try to do that. It's just a beginning, but I hope you'll be interested in looking into it further.

━ ❙❙❙ ━ ❙❙❙ ━ ❙❙❙ ━

Stress is a naturally occurring phenomenon. The only time we know that people don't feel stress is when they're dead! So, to that extent, stress is a good thing to have. Yet most of us, as we grow and develop, don't really learn how to cope effectively with stress-producing situations, and the result is that stress can become so overwhelming that it can interfere seriously with our ability to perform as well as we could. The primary way to manage stress is to replace it with something incompatible with it. For me, the most incompatible thing to stress is relaxation. It's impossible to be tense and relaxed at the same time, and relaxation is a skill that we can learn just like any other skill.

You've learned how to be tense in most stress-producing situations; now you need to learn how to identify the warning signs or symptoms of stress. Then, instead of serving as evidence that stress is gripping you by the throat, such signals can alert you to use your relaxation skills to overcome the stress.

What Happens When You Are Tense

The signs or symptoms of stress are easy to recognize and differ little from person to person. Basically, your rate of breathing will become more rapid and shallower, your heart rate will begin to speed up, and you'll probably notice some tension in your shoulders and forehead, the muscles at the back of your neck, and perhaps even across your chest. You'll probably also notice that your hands and perhaps even your feet become cold and sweaty. There are likely to be disturbances in your gastrointestinal system, such as a "butterfly stomach" or diarrhea and frequent urination. You'll also notice that the secretions in your mouth begin to dry up, that your lips dry out, and that you may have trembling or shaky hands or knees. You may also notice that your voice quivers or even goes up an octave.

A number of changes also occur psychologically during tension. You're more easily confused, your memory becomes confused, and your thinking becomes less flexible and much more self-critical. One of the things your body and mind are designed to do is defend you in times of threat or danger. Here's how that works: The mind, once aware of a threat—which could be as obvious as someone approaching you with a gun in hand, or might involve taking an examination, speaking in front of a group of people, writing a paper, or studying for an exam—reacts in a defensive manner, and the anxiety you typically feel is part of that defensive reaction. In these situations, our adrenal glands produce adrenalin and a group of hormones called corticoids. If the situation persists over a long time, you may also find it difficult to concentrate, and you may experience a general sense of fear or anxiety, insomnia, early waking, changes in eating habits, excessive worrying, general fatigue, and an urge to run away.

The urge to run away is one of the human body's responses to stress. In threatening situations, we want to do one of two things: either to stand and fight or to run away. But many times both urges must be suppressed because they would be inappropriate for the situation. An example would be taking an examination; even though you might like to get up and run out of the room, it probably would not help your grade if you did so, and it's difficult to fight with a piece of paper. So, we often find we must cope with a situation in a way that allows us to stay and face it and to do so using our potential and skills to the maximum. This is where learning how to manage stress can help.

—⫶⫶⫶— ⫶⫶⫶ —⫶⫶⫶—
Managing Your Stress

There are two primary goals for learning how to manage stress effectively. The first is to monitor yourself so that you can be alert to any signs of tension. The second goal is to control that stress using relaxation techniques and imagery, so you can eliminate the stress or, at least, bring it down to a manageable level. Keep in mind that you can never eliminate stress totally; it's not even desirable to do so. Your goal should be to manage that stress at a level that helps your performance. For example, when an athlete goes out to perform, she probably won't do a good job if she's so relaxed that she's just barely awake. On the other hand, if she's so keyed up that she can't contain herself, she probably won't do very well either. An athlete seeks an optimal level of tension. And that's your goal, too.

In any situation where you're trying to perform effectively or better, ask yourself what the appropriate level of tension is in that situation, and try to maintain or bring your level of stress up or down to that point. Relaxation is a skill that you can learn or perfect through practice.

In addition to being relaxed at the appropriate level, you also need to provide yourself with a guide or model of behavior. For example, you might say, "I want to be more relaxed next time I take an examination," or more likely, "I won't be tense the next time I take an examination." It sounds good, but exactly what are you going to do differently? If you've practiced and rehearsed getting tense before, you're likely to behave in just the way you've always done. You must identify the skills of relaxation or the skills of control so that you can see and feel yourself at an appropriate level of tension.

Imagining You're Relaxed

This is where your imagination comes into play. Anything that you imagine in your mind becomes a neuromuscular rehearsal. For example, if you imagine yourself walking down the sidewalk and tripping over each crack, you are much more likely to do so than if you see yourself walking calmly and smoothly along the sidewalk. The same is true of performing. If you say to yourself, "Well, I've always done poorly there," or "I know I'll do poorly there," that's likely what you'll do because that's all that you've rehearsed. The way to get around those awkward performances of the past is to begin thinking and imagining yourself being and feeling exactly the way you would like to feel.

Realize that stress is an internally cued response and can therefore be controlled through the use of imagery. You can simply imagine yourself back in a tension-filled situation and literally feel the same signs of tension building again in your body, which is an excellent example of how that imagery controls your behavior in the present.

What I'd like you to do is to imagine right now the sequence of events or situations that led up to a particular tension-filled situation. To help you get a feeling for how comfortable or uncomfortable you are in the sequence of events, start yourself off at a very low level of tension. We'll call that level zero, although it's never actually zero. Then move through the sequence of events progressively until you reach the most uncomfortable part of that situation, which we'll label as 100.

Example: Taking an Examination

To give you an example, let's take a situation that we'll call "taking an examination." You can imagine yourself on the first day of class, sitting there and listening to the instructor say, "In this course, we'll have four one-hour examinations." Your number on that day might be ten. You might assign a higher number to a situation that occurs during the week before the first hourly exam, when the instructor says, "Now don't forget next week is our first one-hour examination." The next situation might be several days before the exam, when you're studying in your room or the library. The next tense time might be coming to some difficult material while you're studying. The next might be studying the night before the examination. The next might be going to sleep the night before the examination. The next might be getting ready to go to class. The next might be walking to the building in which you're going to have your examination. The next might be seeing the doorway of the room where you're going to take the test. The next might be walking into the examination room. The next might be sitting down at your desk. The next might be looking at other people talking about the test. The next might be hearing the instructor say, "Put all your notes and books away." The next might be seeing the exams come down the aisle toward you. The next might be looking at the examination, and the last might be seeing that the first question is worth 25 points and not knowing the answer to the question.

Each of these particular situations can be lumped together into what we call "test anxiety," and yet each individual situation has its own unique level of tension. It's important that you know how differently you feel in each of these situations and learn what the sequence of your anxiety symptoms or cues are so that you can use them as warning signs.

Levels of Anxiety and Stress

Once you've identified your whole sequence, I want you to go back and to pick out two particular situations. One we'll arbitrarily call the twenty-level, or low stress, scene and the other the sixty-level, or high stress, scene. The distinction between the two is that in the twenty-level scene you know that you're in a stress-producing situation, but you don't feel unduly uncomfortable. In the sixty-level scene, you're starting to feel much stronger signs of stress, but you still feel you're controlling the anxiety—it's not controlling you.

Once you've done that, think of a very relaxed scene, a time in your life when you were someplace where you were calm, relaxed, very much at ease. To help you with this, think also of how all five of your senses experienced that situation. For example, you might be at the ocean, walking along in water up to your knees. As you walk along, you can feel the sand as it gives way beneath your feet. You can feel the coolness of the water on your ankles. You can feel the warmth of the sun on your back and the wind as it blows around you. You can smell that salt in the air and, if you were to lick your lips, you could actually taste it. You can hear the waves as they wash in and out; perhaps you hear some children playing in the distance. You can see the blue ocean, the blue and white of the sky, the yellow sand. And if you put all these together and close your eyes, you can actually feel yourself back there again. Try to describe a situation like that for yourself now. It doesn't have to be at the ocean; it can be anywhere at all. But try to involve all five of your senses as you do.

Once you've developed your relaxation scene, you're ready to learn skills of relaxation. I'm going to take you through an exercise now in which you're going to learn how to recognize the distinction between tension and relaxation. Begin the exercise by sitting or lying down in a comfortable place. Remove any tight clothing, and perhaps your contact lenses or eyeglasses. Dim any bright lights and make sure you're not likely to be interrupted while you do this relaxation exercise. Once you have familiarized yourself with the complete exercise, have a friend read you the instructions while you follow them, or else record the instructions so you can play them back at your convenience.

—ɪɪɪ—ɪɪɪ—ɪɪɪ—

Stress Control Exercise

Settle back and get yourself comfortable. Give yourself a few moments to allow yourself to listen to your thoughts and to your body. If your thoughts get in the way of relaxing, imagine a blackboard in your mind and see yourself writing down all of your thoughts on the blackboard. By doing this you can allow yourself to put those thoughts aside for a while, and you can rest assured that you will be able to retrieve them later.

Now that you are more ready to relax, begin by closing your eyes. Allow your breathing to become a little slower and a little deeper. As you continue breathing slowly and deeply, let your mind drift back into a very calm, relaxed, safe place that you have been in before. In doing so, try to recall everything that you could see back there, everything that you could hear back there, and everything that you could feel back there. Simply allow yourself to reexperience all of the good feelings that you felt back then, as you allow those good feelings to wash away any feelings of tension or discomfort. To help yourself relax even further, take a brief journey through your body, allowing all of the muscles of your body to become as comfortable and as relaxed as you need them to be.

Let's begin that journey down at your feet. Begin by relaxing your feet up to your ankles, wiggle your feet or toes if you like, to help them to relax, then allow that growing wave of relaxation to continue moving up into the muscles of the calves. As muscles relax, they stretch out and allow more blood to flow into them; therefore, they will gradually feel warmer, and heavier, and even more relaxed. The relaxation can continue on up into the muscles of the thighs, relaxing the thighs up to the hips; gradually, little by little, the legs feel more and more comfortable, more and more relaxed.

Then relax all of the muscles of the back up and down your spine, and gradually you can feel the relaxation moving into your abdomen; as you do so you might also feel a pleasant sense of warmth moving out to every part of your body, and you can allow that relaxation to continue moving up into the muscles of the chest. Each time that you exhale, your chest muscles will relax just a little further, just a little deeper, and now the relaxation can flow up into the muscles of the shoulders. Feel the shoulders relax as those nice soothing feelings of relaxation wash away any tightness, any tension in the shoulders, allowing the shoulder muscles to become loose and limp, and relaxed. And now the relaxation can seep out into the muscles of the arms and hands; gradually your arms and hands become heavy, limp, warm, and relaxed.

Now that relaxation can spread up into the muscles of the neck, relaxing the front of the neck, the sides of the neck, and the back of the neck, imagining perhaps that your neck muscles become as limp and floppy as a handful of rubberbands that you toss on a table, loose, limp, and relaxed. And now you can relax the muscles of the face, relaxing the jaw and the mouth, just let the jaw hang loose, and gradually it feels loose, limp, and relaxed. And the relaxation can continue on up into the cheeks and the sides of the face. Now relax the eyes and the nose, and now relax your forehead; any wrinkles in the forehead just melt away as the forehead becomes calm and smooth. And now relax your scalp, and the scalp may feel tingly and relaxed. And now by taking a long, slow, deep breath, you can cleanse yourself of any remaining tension.

Using Visualization

Once you've learned how to relax yourself, practice this exercise once a day for a week or two. You'll find that you can relax yourself quickly and easily, and when you're able to do that, the next step is to learn how to apply that relaxation when and where you want to. You can learn how to use that deep muscle relaxation technique to create feelings of relaxation where you formerly had feelings of tension. Begin to do this by visualizing, or imagining, that twenty-level stress scene that you identified earlier. As you imagine that stress scene, try to feel all of the discomfort that actually occurred when you were there. Remember that the two goals of stress management are (1) to monitor the feelings of stress and (2) to control these feelings. So, in imagining that twenty-level scene, your goal is to find out exactly how your body and mind respond when you're in that situation.

After you understand your body signals or cues of stress during that twenty-level scene, your next goal will be to imagine it once again after you've relaxed yourself, and then to stay relaxed while you imagine it for about twenty seconds. If you experience any discomfort while you imagine the twenty-level scene for twenty seconds, repeat your visualization of the scene once again, and continue that process until you can imagine your twenty-level scene for twenty seconds and not feel any discomfort. Once you do that, imagine the twenty-level scene again without discomfort for thirty seconds; if you feel any discomfort at this length of time, repeat the process until you can visualize it successfully without any tension or discomfort for thirty seconds. When you can do that, your next step is to imagine that twenty-level scene for forty-five seconds, and when you can imagine it for forty-five seconds without feeling any discomfort, move on to imagining the sixty-level scene that you identified earlier.

The steps are the same: First, imagine the sixty-level scene with tension, so you are clear about your body's signs or cues of tension. Then imagine the sixty-level scene for twenty seconds. Your goal is to imagine it without feeling any tension. When you can imagine it without any tension, move on to imagining the sixty-level scene for thirty seconds. And when you can visualize it without any tension, move on to imagining it for forty-five seconds.

Once you can visualize that sixty-level scene for forty-five seconds without any tension, your next step is to move on to what I call a "competency scene." That's where you imagine yourself going through that entire sequence of events, whether it's taking an examination or giving a speech, from start to finish. But see yourself doing it the way you really want to do it. This is your positive, or competency, rehearsal. When you can complete that process from start to finish, seeing yourself thinking, feeling, speaking, moving exactly the way you want to—calmly, competently, and in a relaxed manner—you've achieved your goal. Once you can do that successfully, you may want to repeat the entire process with another situation. But keep in mind that what were formerly stress symptoms for you have now become warning cues.

As soon as you're aware of the first sign of tension, your goal will be to relax by simply closing your eyes for a brief time, taking slow, deep breaths, reachieving that sense of calmness that you can create, and perhaps even imagining yourself back in your relaxation scene once again. You'll probably notice that you are now no longer threatened by being in situations that formerly caused you discomfort. You might be surprised when you find that your level of comfort is enormously greater than it used to be, and you'll find that relaxation becomes a greater part of your life, that you simply don't allow yourself to get out of control any longer because now you have skills that you can use anywhere, anytime. The skills are simply to learn to close your eyes briefly; take a slow, deep breath; and as you exhale, focus on your relaxation scene. The more you practice this technique, the more effective it will be for you.

Suggested Activities

1. Recall your last troublesome experience. What were the anxiety cues you experienced, and in what sequence did they occur?

2. Determine what behaviors and thoughts you would have to go through to get through the event if it happened again.

3. Rehearse the sequence of events thoroughly in your mind so that you have no doubt about what you should do, no matter what happens in a troublesome situation.

Suggested Readings

Benson, H. *The Mind/Body Effect*. New York: Simon and Schuster, 1979.

Benson, H., and M. Z. Klipper. *The Relaxation Response*. New York: Morrow, 1976.

Brown, B. *Supermind*. New York: Harper & Row, 1980.

Bry, A., and M. Bair. *Directing the Movies of Your Mind*. New York: Harper & Row, 1978.

Butler, P. *Talking to Yourself*. New York: Stein and Day, 1981.

Emmons, M. *The Inner Source*. San Luis Obispo, Calif.: Impact Publishers, 1978.

Ferguson, M. *The Aquarian Conspiracy*. Los Angeles: Tarcher, 1980.

Ford, N. D. *Natural Ways to Relieve Pain*. New York: Harian Press, 1980.

Glasser, W. *Positive Addiction*. New York: Harper & Row, 1979.

Green, E., and A. Green. *Beyond Biofeedback*. New York: Delta, 1977.

Jacobson, E. *Anxiety and Tension Control*. Philadelphia: Lippincott, 1964.

Kinser, N. S. *Stress and the American Woman*. New York: Ballantine Books, 1980.

Martin, R. A., and E. Y. Pollard. *Learning to Change*. New York: McGraw-Hill, 1980.

Ornstein, R. *Psychology of Consciousness*. New York: Harcourt Brace Jovanovich, 1979.

Pelletier, K. *Mind as Healer/Mind as Slayer*. New York: Delta Books, 1977.

Shames, R., and C. Sterin. *Healing with Mind Power*. Emmaus, Pa.: Rodale Press, 1978.

20 Standing Up for Yourself — Without Stepping on Others

Ruthann Fox-Hines

COUNSELING PSYCHOLOGIST
COUNSELING AND HUMAN DEVELOPMENT CENTER
UNIVERSITY OF SOUTH CAROLINA

In high school, when I had to talk in front of a class, the paper shook louder than my voice. I have so many "if onlys" when I think back to how I could have handled my college experience differently—how much I missed academically and socially because I wasn't assertive. I didn't question professors. I let folks take advantage of me. I allowed friendships to disintegrate because I wouldn't bring up things that bothered me until they had reached crisis level. I was a beautiful example of the passive person. In graduate school, I switched to the opposite extreme—aggressiveness; nobody was going to push me around. I was going to be tough. That didn't win me many points, either.

It wasn't until after graduate school that I learned about assertivensss and studied and acquired the skills involved. Now I have a Ph.D. degree and am a licensed counseling psychologist in my fifteenth year with a university counseling center. I'm a director and vice president of Resource Associates, Inc., a consulting firm. I'm the mother of a young man with (not "at") whom I can talk. I can get up in front of 300 people and hold their attention. I can get the service I desire in most stores, and I can deal with issues involving friends and colleagues. Assertive behavior has made such a difference in both my professional and personal life that I want to share it with you.

In this chapter, I'll describe the skills of positive communication, often called "assertive behavior." Assertive behavior is always based on mutual respect and on personal responsibility. I hope this chapter motivates you to examine your forms of interacting and to seek further training.

The Importance of Communications Skills

In college and beyond, the skills of standing up for yourself effectively, of communicating your wants, needs, feelings, and ideas in a positive manner are extremely important. Concerned parents or teachers who look out for you may not be around when you need them, and mind readers are extremely rare. It's up to you to communicate your needs specifically, clearly, and with respect for yourself and the other person.

Stop and think a moment of the many occasions when you wished you had such skills! Perhaps you needed to talk to an advisor about getting into a course, or had to ask an instructor to explain an obscure point in a lecture. Maybe you and your roommates have never agreed upon living arrangements and responsibilities. Resisting pressures from overly concerned parents, equitably sharing responsibilities on a committee, having your input heard and valued in classes, handling job interviews successfully, negotiating work requirements such as salary and hours—all these situations call for the skills of positive communication.

Some people find it easy to stand up for themselves, but many find themselves on the receiving end of negative results and reactions. If standing up for your rights is very difficult for you, you may go through life hoping someone else will figure out what you want and do your standing up for you. The sad truth is, someone else rarely will.

Varieties of Communication

Most of us picked up our communications skills in a rather disorganized fashion. We probably began by imitating parents, other family members, and our peers. You might compare this to learning grammar exclusively from everyday conversations, without once consulting a grammar book.

Not standing up for yourself, or standing up in a poor way, tends to cause frustration and poor relationships with others. Generally, if we do our learning in the pick-it-up-as-you-go-along school, our communication of feelings, and needs, will tend to fall into one of three categories, or some combination of all three.

1. *Passive:* not speaking up, hinting, whining, poor-me routines.

2. *Aggressive:* speaking up in a put-down way, demanding, pressuring.

3. *Passive-aggressive:* speaking up in a confused way, saying one thing and doing another ("Sure, I'll be there on time," and showing up late).

None of these attempts at communication is particularly well received by other people. The poor communicator is frequently disappointed, rejected, or even avoided.

—III——III——III—
Assertive Behavior

The most effective and positive ways of standing up for yourself and of communicating your needs and feelings properly are referred to as assertive behaviors. *Assertiveness* is clear, direct, respectful, responsible communication—verbal and nonverbal. It can be so much more effective than passive or passive-aggressive forms of communication because your chances of being heard and understood are greater, and the chances of the receiver of your communication drawing away, closing his or her ears to what you have to say, or coming back at you fighting are less. If others hear and understand you, and don't feel the need to protect themselves from you, your chances of getting an acceptable response are much greater.

One definition of assertiveness labels it as behavior that permits a person to stand up for his or her rights without denying others their rights. This definition is extremely important. If we simply stand up for our rights, we'll probably come across as aggressive. If we focus exclusively on the rights of the other person, we become passive. Attention to our own *and* others' rights is important in learning to be assertive.

And what are those rights? They include personal rights, such as the right to your own feelings, and interpersonal rights, such as the right to ask others for what you want or need. To avoid denying others their rights, you need to be aware of, and consciously acknowledge, the rights of others. For example, although you have the right to ask a favor, other people have the right to tell you that they refuse to grant it.

—III——III——III—
Mutual Respect and
Personal Responsibility

To stand up assertively for your rights, two conditions completely or partially missing from other forms of communication must be present: mutual respect and personal responsibility.

Basically, these conditions can be expressed in the following manner: I respect myself and my right to my ideas, feelings, needs, wants, and values, and I respect you and your rights to the same. I take responsibility for myself. I don't require you to be responsible for me and for figuring out what I am; I'll figure it out for myself.

Passive, passive-aggressive, and aggressive behaviors tend to lack respect for the self and/or the other person, and all three tend to be irresponsible forms of behavior.

Examples of Inappropriate Behaviors

An example may help you distinguish the various behaviors. You are serving on a class committee, and one of the other students isn't doing her share of the work. You're becoming extremely frustrated and worried about the grade you may receive on the project if this other person doesn't come through. The *passive* approach might be to hint about the deadline, and leave it up to the other person to figure out that you're concerned. Using this approach, you show that you're not respecting your own feelings and needs enough to make them known and that you're putting the major responsibility for figuring out what you mean on the other person.

The *passive-aggressive* approach might be to complain to another committee member. This shows a lack of respect for the person you should be addressing. Haven't you often said, "I wish he would respect me enough to come to me instead of talking to others about me." This behavior is irresponsible because you probably hope that the person you complain to will take the responsibility of saying something to the individual at fault.

The *aggressive* approach might be to confront the individual in this manner: "You're messing it up for the rest of us. How can you be so inconsiderate? If you don't have your part ready by tomorrow, I'm telling the professor!" This attack ignores the other person's feelings entirely and possibly overlooks mitigating circumstances of which you may be unaware. Thus, it is disrespectful.

If these three forms of address are incorrect and inappropriate, what is the assertive, or proper, approach?

The Assertive Approach

The *assertive* approach respects the other person and does not attack her, yet still deals with the issues and is responsible enough to express feelings and wishes clearly (in specific words, not by implication or tone of voice).

Such a communication might sound like this: "Mary, I have a problem. Our project is due next week, and I'm worried we won't have it ready on time. I had my part ready yesterday, the day we agreed on. I figure you probably have a heavy load and may have forgotten we agreed on that date. Still, I'm sort of frustrated and worried that we won't have a good project. Would you please make this a priority, and do your part so we can meet either tomorrow afternoon or noon the next day at the latest? I'd very, very much appreciate it."

The other person may feel embarrassed, but there's a good chance she won't feel as if you attacked her, and therefore won't be forced to take a defensive position. When people are attacked, they defend themselves either by "flight" or "fight." Using flight, they passively comply to another's wishes, but resentment builds inside them. Using fight, they openly throw back accusations or fight subversively (passive-aggressive) by getting the work done, but in a rather slipshod fashion.

On the other hand, when you approach people in a respectful and open manner, chances are they'll hear you more clearly and respond in a more positive manner.

—III—III—III—

Formula for Assertiveness

To make assertive communication your method for standing up for yourself, you may find the following formula helpful: R→, R←, S.

Respect the Other Person

R→ reminds you to communicate respect for the other person. Incidentally, respect does not necessarily mean liking, admiring, or agreeing with that person. It simply acknowledges that the other person *is* a person with the same basic rights as you. In other words, you can dislike someone's behavior or disagree with her or him and still offer basic human respect.

We communicate respect both in speech and in actions, in the words we choose to use, and in the nonverbal expressions that accompany the words. The verbal expression may be as simple as saying, "Excuse me," as you move through a crowd getting off an elevator, instead of pushing your way through silently. Your words may acknowledge that the other person has his or her own set of values and needs: "I realize you have established certain criteria for grades in this class . . ." is a good opener when you're about to discuss a possible grade change with a professor.

The verbal communication may even express empathy: "I realize you have a heavy load." It may offer the benefit of the doubt: "I'm sure it probably just slipped your mind." Respect for other people means giving them what we want to receive: courtesy, acknowledgment, and empathy.

Nonverbal communications of respect for others may be expressed in gestures, facial expressions, and tone of voice. Such communications may be more significant than words. Said in the wrong tone of voice, "I realize you have a heavy load" could have an opposite and sarcastic meaning. Attention to your nonverbal communications becomes essential to learning effective and positive methods of standing up for yourself.

Nonverbal expressions that communicate respect for others include a clear, relatively gentle, and unhurried manner of speaking, eye contact when another person is talking, uncrossed arms to signal openness, and giving others appropriate physical space so they don't feel crowded or intimidated. Cultural differences exist in nonverbal as well as verbal communications. Because of this, you should not take certain nonverbals as signs of disrespect when the individual expressing them is of a different cultural background. For example, Mediterranean, Latin American, and Middle Eastern people need much less space between themselves and others (as little as twelve inches) than their Northern European or North American counterparts (who require as much as three feet). Unless we're aware of differences like these, we could interpret such behavior as intimidating and disrespectful.

Respect Yourself

R← reminds you to respect yourself and to accept personal responsibility for your feelings, wants, and actions. A major way to accomplish this verbally is to use the first-person singular pronoun: I, me, my—especially the "I." Say "I feel . . . ," not "You make me feel . . ."; "I need more time," not "That's not a lot of time" (indirect, almost a hint) or "Give me more time" (a demand). Say "I don't want to . . . ," not "Wellllll, maybe . . . ," or "No! How could you ask me that?"

Nonverbal communication of self-respect also includes such things as eye contact and open body movements. Both imply that you believe what you say and have nothing to hide. Holding your head up instead of lowering it tends to communicate assurance rather than fear. Ending a spoken sentence with a softened, slightly lowered voice instead of an "up in the air" question mark shows that you have confidence in what you're saying.

Be Specific

S stands for specificity, or being specific, which develops from personal responsibility and respect for the other person. Specificity means being responsible enough to figure out your views, feelings, and wants and being able to communicate them as clearly as possible. It means avoiding labels or generalities about other people and their behavior. Instead of saying, "How can you be so inconsiderate?" when a smoker allows smoke to blow in your direction, you might try this: "I'm having a problem with the smoke from your cigarette. Would you please blow it in the other direction?"

Avoid labels such as "inconsiderate," "lazy," and "poor attitude." Don't you feel attacked when others use these labels on you? Talk about the behaviors that lead you to think about those labels. Avoid generalities such as "love," "attention," and "respect." Instead, determine the specific behaviors you include in your definitions of those vague terms, and talk about those behaviors. For instance, if you don't like someone to keep looking at a magazine when you're talking to her, don't say, "You don't respect me." Instead, you might try saying, "I'm uncomfortable when I talk to someone and don't get eye contact. When we talk, I'd appreciate it if you'd put your magazine down. It would help a lot."

—|||——|||——|||—

Choosing the Proper Response: An Example

To see the formula at work, let's go through an example. Mark is a relatively conscientious student. His roommate John seems to be majoring in partying. John cuts classes and regularly borrows Mark's notes from the two classes they share. Although Mark has been rescuing John by giving him his notes whenever John asks (being the "good guy"), he is beginning to feel used. One important lesson from this example is that "rescuers become victims." If you do for others what they can and should do for themselves, they tend to demand more and more and value what they get less and less.

Mark's first mistake was not to make his position clear at the start. A suggestion I can't stress too strongly is: The more you take responsibility for yourself—know what you feel and what your priorities and wants are, and make them clearly known to others—the fewer problems you'll have down the road.

The first time John asked to borrow the notes, Mark could have said, "I know you missed class and need the material (*acknowledging John's plight: R→*). But I don't usually lend my notes. I'll let you use them this time, but in the future, please don't ask. Find someone else or talk to the instructor" (*"I" statements of a clear policy and Mark's wishes: R← and S*).

If John pressures him, Mark may need to protect himself by tightening his communication and using what is sometimes referred to as a "broken record": No matter what John says, Mark responds by repeating the major message: "I don't lend my notes." Here is an example:

JOHN: Ah, come on. I thought we'd be able to take care of each other in classes (*a guilt trip*).

MARK: (*resisting the guilt and focusing on the major issue*) I don't lend my notes out. This time I said okay, but from now on, no.

JOHN: Hey, what kind of buddy are you? I thought we could count on each other.

MARK: John (*using the other person's name may make him more attentive*), I don't lend my notes. I hope you'll respect that and not use it to judge whether or not I'm a good buddy.

At this point, John may start to head out of the room in a huff.

MARK: Hey, John, I'm sorry you've taken my not lending out notes that way. I hope later you'll accept my position.

Since Mark didn't take care of this issue at the outset, he's reaching a frustrating point and probably establishing a negative pattern of interaction with John. He could slip into a passive approach easily, avoiding his room as much as possible so he can avoid John. Or he could become passive-aggressive and let his frustration show in his voice, make sarcastic remarks, or even give John the wrong notes. Finally, he could explode in an aggressive outburst: "Don't you ever take your own crummy notes? I'm sick and tired of doing all your work for you. Find someone else to mooch off. And, by the way, I'm also sick and tired of. . . ." Here, all Mark's other little frustrations with John may come pouring out.

Any of these alternatives will result in added frustration on Mark's part, distancing between the two, or even fight or flight on John's part: a loud argument, sneak attacks, or stony silences. There's a good chance that both will be seeking new roommates at a time when reshuffling may be difficult.

The Assertive Approach

The assertive approach, while not guaranteeing that Mark will get what he wants from John, at least opens the door for such a possibility. First, Mark needs to separate the issues he has with John—notes, noise, privacy, or whatever—and decide which issues he wants to deal with first. Dealing with individual issues is better than dumping a whole load of complaints on a person all at once. Mark should also find a time when he can talk to John alone. Complaints made in front of others tend to be disrespectful and cause the other person to be more defensive. Then he might say, "John, I know I've been lending you my notes for X and Y classes. (*By acknowledging his own part, Mark is showing respect for John: R→.*) But I'm beginning to feel used. I don't mind lending my notes if someone is sick, but I really don't like doing it on a regular basis (*"I" statements and clarity of feelings and wishes: R← and S*). I know I should have said something earlier (*again, R←, accepting responsibility that isn't John's*). I want to break that pattern. From now on, I'm not lending my notes, and I'm asking you not to ask me for them. Find someone else or talk with the instructor" (*more "I" statements and a clear statement of what he doesn't want and what he wants from John: R← and S*). If John pushes, Mark can resort to the "broken record" described earlier.

—|||—|||—|||—
Learning Effective Communications Skills

Since assertiveness, which encompasses standing up for yourself effectively and communicating in a positive manner, is a behavior patten, we can learn these methods of interacting as skills. Learning communications skills is similar to learning to drive a car. First, you practice in "safe" places such as the driveway or empty parking lots. Later, as you feel more comfortable with your skills, you try driving on the streets and, eventually, in five o'clock traffic. When you first learn to drive, such skills as braking smoothly feel unnatural and awkward. Later, after practicing, you reach a point where you don't even have to think about it.

The same is true with communications skills. First, you try simple skills in such places as a training group. When you first try these new communications, they may feel funny (uncrossing your arms, for example, if you're in the habit of keeping them crossed). Later, with practice, you find you can use these behaviors in the "real world." Still later, you'll find you don't have to think much about them. At that point, they've become natural.

The best way to learn assertive behavior skills is through special training seminars. Most colleges and universities, through their counseling centers or continuing education programs, and many community organizations such as the YWCA and YMCA offer workshops, short courses, or seminars in assertiveness. Books listed at the end of this chapter may also be useful to you. Remember, though, that reading and learning aren't enough. Practice is the essential ingredient.

Suggested Activities

1. Explain to a friend outside of class that assertiveness is not the same as aggressiveness.

2. Indicate the type of communication in each of the following examples: assertive (AS), passive (P), passive-aggressive (PA), aggressive (AG).

_____ a. A mother indicates she would like her daughter, a college student, to come home each weekend. The student replies: "Mom, I know you love me and want what's best for me. Right now, with studies and the friendships I'm trying to establish, what's best for me is to have most of my weekends here. I won't be coming home except at breaks, but I promise I'll write or call at least once a week. Thanks for understanding."

_____ b. You're asked to do a favor. Your reply: "Are you kidding? Hell, no!"

_____ c. You're a student and need to borrow a classmate's notes. You say to her: "I don't know what I'm going to do. I missed Carter's class last Friday and that test of his is next week. Oh, Lord, I know I'm going to do awful. I'll probably flunk."

_____ d. Someone pays you a compliment. You reply: "Thank you. I appreciate your noticing."

_____ e. You're upset with a friend who usually walks in late for meetings. He does it again. You say: "Oh, look. Sam's on time for a change!"

_____ f. You'd like to ask your roommate to play the stereo more softly. You say: "Mark, I don't have any problem with the fact that you enjoy the stereo loud. What I have a problem with is that, when I'm here and trying to study, the loud stereo breaks my concentration. When I'm out, do as you like. But, please, when I'm here, keep it lower. I'd appreciate it a lot."

Answers: a. AS   b. AG   c. P   d. AS   e. PA   f. AS

3. This classroom exercise can help both in the practice of assertive nonverbal behavior and in the personal coaching and cheering needed to remember we have certain rights. This exercise will take from thirty to sixty minutes of class time; parts a and b can be done ahead of time outside of class.

   a. Mark the rights listed below that are especially important to you and which you have some difficulty affirming:

   _____   1. To lead my own life, make my own decisions, make choices, and take the consequences.

   _____   2. To have my own values and to act on those values in a responsible manner.

   _____   3. To control my own body, time, money, or property.

   _____   4. To have all my feelings, positive and negative, and to express these feelings in a responsible way.

   _____   5. To have my own opinions, ideas, and perceptions and to express them in a responsible, nondogmatic way.

_____ 6. To have needs and act to meet them.

_____ 7. To express my needs, make requests, ask for information, ask for special consideration.

_____ 8. To refuse requests and invitations.

_____ 9. To *not* feel what others would like me to feel. To not share values and perceptions that others would like me to share.

_____ 10. To be imperfect, make mistakes, and act to correct them.

_____ 11. To change feelings, values, opinions, ideas, and behaviors.

_____ 12. To stop and think when confronted, invited, or asked to do a favor.

All these rights depend on your willingness to allow them to others; for example, you have the right to say no if you permit that right to others.

b. Pick out one right that is the most important to you—that is, if you worked on remembering you had that right and began behaving in terms of possessing it, your life might be improved. Write it out in the space provided. (You may think "I want all of those rights"; if so, for now, for the purpose of the exercise, focus on one. As that one becomes yours through affirmation, go on to the others.)

_____

_____

c. (approximately 10 minutes) In class, pair up and practice assertively reading and saying the following sentence plus the right you chose to work on. To practice assertively:

1. sit up straight; feet flat on the floor (well-balanced); head up, not lowered.

2. make eye contact with your partner (hold the paper or book up so you don't have to keep looking down at the desk or your lap).

3. keep facial expression serious and don't laugh either during or after.

4. make sure your voice is strong and goes down at the end of the affirmed right.

5. go slowly enough to be meaningful; don't rush.

I _____ (your name), as a worthy human being, who respects the rights of others, have the *perfect* right to: (read the right you have written out in part b).

As you practice with a partner, give each other specific feedback, such as "Your eye contact was good" or "It would be better if you slowed down a bit." Practice several times until you accomplish an assertive affirmation.

d. (approximately 10 minutes) Pairs join other pairs (form groups of four or six) and go around the group, each doing an assertive affirmation.

e. Practice assertive affirmations at home, making eye contact with yourself in a mirror. (During the next class, each person could then do an assertive affirmation after home practice.)

f. The instructor may want to lead a discussion about how things would be different if all students allowed themselves to have the right they have not let themselves have until now.

4. In this class exercise for role-playing practice, divide the class into teams of threes (one or two teams of fours, if necessary).

a. Each team should write up one or two situations that call for assertive behavior: roommate or dating issues, interactions with professors, resisting pressures, and interactions with parents, for example. Students could do this individually ahead of time, and teams could choose from among the situations brought in. Put the situations in a pile and have each team draw a situation.

b. (approximately 15 minutes) Teams plan a role-playing demonstration of assertive handling of the situation they draw. One member might play the roommate, friend, or professor; another plays the person who assertively handles the situation; the third (and fourth) member would serve as a helper to the one being assertive, reminding the assertive member of the rights involved and suggesting R→, R←, S phrasing and nonverbal behavior.

c. (approximately 5 minutes per role play) Each team presents its role play to the class.

d. Class can then follow each role-playing demonstration with some discussion of how it was handled and suggestions for improvement (approximately 5 minutes for each role play). For further practice, teams could later switch situations and redo them or come up with new ones to practice.

A word about role playing: Have fun. This kind of practice is necessary. Skills are not learned through mere reading. Trying them out is necessary. Since the skills are new, it is natural to feel a bit awkward. Feeling "natural" only comes with practice.

5. Contact your college or university counseling center or continuing education department for information regarding workshops or seminars on assertive behavior.

6. Get together with friends or fellow students who are interested in developing these skills. Use the workbook *Assert Yourself* by Galassi and Galassi (see Suggested Readings) as a guide, or your instructor or college may be able to acquire the game, Assert with Love, High Consciousness Games, Inc., PO Box 3206, Kansas City, Kans. 66103.

Suggested Readings

Butler, Pam. *Self Assertion for Women.* San Francisco: Canfield Press, 1981.

Emmons, M. L., and R. E. Alberti. *Your Perfect Right.* San Luis Obispo, Calif.: Impact Publishers, 1974.

Galassi, J., and M. Galassi. *Assert Yourself.* (workbook) New York: Human Sciences Press, 1977.

Jacubowski, R. and A. J. Lang. *The Assertive Option.* Champaign, Ill.: Research Press, 1978.

21 Dollars and Sense: Dealing with College Costs and Money Management

Ray Edwards

DIRECTOR OF STUDENT FINANCIAL AID
EAST CAROLINA UNIVERSITY

In many ways, the trappings of the academic world haven't changed much since my own undergraduate days in the sixties. When I observe the daily rituals occurring on campus, I am struck by the numerous similarities to the collegiate community in which I grew into adulthood. For those of us who are now what we never thought we'd ever be—middle aged—it is comforting to know that contemporary college life still resembles much of what we remember, or at least think we remember, about our own experiences.

Nevertheless, there are also clear and striking differences between the post-secondary worlds of twenty years ago and today. Among the most significant differences are those in the economics of higher education. The harsh economic realities of the eighties have taken a serious toll on both institutions and American families. Indeed, from today's vantage point, the old adage concerning the inevitability of death and taxes can easily be amended to include rising college costs as well. With typical costs rising at an average annual rate of 6 and 8 percent for public and private institutions, respectively, the cumulative impact has been alarming.

This was not the case when I went to college. Costs were relatively stable, and my parents were able to finance my attendance at our hometown state university by small bank loans. I earned money for my clothes and social activities by selling newspapers to patients at a hospital. And while paying for a college education wasn't a piece of cake for my parents even then, they managed it without too much long-range hardship. But then, my tuition was only $100 per semester. Today at *that same institution, tuition is over $1,000 per semester—a tenfold increase in under twenty-five years. Unfortunately, you and your family are likely to see costs continue to increase at a rate exceeding overall inflation, and many of you will have to incur significant loan indebtedness to foot the bill. The task of financing a postsecondary education in today's world can be sobering, indeed.*

This chapter aims to help you successfully cope with this many-faceted challenge of paying for your college expenses and managing your money effectively. Obviously, one chapter in one book cannot hope to provide all the answers for everyone—we both know that. However, the information contained here will provide you with a good understanding of the options available to you and may enable you to keep your loan debt to a reasonable level and make the most of what you have. With a bit of planning and common sense, you can be successful. It may not always be easy, but you can do it!

━ⅠⅠⅠ━ⅠⅠⅠ━ⅠⅠⅠ━

In meeting the varied challenges facing you as you begin your college career, none may be more challenging or important than dealing with your finances. For the first time in your life, you may find yourself totally responsible for a "household of one." While this can present frustrations and anxieties, especially if you're away from home for the first time, don't let the innumerable demands that will tug at your purse strings overwhelm you. Managing your finances, like most other things in life, can be learned, and the more you learn about how to manage your money, the better at it you will become.

Managing your money is only one aspect of the larger picture of paying for your college education. First you must ensure that you have adequate resources to manage. Paying for college doesn't just happen—it must be planned. For most students the task is more complicated than simply paying tuition.

In recent years, financial aid programs have meant the difference between going and not going to college for many students seeking higher education. In fact, approximately 50 percent of all students nationwide qualify for some type of financial aid each year. With educational costs what they are, and with the likelihood that inflation and other economic factors will continue to force them even higher, it's increasingly important that you familiarize yourself with the process for obtaining financial aid. Millions of students apply annually for the billions of dollars available in federal aid, and although this process can appear to be somewhat confusing and complex, there's really no need to be intimidated by it. Indeed, with a little effort on your part, the mystery often associated with financial aid will easily disappear. Whether you need to apply as a freshman or later in your academic career, the time and effort required are small when you consider the possible payoff.

Financing a College Education

In the task of paying for your college education, no single factor is more crucial than planning. It would be nice to think that every family begins planning for their children's college education years ahead, but this is often not the case. Many families are simply not in a position to save much toward the day when their children are ready for college. And many of those who do find that their savings, because of recent economic conditions, are inadequate for current costs. It becomes critical, then, for you to approach the financing of your education in a comprehensive and creative way.

Costs

To deal effectively with college costs, you must first establish what those costs are. In doing this, it's essential that *all* costs be identified. Tuition and academic fees are obvious and generally easy to determine, but many other expenses are also involved, and some of these are more difficult to assess. The following list includes most of the typical costs you'll have to deal with:

- Tuition/academic fees

- Books

- Equipment and/or supplies

- Room

- Board

- Transportation

- Personal or miscellaneous

To determine these costs, seek help from your college catalog, admissions office, and financial aid office. The aid office of almost every institution will be able to provide you with a copy of what it considers the average comprehensive educational costs most of its students face for the current academic year. Based on such average expenses, you can then construct a personalized list of costs. In doing this, you should be conscious of possible ways to keep expenses to a minimum.
Here are some examples of ways to save:

- Purchase used books rather than new ones whenever possible.

- Carpool or use public transportation instead of driving your own car.

- Earn course credit by advanced placement exams, thereby reducing the number of courses you must take and pay for.

- Save money by accelerating your program and attending summer school.

- Buy a board plan instead of paying for your meals on a daily basis.

These and other techniques can help you get the most for your money, as well as keep your expenses at a level that's as reasonable as possible. Once you have a handle on the expenses facing you, it's much easier to relate costs to the resources you have available. After all, the real question is not simply how much an education costs or how much you have available. It's how much you need versus how much you have that counts. In order to answer that question, you must analyze your resources just as you did your costs.

Resources

Personal/family resources. In assessing resources, you should first identify personal and, if applicable, family finances available to help you pay for your education. Parental savings, insurance policies taken out for you when you were young, personal savings, trust funds, and summer employment are examples of resources. In addition, relatives are sometimes willing to help you pay for school through direct contributions or loans. Savings from part-time jobs can also help. Although financial aid programs and scholarships may be available to you, remember that the ultimate responsibility for financing your college education rests with you and, to the extent possible, with your family.

After identifying the funds available to you from personal and/or family sources, it's a simple matter of comparison to determine if you need further finances. If there's a gap between what you have available and what you need, it's time to think about applying for financial aid.

Financial aid resources. Once you have determined that you're going to need aid to help pay for your educational expenses, you must successfully negotiate the financial aid application process. Whether you are a freshman or upperclass student, you'll have to reapply for financial aid each year. Negotiating this process is primarily an exercise in completing forms, so expect to spend some time filling in spaces and checking boxes. The process may appear confusing at times, but it's really quite straightforward. Familiarize yourself with the application procedures and necessary forms, and you should have a fairly easy time completing the process.

Before outlining the basic steps in the application process itself, let's first look at some points about financial aid as a whole. What is financial aid? What is it based on? What types of aid programs are available? The answers to these three questions will provide you with a general orientation to the ins and outs of financial aid.

What is Financial Aid?

Quite simply, financial aid is any type of financial support that's available to you to help pay your educational costs. The term *financial aid* may refer to anything from a federal grant to an institutional scholarship. Typically, it can be categorized as either gift aid or self-help aid. *Gift aid* generally means that the student receiving the funds doesn't have to repay the award; *self-help* implies that the student must do something to receive the aid, such as work or repay it. In both types of aid, financial need may or may not be a factor.

The criteria on which financial aid is awarded vary according to the type of aid under consideration and the college. All aid programs require that you meet some sort of eligibility standards. Typically, the criteria are academic merit and financial need, or a combination of these two factors. For the large federal aid programs, the major eligibility factors are financial need and maintaining satisfactory progress toward your degree.

What Types of Aid Are Available?

Regardless of how financial aid is categorized (gift or self-help) or on what criterion it's awarded (need and/or merit), there are five basic types of aid programs generally available: grants, loans, work, scholarships, and cooperative education programs.

Grant programs don't require any repayment from you, while loans, as the name implies, do require that you repay the amount you received when you leave school. A college work-study program is a need-based financial aid program that provides you with the opportunity to work part time while going to school, thereby earning part of the money you'll need to pay for your educational expenses. In addition to college work-study jobs, many schools also offer regular part-time student assistant jobs. In considering whether to work while going to school, remember that your first priority is to succeed academically. If working will not adversely affect your grades, you can gain marketable job experience by working part time. In fact, several national studies indicate that part-time work actually enhances academic performance.

In addition to these types of aid programs, many civic organizations, local clubs and churches, high schools, and private foundations provide monetary assistance in the form of scholarships or loans. Furthermore, many institutions offer cooperative education programs that allow you to combine an academic program with employment in your area of study. By co-oping, you not only gain valuable work experience that will pay off when you graduate and begin job hunting but you also have the opportunity to earn money, some of which you may be able to put toward your remaining educational costs.

A number of helpful publications can help you identify financial aid opportunities; some are listed at the end of this chapter. However, the best source of information concerning the types of programs offered by your college is the financial aid office. There you should be able to obtain information about all aid programs for which you might be eligible.

Financial Aid Application Process

Just as there are various eligibility criteria for the different financial aid programs, there are also various application procedures that depend on the type of aid you're considering. It's impossible to cover all conceivable application requirements here because they vary as widely as types of colleges. Nevertheless, three basic elements are common to almost all application processes.

1. *Needs-analysis document.* Most aid programs are based on need and require that you complete some type of financial statement. This document may take the form of a local organization's simple one-page approach or a more thorough multi-page form. The large federal aid programs require that you complete one of the federally approved needs-analysis forms. These forms are available in the aid office of all institutions that participate in the federal student aid programs.

2. *Institutional financial aid application.* Many colleges require some type of institutional application for aid in addition to the needs-analysis form just mentioned. This form generally asks for information that the school uses in determining its aid awards, information not obtained on the needs-analysis document.

3. *Scholarship application.* Almost all institutions or organizations that award scholarships based on scholastic merit require you to complete a special scholarship application. These forms usually ask about your past academic record, college entrance examination scores, class rank, offices

held, and honors received. In addition, as a part of the application process, scholarship applicants are often required to interview with the awarding unit.

In tackling the financial aid application process, keep several things in mind. First, early planning is essential. Make sure that you begin as early as possible to determine what application procedures are required for the aid programs you're going to apply for. Remember that deadlines can vary widely, with scholarship application deadlines generally earlier than those for need-based aid programs. Also keep in mind that some forms will require financial information that you may have to gather before you can accurately complete them.

Second, it takes time for your application(s) to be processed. Depending on the type of program, the processing may take anywhere from several weeks to several months. Find out how long the processing normally takes so you'll be able to check on it if necessary. After your application has been received, you may be required to either clarify some data you provided or submit additional information. To prevent unnecessary delays in the process, it is essential that you respond as quickly as possible with the additional information or clarification.

Finally, to avoid costly delays, confusion, or other unforeseen circumstances, you should *always* make a photocopy (with the data noted) of everything you complete or send with your application. This simple precaution may save you untold time and agony.

Managing Your Funds

Now that we've covered the basic aspects of financing a college education, it's time to address the second major issue—money management. Whether you are receiving need-based financial aid or paying your way entirely on your own, you must successfully manage your financial resources.

As with financing a postsecondary education and dealing with the financial aid process, the key to managing your money is planning. You *must plan* how you're going to spend your money. If you don't, you risk facing some serious problems as the year progresses. And the keys to planning your finances successfully and preventing unpleasant surprises can be summarized in two words: budgeting and discipline.

As I mentioned in the introduction to this chapter, you can learn to manage your finances. Fortunately, learning the techniques of sound money management is not a difficult task. Basic common sense and reason are the foundations for learning how to budget. So let's turn our attention to the money management process.

The Money Management Three-Step: Budgeting Made Simple

To establish a reasonable budget for yourself, you must determine three basic facts. First, how long a period of time do you want your budget to cover? One semester, two quarters, an entire year? Second, what items must your budget include? In other words, how comprehensive must it be? Are you going to be responsible for handling your total costs or only ongoing living expenses, while Mom and Dad pay your tuition and pay room costs directly? Third, how much money do you actually have?

In constructing a budget, you should make it as comprehensive as necessary. The whole point of a budget is to establish a plan for allocating the financial resources you have available. It's nothing more than a systematic way of preventing confusion and uncertainty about how you'll spend your money. By planning how you will spend, you can prevent impulsive spending and ensure that you make it to the end of your budget period without going into the red. The following simple steps will guarantee a reasonable and comprehensive budget.

Itemize your expenses. The first step in setting your budget is to list all the expenses you can think of. In doing this, keep in mind that you should take *all* anticipated expenses into account. Begin by listing costs for such things as tuition, fees, books, and supplies. Once you feel satisfied you've accounted for your educational expenses, begin to itemize your anticipated living costs; in this area you must really be deliberate in your approach. You must include not only such things as food, laundry, clothing, and toiletries/cosmetics but your social life as well. If you fail to allow for the latter, you may nickel and dime your budget into the red with such small expenses as going to the movies. They may not seem like much, but they can mount up. Remember, the whole point here is to be in control of your money. You can be in control only if you know how much you're going to need to spend and for what. Chart A should help you in this task of itemizing your expenses.

Chart A   *Itemizing Your Expenses*
Time Period: (Example) Academic Year

A. EDUCATIONAL EXPENSES:

Tuition	$ 500
Fees	$ 700
Books	$ 250
Supplies	$ 50
SUBTOTAL	$1,500

B. LIVING EXPENSES:

Housing	$ 850
Board	$1,475
Personal	$ 75
Transportation	$ 300
Clothes	$ 225
Entertainment	$ 175
SUBTOTAL	$3,100
TOTAL	$4,600

Itemize your resources. Once you have a handle on your expected costs, you must tackle the issue of how much money you will have and how and from what sources you will receive it. This is the second crucial step in establishing a budget.

There are any number of possible and effective methods for listing your financial resources. For simplicity and comprehensiveness, however, one extremely effective way is to list the money you'll have available by categories, such as part-time work, money from parents, savings, and student aid. This way, you'll get a total perspective of what you'll have available, which will help when it comes time to actually write out your budget. Chart B should help you in this process.

Chart B *Itemizing Your Resources*
Time Period: (Example) Academic Year

A. SAVINGS:

Yours	$ 400
Parents	$ 200

B. PARENTS:

Cash	$ 300
Bank loans	$1,000

C. WORK:

Summer	$ 0
Part time during year	$ 0

Social Security	$ 0
Veteran's	$ 0
Other	$ 0

E. FINANCIAL AID:

Grants	$1,200
Scholarships	$ 400
Student loans	$ 600

F. OTHER:

ROTC	$ 900
Relatives	$ 0
Trusts	$ 0
TOTAL	$5,000

Order your expenses. Now that you've itemized all your anticipated expenses and resources, it's time to begin analyzing the budgeting process. This third step requires putting your costs into a common sense perspective. In doing this analysis, you must approach your expected costs from a cold, objective point of view. For clarity and perspective, go through all the costs you've listed and determine whether each can be categorized as discretionary (that is, avoidable, unfixed costs) or nondiscretionary (unavoidable, fixed costs). The purpose of this exercise is to focus on those expenses such as tuition, books, and residence hall costs that are fixed (those you *must* pay for) and those such as food, clothing, and entertainment that are not fixed (those you have control over).

By categorizing your expenses as to whether or not you have discretion over them, you're in a better position to put your financial situation in perspective. After you have identified your fixed, nondiscretionary expenses, you know exactly how much of your money must be allocated to them. You then face the easier task of reviewing your discretionary, more controllable costs in light of your remaining sources.

To deal effectively with discretionary expenses, you must first go through all your expected controllable costs and rank them in order of importance. Obviously, there are a few expenses for which you must allocate part of your resources—food and transportation, for example. You can't stop eating or transporting yourself to campus for classes. Therefore, you should rank these costs at the top of the list; rank others in descending order of importance. Remember that you have much greater latitude in deciding how much you're going to spend for these items. You can eat or you can really dine, for example. By the same token, if you must commute to class you may be able to use public transportation rather than driving your own car. And if public transportation isn't available, a carpool can reduce your commuting costs. In putting discretionary items into perspective, the following questions apply:

1. Must you dress to impress? Alligators can eat your budget!
2. Is anything morally wrong with a cheap date?
3. Are campus activities available that are cheaper than those off campus?
4. Is a Dutch date really foreign?
5. Can you sacrifice a color TV and 500 watts of stereo for something a bit more modest?

Once you have completed this exercise you can begin to construct your budget.

Constructing Your Budget

If you've completed the steps just outlined, constructing your budget should be easy. You should actually make up two versions of your budget. The first should put your financial picture into overall perspective, and the second should be an actual monthly or weekly version of how you are going to spend your money. Based on the previous two charts, Chart C (p. 288) is an example of an overall budget and summary for a student attending a college that operates on the typical two-semester (fall/spring) academic year calendar. This student lives on campus and travels home (which is in-state) for visits and holidays three times each semester. Notice how easily you can put your overall financial situation into perspective by this approach.

An overall perspective is essential if you're going to deal successfully with expenses versus resources. This approach helps you arrive at the bottom line—and that, after all, is what it's all about. However, the second version of your budget—the actual expenditure budget—is equally important if you are going to be in control of your money. Chart D is a monthly expenditure budget for the same student. Keep in mind that the large expenses for tuition, books, and room occur at the beginning of the semester, while continuing expenses are handled on an ongoing basis. The monthly approach is used here because it's the most common method for dealing with expenses and because it's a convenient basic structure for dealing with these expenses. It provides you with a continuing mechanism for keeping track of your money without becoming overly complicated, and

Chart C   *Expense/Resource Budget Summary*

I. ITEMIZED EXPENSES		II. ITEMIZED RESOURCES	
A. EDUCATIONAL:		**A. SAVINGS:**	
Tuition	$ 500	Yours	$ 400
Fees	$ 700	Parents	$ 200
Books	$ 250	**B. PARENTS:**	
Supplies	$ 50	Cash	$ 300
SUBTOTAL	$1,500	Bank loans	$1,000
B. LIVING:		**C. WORK:**	
Housing	$ 850	Summer	$ 0
Board	$1,475	Part time during year	$ 0
Personal	$ 75	**D. BENEFITS:**	
Transportation	$ 300	Social Security	$ 0
Clothes	$ 225	Veteran's	$ 0
Entertainment	$ 175	Other	$ 0
SUBTOTAL	$3,100	**E. FINANCIAL AID:**	
TOTAL	$4,600	Grant(s)	$1,200
		Student loan(s)	$ 600
III. SUMMARY		Scholarship(s)	$ 400
A. TOTAL RESOURCES	$5,000	**F. OTHER:**	
B. TOTAL EXPENSES	$4,600	ROTC	$ 900
C. DIFFERENCE +/−	$+400	Relatives	$ 0
		Trusts	$ 0
		TOTAL	$5,000

since checking accounts run on a monthly basis, it's convenient for balancing purposes.

In establishing your monthly expenses, enter the fixed costs first, with the discretionary items after. To arrive at the amount you're going to allow yourself for discretionary expenses, simply divide your total anticipated costs for those items by the appropriate number of months for which you're budgeting. This way, once you have compared that month's costs to resources, you can go back and adjust your discretionary expenses as needed.

Chart D   *Monthly Expenditure Budget*
Month: September

EXPENSES			RESOURCES	
Fixed:			My own	$ 400
Tuition	$ 250		Mom/Dad	$ 200
Fees	$ 350		Federal grant	$ 600
Books	$ 125		Student loan	$ 300
Dormitory	$ 425		Scholarship	$ 200
			TOTAL	$1,700
Discretionary:			BOTTOM LINE	
Supplies	$ 35		Total resources	$1,700
Food	$ 195		Total expenses	$1,415
Personal	$ 15		Balance	$ 285
Entertainment	$ 20			
TOTAL	$1,415			

Again, this is simply an example of one way of budgeting for your expenses. Whatever specific approach you take, make sure that you use a technique that is comprehensive and provides you with an ongoing way of tracking your spending. If you don't keep your financial health and well-being in perspective, you could find yourself writing one of those "having a wonderful time, send money" letters before the end of the semester.

━ııı━ııı━ııı━
Student Loans: Avoiding a Future of Indebtedness

For many students today, borrowing through one or more of the low-interest, long-term student loan programs is an unavoidable part of paying for their college educations. These programs have made it possible for millions of students to obtain the money they needed to get a college degree, and you may very well find yourself joining their ranks before your college career ends. There is little doubt that the availability of these federally subsidized programs had contributed much to the cause of educational access in this country. But, as with so many other things in life, there is a good news/bad news aspect to the student loan issue. Many students now find themselves facing a significant amount of loan indebtedness upon graduation—a burden it may take them years to pay off.

If you find that you must consider borrowing to pay for your education, do so wisely and with thought. Remember, when you borrow, you must repay. Therefore, consider all available alternative options (such as part-time work and co-op programs) before you borrow. If you ultimately decide that your only practical option is to borrow, do so with not only your present but also your future in mind. That is, don't bite off more today than you are going to be able to chew tomorrow.

In making the decision to borrow through one of the available student loan programs, consider the following basic but critical questions:

1. How much do you expect that you will need to borrow throughout your college career (including graduate school, if that is in your plan)?

2. How much will your monthly repayment obligation amount to based on your answer to the first question, and for how long a period will you be repaying your loan?

3. Given your career goals and the likely range of your starting salary, how much will you realistically be able to afford to repay monthly?

The answer to the first question may be a bit difficult for you to project at this point, but it is essential that you attempt it. By following the process for identifying costs and resources (outlined earlier in this chapter) for your entire anticipated academic career, you can estimate the approximate amount of total student loan you will need. Once you have this estimated figure, you can determine the answer to the second question. Your monthly repayment will be no less than the minimum required by the type of loan program through which you borrowed, but may be higher than the required minimum if your total indebtedness requires it. For example, the minimum monthly payment required by the National Direct Student Loan program (NDSL) is thirty dollars, while for the Guaranteed Student Loan program (GSL) the minimum is fifty dollars per month. Similarly, the length of time you have to repay will vary according to the total amount of loan obligation you have assumed. Under normal circumstances, the maximum allowable length of time you will have to repay under both the NDSL and GSL programs is ten years (120 monthly payments). You will have less time if the amount of your loan can be paid off in less than ten years at the minimum monthly payment. For example, if you have borrowed $2,000 through the GSL program, you will have 47 monthly payments of $50. On the other hand, if you have borrowed $5,000, you will have up to the full ten years— 120 payments of $60.97. You can compute your approximate monthly repayment by using Chart E; your lender can also provide you with this information.

Chart E   *Monthly Loan Repayment Calculation*

Interest Rate	Total Loan Principle		Repayment Multiplier		Per Month Payment
5%	×		.0106065	=	
6%	×		.0111080	=	
7%	×		.0116108	=	
8%	×		.0121328	=	
9%	×		.0126676	=	
10%	×		.0132153	=	
11%	×		.0137753	=	
12%	×		.0143473	=	

Example: $10,000 total loan at 7%
$10,000 × .0116108 = $116.10 per month

Once you have computed the amount of your monthly loan repayment based on your estimates, determine whether or not you will be able to afford that amount upon graduation. Doing this will take some research on your part. But again, it is essential that you do so if you are going to make reasonable decisions about borrowing today that you will be able to live with later on. To predict the level of loan repayment you can handle once you enter the work force, you must estimate your expected starting salary and expenses. One of the best sources of data on starting salaries is the *Occupational Outlook Handbook,* published annually by the Department of Labor's Bureau of Labor Statistics. This publication should be available in your school's library or career education/career planning center.

After you have determined your likely starting salary, subtract projected federal, state, and local taxes, which will be deducted from that salary, and divide the result by twelve. This will give you your estimated monthly after-tax income. This is the amount of income you will actually have available for *all* your monthly expenses, including your student loan debt.

The last step in this process is to develop an estimated monthly expense budget for yourself. In doing this, keep in mind that upon graduation you will not only confront a new career but a new life-style as well. The financial challenges of setting up this new life will be great, and you will have to be disciplined in setting your priorities. You can develop your future budget in the same way you developed your college expense budget in the previous section of this chapter. And again, be as realistic as possible. When you have completed this budget exercise, you should have a much better idea of what level of loan burden you can reasonably afford. In making your decision, be careful not to fall prey to what I call "deferred responsibility syndrome." It's very easy to assume a burden today that you won't have to actually face for several years. As a rule, banks generally advise undergraduates not to assume a loan debt that will exceed 8 percent of their first year's anticipated gross income. Making a reasoned and realistic decision about loan debt now could be the best decision you make in the next ten years.

Financing your college education, successfully managing your money during your college years, and guarding against excessive loan indebtedness are formidable undertakings. Recent economic developments have made it increasingly difficult for students and their families to cope with these challenges. Nevertheless, millions of American young people are doing it.

In approaching these challenges, you must, above all else, *plan* for what you're going to do. Systematic thinking and planning are absolutely essential if you are going to succeed. Be flexible in your thinking and creative in your approach. You may have to change a decision or alter a previously desired plan as a result of this process, but if you do, don't be overly discouraged. As long as you keep your ultimate goals in front of you, you can make it.

Keep in mind that on every campus there are people and resources available to help you. Use them! The challenges are great, but the payoff is even greater. Above all else, once you've developed your final plan, stick to it. Be confident in what you've done and disciplined enough to make it work. For after all else is said, the only person who can make it work is you. Good luck!

Suggested Activities

1. Determine how much it costs to attend your institution for each term and for the entire academic year.

2. Determine whether you have adequate financial resources to pay for your college education.

3. Explore the types of financial aid programs available at your institution and determine the application procedures and deadlines for applying.

4. Itemize your expenses and resources for the current year using the example included in this chapter as a guide.

5. Construct an overall expense/resource budget for yourself for the current academic year.

6. Construct a monthly expenditure budget for yourself for each month in the current academic year.

7. Visit the financial aid, student employment, career planning, and co-operative education offices at your school and find out as much as you can about the services they offer.

8. Plan for your student loan repayment obligation by following the exercises included in this chapter.

Suggested Readings

The College Cost Book. Published yearly. Princeton, N.J.: College Scholarship Service of the College Board.

College Planning/Search Book. Published yearly. Iowa City, Iowa: American College Testing Program.

Directory of Special Programs for Minority Group Members. 3rd ed. Garrett Park, Md.: Garrett Park Press.

Fabisch, Victoria. *The A's and B's: Your Guide to Academic Scholarships*. Published yearly. Alexandria, Va.: Octameron Associates.

Feingold, S. Norman, and M. Feingold. *Scholarships, Fellowships, and Loans*. Vol. 6. Arlington, Mass.: Bellman, 1982.

Guide for Students and Parents. Published yearly. Iowa City, Iowa: American College Testing Program Needs Analysis Service.

Keeslar, Oreon. *Financial Aids for Higher Education*. Dubuque, Iowa: W. C. Brown.

Kennedy, Joyce, and Herm Davis. *The College Financial Aid Emergency Kit*. Published yearly. Cardiff, Calif.: Sun Features.

Leider, R. *Your Own Financial Aid Factory*. Alexandria, Va.: Octameron Associates, 1984.

Lovejoy's College Guide. Published yearly. Red Bank, N.J.: Lovejoy's College Guide.

Moore, Donald R. *Money for College! How to Get It*. Woodbury, N.Y.: Barron's Educational Service, 1982.

Need a Lift? Published yearly. Indianapolis: American Legion, National Emblem Sales.

Schlacter, Gail A. *Directory of Financial Aids for Minorities*. Santa Barbara, Calif.: Reference Service Press, 1985.

Schlacter, Gail A. *Directory of Financial Aids for Women*. Santa Barbara, Calif.: Reference Service Press, 1985.

U.S. Department of Education. Published yearly. *Student Consumer Guide*. Washington, D.C.: U.S. Government Printing Office.

22 Welcoming the Returning Student

Dorothy S. Fidler

DIRECTOR OF MATURE STUDENTS PROGRAM
ASSOCIATE DIRECTOR, NATIONAL CENTER FOR
  THE STUDY OF THE FRESHMAN YEAR EXPERIENCE
UNIVERSITY OF SOUTH CAROLINA

After fourteen years as a housewife, I returned to college to continue my own education, so I feel a certain kinship with those of you who are also returning to an academic setting after a long absence. On the night of my first college class, I can remember sitting in the classroom and waiting for the professor. I turned to a stranger seated next to me and said in a loud voice: "What in the world am I doing here? I have a baby at home in diapers. She probably needs to be changed right now. I should be at home this minute taking care of my baby." I vividly recall the rush of anxiety, the feeling of being out of place, the confusion of not knowing where I should be or what my proper role was at that moment. Besides, I was afraid I could never learn statistics. I literally had to hang onto the desk to stay seated until the professor entered the room and greeted the class. That was only the first of many anxiety attacks. Many other times during the years it took to earn my degrees, I gritted my teeth and concentrated on channeling the energy generated by anxiety into productive work. Finally, I earned a Ph.D. degree in psychology.

These feelings of anxiety, inadequacy, and confusion engulf all of us at one time or another, regardless of age. However, they may be more typical of adult students. Because I've experienced them firsthand, I can identify with those of you who feel sheer panic as you begin college. I hope this chapter offers you the encouragement to continue the intellectual growth and personality development that is really an integral part of going to college, regardless of age.

—III—III—III—

All over the country, adult students (usually defined as those over 25 years old) are enrolling in college courses in record-breaking numbers. Some statisticians predict that by the end of this decade, one out of every three college students will be over 25 years old; other experts predict one out of every two will be an older student. Educators are watching this trend with great interest, for they recognize that older students are changing the face of higher education as campuses adapt to meet the demands of their new clientele.

This chapter is dedicated to helping older students acclimate to campus life more quickly. Younger students should also find in this chapter ways that they can assist in this process while learning more about our expanding population of adult students.

On campus, younger and older students can learn from each other. Each sees the other as a reflection of himself or herself at a different stage of life. Yet at the beginning of college, younger students often feel threatened by older classmates, and older students fear they can't compete with bright young teenagers fresh from college preparatory classes. After several weeks, older students find that their high motivation enables them to compete for good grades, and younger students learn to appreciate the multiple roles of spouse, parent, or employee that many adults play in addition to their role as student.

—III—III—III—
Assets of Adult Students

Most educators and younger students heartily welcome older students to college campuses, for they bring many assets to the classroom. One asset characteristic of adult students is a high level of motivation to learn and perform well in college. If you are an older student, you probably feel greatly motivated to succeed in your college course work. Because professors enjoy teaching students who really want to learn, you will surely be appreciated. Most faculty feel that your motivation to learn is a definite asset in the classroom with residual benefits for younger students as well.

Another plus that you as an adult bring to college is your real-life experience: your personal experiences in working in the community, holding a job, raising children, or managing a household. These day-to-day practical experiences enrich the theoretical concepts presented in the classroom. You can learn to relate general theories to specific examples in your own life. Your own experiences are a vast resource of relevant material for written assignments and classroom discussions.

Recent research suggests a third asset for older students: a definite increase in verbal skills. In recent studies, hundreds of individuals took tests of learning ability at ten-year intervals. Results of these tests showed that, contrary to popular belief, learning ability does not decline with age. In fact, these studies found that verbal ability actually increases, rather than decreases, with age.

So in some ways, you're smarter now that you're older, for you have better verbal skills, heightened motivation to learn, and a vast wealth of experiences. As lifelong learning becomes a social reality in our own culture, we can point with pride to these assets that older students bring to the college classroom.

Who, Me Worried?

In spite of these assets, you may feel a great deal of anxiety as you begin your college career. This is a venture that literally can change your life! You will learn new skills that can open the door to new opportunities, new goals, and new directions for yourself. You may experience spurts of intellectual growth and personality development. You may begin to reevaluate long-held beliefs and values. Any apprehension that you feel at the beginning of such a challenge is genuine.

In fact, apprehension is a universal characteristic of adult students. For example, the following journal entry was written by a 32-year-old freshman on his first day of classes:

> I was so restless for the past month thinking about what going to college would be like. Every day I got a little more excited. As the time grew nearer I lost my appetite, I found myself daydreaming and basically "out to lunch" a great deal of the time. My thoughts centered around: Would I do well? Am I smart enough? Can I handle the change from having been out of school for fourteen years and definitely out of shape when it comes to brain power? Do I even remember what it is like to study? Will I be adequate?
>
> Well, what it boils down to is that I have been psyching myself up and out. I have questioned my own ability to the point to where I am suffering from extreme anxiety tension.

One of your tasks in the days ahead is to learn how to manage your own anxiety so it acts as a positive, rather than a negative, force in this new venture. Anxiety is merely a name, a label used to describe a feeling. The feeling itself is caused by heightened levels of adrenaline in the body. When you wish to perform well, adrenaline levels in your body rise to meet the challenge. Increased adrenaline generally improves performance. However, some researchers suggest that too much adrenaline might "blow the circuits" and be detrimental to performance.

You usually select different labels to describe the feelings associated with different levels of adrenaline in your system. For example, if your adrenaline level is only slightly raised, you may label this physiological fact as "feeling excited." If the adrenaline level becomes moderately high, you may say you're "a little worried or apprehensive." If your adrenaline level is very high, you'll probably label this feeling as "intense fear" or "dread." You can alter the level of adrenaline and the label you use to describe your feeling.

A variety of stress-reduction techniques will reduce the amount of adrenaline to a manageable level. One such technique is to relabel the feeling itself. Relabeling "apprehension" as "challenging excitement" improves your outlook and your ability to cope. It may even reduce the actual amount of adrenaline in your bloodstream! You may want to practice this technique of relabeling as you face the challenge of beginning college. See also Chapter 19 for help with managing stress.

The remainder of this chapter provides additional ways to help you reduce stress and successfully meet the exciting challenges in your new college environment. Some of these hints may not apply to your particular situation, but they represent bits of wisdom passed on by others who are old hands at being older students.

—||||——||||——||||—
Helpful Hints from Adult Learners

1. *Enroll part time.* At the beginning, consider enrolling as a part-time student. As in any new venture, getting started is the hardest part! Returning to an academic setting is a time of great change for you. Small colleges and large universities alike have subcultures: a new language (semester, quarter, grade-point ratio), new regulations, new expectations. In learning the lingo and becoming part of the college culture, you may undergo a bit of culture shock. Some researchers argue that any change (even good change) is stressful. Learning to gauge the optimal amount of change for you is part of learning stress management. Too much change can lead to physical and psychological stress, which, in turn, can lead to physical illness. Enrolling as a part-time student and taking only one, two, or three classes reduces some of the stress. A reduced course load allows you the extra time to relax and enjoy the challenge of learning. After adjusting to the new culture, you may want to increase your course load and become a full-time student.

2. *Take a course in how to study.* Many colleges offer credit or noncredit courses in study skills. Most adults have not studied since high school and have very rusty study habits. Studying isn't merely reading for pleasure; studying involves organizing, storing, and retrieving great chunks of infor-mation. How to organize material meaningfully to aid memory retention, how to study for different kinds of exams, how to read textbooks and take notes in class—these are processes you can learn. You'll develop a few study skills on your own, but a course in study skills helps you become a more

efficient student more quickly. With increased efficiency, you can become a more productive student with less effort.

3. *Look for review courses.* If you learned French or algebra years ago but have had no need to keep in practice, you probably forgot much of what you once knew. You may need to review basic math, language, or writing skills before beginning upper-level courses. The good news is that relearning material you once knew is much easier than learning new material. There are several ways to review basic skills. You may try studying on your own or attending adult education courses through the local public schools. Many colleges now offer credit or noncredit courses to review math, grammar, and writing skills. So take time to brush up on the basics before enrolling in upper-level courses.

4. *Learn good time management techniques.* As for most students, but especially because you're older, time allocation is the single most critical problem you will face. A college education requires a serious time commitment regardless of age, but for a mature student with prior commitments, time pressures are relentless. Because demands from family, job, friends, and school often occur simultaneously, you may well experience serious role conflicts. Such conflicts require you to set priorities and carefully allocate your time. The following excerpt from a mature student's English paper highlights role conflict and her resulting time management decisions.

> My greatest difficulty in going back to college has been scheduling my time. One has to schedule so many activities in a limited time period and the following is on my schedule: time for my son, time for studying, time for housework and cooking, and time to relax. There never seems to be enough time to do everything, so I have to do things that I think are most important first.
>
> I always take time to help my son with his homework, read to him, and play with him because I think he should be first in my list of priorities. Studying comes next on my time schedule. I have discovered if I get behind in my studies, it is nearly impossible to catch up, and I study every day. Although I should cook more and prepare better meals, we have been eating out a lot. A woman and a small child can eat out almost as cheaply as she can cook. We also have more soup and sandwiches than we did before. My house is a disaster area and I hate to live in a messy house, but I avoid looking at messy bedrooms by simply closing the bedroom doors. Washing the dishes is my hardest task, so I buy paper plates and paper cups. Having time to relax has been my most difficult task. This is something I have not been able to do. The only time I relax is when my son goes to sleep, but sometimes I use this quiet time to study.
>
> I will continue taking up time with my son because he is young only once, and I know he needs me. Studying is still very important to me, so I will continue to put study time before housework and

cooking because I believe I can make up for that by cooking good meals when I have more time, by getting help with the housework, and by thoroughly cleaning my house on the weekend.

Going back to school has been a wonderful experience, and I hope I can learn to manage my time more effectively.

It's clear that this mature student has already learned a great deal about effective time management. Her priorities are set: first her young son; second, schoolwork; third, housework. She lacks the time to excel in all three categories simultaneously, so she contents herself with doing well in the first two. For her, housework can wait. Setting priorities and sticking by them requires enormous self-knowledge and self-discipline, but these skills can be learned and fine tuned. Chapter 4 of this book has time management suggestions. As you learn to allocate time effectively, you may find that some tasks just have to wait. Striving for perfection in every facet of your life every day can create enough stress to produce illness. Deciding what's important enough to do well is a necessary ingredient of good time management. While setting priorities for what's essential in your own life, your values may shift. Things that were important before college may fade into the background as new priorities emerge. Having a peer group of mature students experiencing this challenge together can be an invaluable aid as you reaffirm some values and discard others.

5. *Be realistic about expectations.* You don't have to be a super hero to enroll in college, but you do need realistic expectations. Some students expect to make all A's by simply attending class, so the following rule of thumb may help you set realistic goals and allot adequate time for study: *On an average, students spend two or three hours of outside preparation for every hour in the classroom to obtain a grade of C.*

By this rule of thumb, a class that meets three 50-minute sessions a week requires six to nine hours of preparation per week. Depending on your own special abilities and past experiences, you may need to spend more or less preparation time per week to maintain a grade of C. And, of course, if you expect A's in every class, you may need to spend even more time reading assignments, outlining notes, studying for exams, and writing papers. Many adults push themselves to make all A's in every course. Such high expectations may create severe sacrifices in other important areas of life.

━ⅢⅠ━ⅢⅠ━ⅢⅠ━
Support Systems on Campus

Support and encouragement to pursue goals can come from several sources: from your peers (that is, other older students), from faculty, and from administrators. You should be able to find encouragement from all three of these sources on your campus.

Peer Support Groups

Educational research has shown that developing friendships in a peer group helps students stay in school. If you become friends with at least one other student you can confide in, study with, and call in emergencies, you'll be more likely to enroll in college classes again next year. For example, you can exchange lecture notes if you miss a class or entrust your friend with your cassette recorder to tape a lecture if you know ahead of time that you're going to miss it. By simply sharing thoughts over coffee together, you can monitor your own reactions to the college environment.

To help in the development of peer support groups among older students, some colleges offer special orientation programs designed to meet the needs of adult learners. Such orientation programs represent the first chance for older students to meet on campus and begin developing the rudiments of peer support groups. These orientations also deliver information such as availability of special courses, services, facilities, and organizations for adult students as well as the availability of on-campus child-care facilities.

Several large universities reserve sections of courses for mature students only. At some universities these mature students' classes feature a unique curriculum adapted to the needs and interests of adult learners. At other universities, special sections of courses that maintain the regular curriculum are set aside for mature students.

Classes, orientation programs, and student organizations designed specifically for adult learners provide opportunities for you to meet other older students who share your interests and concerns. If no such services exist in the college where you are presently enrolled, you might place an announcement in the college newspaper and form your own group. After all, younger students have many ways of forming mutual support groups: fraternities, sororities, student organizations, dances, and roommates. If your college doesn't provide opportunities for older students to gather and develop friendships among peers, you may need to find a way on your own to build this into your college experience. There's no doubt that peer support is important to staying in school.

Faculty/Academic Advisors

Finding a good advisor is another critical factor in your college education. At the very least, academic advisors provide information on degree requirements and courses needed in your major. Some universities now designate special academic advisors for mature students. Such advisors must be attuned to the conflicting demands of job, home, and school as well as to the course scheduling problems of adults who work full time. Knowledge of weekend and evening courses, assistance with registration, and recognition of mature students' time constraints are hallmarks of an excellent adult advisor. If no special advisor on your campus is identified for mature students, ask your favorite faculty member to help you select courses, schedule classes, and plan your college career.

Administrator/Ombudsman

The "royal runaround" in administrative procedures probably exists in some fashion on every college campus. Bureaucratic red tape is a major hurdle to older students with limited time and lack of experience in dealing with such challenges. Campus procedures were originally established to serve faculty, administrators, and younger students. In order to adapt procedures to serve adult learners as well, many campuses now have an administrator designed as advocate or ombudsman for mature students. In large universities adult advocates are often found in the division of student affairs or in continuing education programs, which schedule evening or weekend classes. The larger the campus, the more likely it is that you'll need help from an administrator who understands procedures, knows how to get things done, and is sympathetic to the special needs of the adult learner.

Some colleges and universities are beginning to change to meet the needs of mature students. These days, you should be able to find support and encouragement on your campus from students, faculty, and administrators. If you encounter obstacles rather than encouragement, remember that a college education requires persistence as well as intelligence!

Student Services

In an effort to retain students with high potential, most colleges have established counseling centers, writing labs, centers for academic skills development, career and life planning, academic advisement, and a host of other student support services. These services exist in addition to regular credit courses. Research on student retention shows that the more support services a student uses, the more likely it is that he or she will reenroll for subsequent course work. Thus, you should seek out and use the student services on your own campus. If you need help in selecting a major, ask for the career planning or academic advisement center. If you have a personal problem that interferes with your studies, seek help from the counseling center. If you need help with study skills, look for an academic skills development center. Active use of such student services will improve your own chances of survival in this new subculture of academia.

On many campuses, student services may not be available to adults. Such support services may not exist, or they may not be available to part-time students or to adults who must work full time and need access to services on nights and weekends. If a vital support service is not available to adult students on your campus, consider requesting that it be made available. Some colleges are still adjusting to adults as a new clientele and will welcome formal petitions to extend support services to older students.

—III—III—III—
Spouse Support

If you're currently married and living with your spouse, his or her support for your educational goals is crucial. A nonsupportive spouse who interferes with study time will greatly reduce your chances of success in the classroom. In contrast, an actively supportive spouse will willingly adjust household routines and family responsibilities to accommodate exam schedules. The degree of support from your husband or wife is probably the most important factor in your pursuit of a college education. Enrolling in classes and accepting the challenge to assimilate new ideas and develop new skills may threaten a spouse, and he or she may attempt to sabotage your college career. If this occurs, you'll be forced to make a difficult decision: to enroll in classes and deal openly with the sabotage; to forfeit your education; or to leave your spouse. These are tough choices, but you're poised at the beginning of a period of great intellectual and personal development. Adjustments in relationships between spouses often go hand in hand with any period of enormous growth. The pursuit of a college education is no exception.

—III—III—III—
Financial Aid for Mature Students

Like much else about higher education, financial aid eligibility and procedures were designed for younger students who are dependent on their parents. Older students often do not meet the eligibility criteria established for younger students. And yet, an adult with adequate income to support a family may not also be able to pay tuition for college courses. On campuses across the nation, administrators of financial aid programs recognize the unique circumstances of mature students. But cutbacks in state and federal student aid have delayed progress in meeting the needs of adult learners.

In spite of this gloomy outlook for financial aid, you'll want to check out all resources on your own campus. For example, some states allow free or reduced tuition to retirees over 60 years old enrolled in state-supported schools. If you're working, your own company may pay college tuition to encourage its employees to upgrade job skills or complete a degree. You may qualify for a loan or scholarship from a local or national civic club or women's organization. The student financial aid office on your campus is a clearinghouse for information on federal and state aid programs as well as on local and national scholarships from business, industry, and civic clubs. If rising costs threaten your continuing education, investigate all possibilities for financial aid. Lack of financial resources is one of the biggest hurdles of adult students. See Chapter 21 on financial aid.

—ııı—ııı—ııı—
Adult Development

You may be feeling guilty about the money you're spending on your own education. This guilt is particularly sharp among spouses who are using family resources to pay tuition costs. Perhaps a look at the reasons older students enroll in college courses can help alleviate those guilt feelings. For both men and women, whether married or single, any one of the following reasons is legitimate for making this financial investment in yourself.

Self-Fulfillment

The ultimate reason you choose to attend college is self-fulfillment. This is the single most legitimate reason for you to make this investment in yourself. To take courses for the pure pleasure of learning needs no other justification. Expanding your horizons through the study of genetics or political science, anthropology, literature, art history, or psychology for the pure pleasure of learning is the epitome of self-fulfillment and personal development.

Job Advancement Skills

In addition, some adults take a few specific courses to acquire skills for job advancement and promotion in their present careers. Others enroll in degree programs to obtain credentials in the marketplace. Older women, for example, often seek a college degree as a way to enter the job market for the first time. Many working women and men seek a degree to implement a career change into an entirely new field. Of course, reasons that lead directly to financial gain are simple to justify. But the reasons that fill deep human needs are just as legitimate as financial gain.

The Need to Grow to Full Potential

Some adults seek a college education to fill a vacuum in a stage of adult development. For example, some women and men feel a loss of identity, a sense of stagnation or isolation during certain stages of adulthood. At such times, adult development is somewhat out of kilter, as familiar roles erode.

For example, a mother whose children have grown and left home may experience the "empty nest syndrome." Her role as full-time caretaker has evaporated and she may no longer feel needed. Another example is the man who has recently retired or lost his role as breadwinner.

Such major changes in one's life can produce feelings of disequilibrium, an uncomfortable sense of being psychologically off balance. Some psychologists, however, suggest that stages of disequilibrium are necessary for further development. From the discomfort, a new stage of personality can emerge. To assist emergence into a new stage, some adults find that the goal of a college education fills a void and reduces isolation or stagnation.

If you have never experienced serious bouts of isolation or stagnation, and your development has been rather smooth and uneventful, you can still expand your horizons and implement growth through a college education. You may find that learning new concepts or new philosophical systems of thought can trigger a period during which you may begin to question long-held beliefs. Long-cherished values may begin to erode in the face of new information. If so, be assured that you may be on the brink of a new and more advanced stage of adult development.

Of course, a college education is not a panacea for everyone; it offers no guarantees that you'll reach your goals. But for whatever reasons you decide to continue your education—to fill a void, to expand horizons, to enter the job market, or to advance in the marketplace—those reasons are valid because they're your reasons. You can get rid of any guilt about using time, energy, and money to pursue your goal. You're making an investment in yourself during a critical stage of your development. This investment also benefits those around you as you strive to attain your fullest potential.

The Adult Learner's Impact on Higher Education

Because you're making an investment in yourself and the stakes are high, approach a college education as a good consumer. You have a real interest in the quality of classroom instruction and the availability of student support services suitable for adult learners. You are here because you want to be. You are probably paying your own way, and you want your money's worth.

This consumer approach is typical of adult students and has the potential of altering institutions of higher education for the better. Already the structures of colleges and universities are changing (although at uneven rates) to meet the demands of adult learners. By their sheer numbers, older students are changing programs and procedures, and depending on how prevalent and how vocal adult students become, they may make a lasting positive impact on the quality of higher education.

If you're one of these pioneers reshaping the structure of American colleges and universities, be proud of your accomplishments! Along with your own growth and personality development, you and many others like you offer to institutions of higher education across the nation the promise of a period of renewed growth and revitalization. It's a worthy challenge!

Suggested Activities

1. Invite an outside speaker to your class to discuss the nature of stress and techniques for reducing stress such as biofeedback or self-hypnosis. Practice these techniques yourself.

2. Discuss your strengths and weaknesses in basic skills such as reading, writing, and math. Determine what kind of help you need, and find out where you can obtain that help on your campus. Follow through on this, either individually or as a class. Other class members with strengths in your weakest areas may also be willing to provide you with training and support, just as you might do for others.

3. Prepare an oral or written report on several theories of adult development.

4. On sheets of poster-sized paper, draw your lifeline depicting important milestones throughout your life. Describe your lifeline aloud to the group.

Suggested Readings

Beal, Philip E., and Lee Noel. *What Works in Student Retention,* Iowa City, Iowa, and Boulder, Colo.: American College Testing Program and National Center for Higher Education Management Systems, 1980.

Erikson, Erik. *Childhood and Society.* New York: Norton, 1964.

Erikson, Erik. *Identity: Youth and Crisis.* New York: Norton, 1968.

Friedan, Betty, *The Feminine Mystique.* New York: Dell, 1962.

Lenning, Oscar T., Philip E. Beal, and Ken Sauer. *Attrition and Retention: Evidence for Action and Research.* Boulder, Colo.: National Center for Higher Education Management Systems, 1980.

Sheehy, Gail. *Passages: Predictable Crises of Adult Life.* New York: Dutton, 1974.

Glossary

College Terms

Ed Ewing

One way in which college is different from other institutions is in the vocabulary its residents and employees use. Many of the terms you'll find in your admission materials, orientation information, handbooks, and catalogs were taken from the literature of the first colleges and universities in Europe and are used today more out of custom and tradition than for any practical reasons. This glossary will help you understand the unusual language you may encounter from faculty, deans, and your college administration.

To show you how difficult college jargon can be, look back at the paragraph you've just read, particularly at the terms college, university, faculty, and dean. What do you think these mean? Think of a definition for each of them and compare your definitions to those you'll learn here. We'll begin by helping you with the two most difficult words, college and university.

A university is a group of colleges, and the degree programs (majors) are within the various colleges. The college is the degree-granting component of a university, but different types of colleges exist. Some offer only undergraduate degrees. Some offer both undergraduate and graduate degrees, and others—such as a law school—may offer only graduate degrees. In the following glossary, we've defined some common words or terms you may encounter during your college years. We hope it will help you better understand your college life.

- ☐ **Academic Advisor** Colleges have many people who carry the title of advisor or counselor. Your academic advisor may be a faculty member in the academic field you've chosen or a full-time administrative employee who works in a counseling office of the school. You'll be assigned an advisor once you begin college, and this person will serve as your resource to all academic and nonacademic services. While academic advisors will help you plan your college schedule or choose a major, they can also offer much more. Ask about anything that puzzles you, and you may save both time and money.

☐ **Accreditation** Colleges and universities are judged, or accredited, either by an organization of other colleges and universities or by professional organizations. Accrediting teams visit on a regular basis and judge schools on faculty, degrees offered, library facilities, laboratories, other facilities, and finances. Southern schools are accredited by the Southern Association of Colleges and Schools. A law school may be accredited by the American Bar Association. A college of business must be accredited by the American Association of Collegiate Schools of Business, and colleges of communications or journalism may be accredited by the Association for Education in Journalism and Mass Communication. You should seek accredited schools and programs because these are usually the best of their kind and are recognized as such by many future employers.

☐ **Admissions** The first contact you may have with a college or university may be with its admissions office. The people who work there are trying to "sell" their school and its programs to you, and they'll send you many forms. Read these forms carefully and note all deadlines. Send your application to them early, because some schools may assign dormitory space on the basis of the date you're accepted for admission. Some schools offer more than one type of admission status. You may be permitted entrance to one college or major program, but denied entrance to another. Acceptance to a university does not always guarantee acceptance into all of its programs. *See also* Associate degree; Bachelor's degree; Major.

☐ **Alumnus** A graduate of a college or university. Schools have alumni offices, which may ask you for money or other support after you graduate.

☐ **Assistant Professor** *See* Professor.

☐ **Associate Degree** May be an associate degree in arts or an associate degree in science (A.A. or A.S.). Although many terms used by American universities were taken from European schools, this term is an exception. An associate degree is a two-year degree. Many associate degree programs are offered at community and junior colleges and at technical schools, but many large universities also offer such programs. Just because you earn an associate degree does not mean you're halfway toward a bachelor's degree. Some states have agreements that require state colleges and universities to accept all classes satisfactorily completed toward an associate degree and to count those credits toward a bachelor's degree. However, this is not true in all states.

☐ **Associate Professor** *See* Professor.

☐ **Bachelor's Degree** The formal name for a four-year college degree. Two major types are the bachelor of arts (B.A.) and Bachelor of Science

(B.S.). Requirements for these degrees vary, depending on the standards of the school or college.

- **Bookstore** More than a place that sells textbooks, a college bookstore may also sell running shorts, pens and pencils, greeting cards, and a host of other items. Be certain you purchase the proper edition of required texts, and see if used copies are available at a reduced price. Always keep your book receipt, and do not mark in the book until you're sure you'll keep it, or you may have trouble obtaining a refund. Bookstores are usually located in student centers or college university unions.

- **Cafeteria or Dining Hall** These terms mean the same thing on some campuses but different things on others. The dining hall may be part of a dormitory, and your food may be prepaid if you purchased a meal card or board plan. In a cafeteria you pay for each item you select; it may be located in the student center.

- **Career Counseling/Planning** Most campuses began offering this service in the 1970s because students saw a direct relationship between what they were studying in college and the job market. Students wanted to know where the jobs were and what they needed to achieve to be eligible for them. Career planning services include but are not limited to self-assessment and interest tests, job search workshops, decision-making workshops, and résumé workshops. These services are usually located in counseling centers, student affairs offices, or placement offices.

- **Carrel** A study room or numbered desk and chair in the college library that can be assigned to students. Not everyone is eligible for one, and you must request a carrel from the college librarian.

- **Chancellor** Title given to a high academic officer at some colleges and universities. The chancellor is usually just below the president in importance.

- **Class Card or Course Card** Usually required for registration unless you register by computer. At registration, you pick up one card for each class approved for you by your advisor. The card usually lists the name and number of the class, number of credits, days, times, and name of the professor. If more than one section of the same course is offered, a section number will appear. *Always check your course cards carefully.* Once these cards are fed into the computer, you are assigned a seat in the class, and your name will appear on the class role for the card that you submit. *See also* Section.

- **Class Standing** Most colleges link your standing to the number of hours you've earned, not the number of years you've attended school. A freshman is enrolled in the first quarter of college work. A sophomore is in the second quarter. A junior has passed the halfway point, and a senior has three-fourths of his or her requirements completed. This rule applies to students on the quarter and semester systems in four-year undergraduate programs. *See also* Quarter system and Semester system.

- **CLEP** Stands for College Level Examination Program, a series of tests you may take to demonstrate proficiency in various college subjects. If you pass the test, you will earn credit for certain college courses. CLEP subject exams cover individual courses, such as Introductory Psychology; CLEP general exams incorporate several courses, such as the one for social studies. Be aware that some colleges will accept CLEP subject exams, but not CLEP general exams. CLEP tests are usually administered through the college testing office. You can also obtain information about CLEP tests from your admissions office and/or your advisor.

- **Coeducational** A school that admits men and women. Most colleges are coeducational. Some schools have coeducational residence halls where men and women live in the same building, but not in the same room.

- **Cognate** A group of courses related to a student's major and approved by his or her advisor. Such courses are required for graduation at many colleges. Cognates are junior- and senior-level courses. Colleges that don't require a cognate may require a minor. *See also* Minor.

- **Commencement** A day set aside by colleges to award degrees to graduating students. Some schools hold two or three commencements annually, but the most popular ones are held in May or early June.

- **Community College** A two-year college that may also be known as a junior college or technical school. These colleges award associate degrees, and technical colleges may offer other types of degrees or certificates as well. Be certain that the community college you select is accredited, and remember that there's no guarantee that all courses you take at a two-year college will transfer to a four-year college or university.

- **Comprehensive Examination** Some schools use this term to describe final exams, which are given during the last days of the term. The word *comprehensive* means that all material covered during the term may be included on the exam. Graduate students may also take comprehensive exams to earn the master's or doctoral degree.

- **Continuing Education** Over the years, the meaning of this term has changed. Some schools may still refer to such programs as "adult education." Continuing education programs enable the nontraditional college student to take classes without having to be admitted as a degree candidate. While continuing education students may take college courses for credit, some colleges have established noncredit learning programs under this name.

- **Core Courses/Distribution Requirements/Basic Requirements/ General Education** These terms all mean the same thing. Colleges require that all students complete specific groups of courses. These courses usually occur at the freshman and sophomore levels and include English, math, science, and history requirements. Since many of these lower numbered courses must be completed before other courses can be taken, it's wise to complete your core courses as early as possible. *See also* Prerequisite.

- **Counseling Office** Counseling is provided by trained professionals at your college. Counselors can help you with various adjustment problems and may refer you to other services. There are many types of counselors; you'll find them in the following offices: Admissions, Financial Aid, Residence Halls, Career Planning, Placement, Veteran's Affairs, Study Skills, Academic Advising, and Counseling Centers. Counselors treat in confidence whatever you tell them. Once you determine that you need some type of counseling, seek it out. Your tuition is paying for it.

- **Course Number** Different colleges number their courses in different ways. Most undergraduates take courses at the 100 level through at least the 400 level, but this will vary on different campuses. Graduate-level courses carry higher numbers. The 100-level courses are usually survey courses introducing that subject, while upper-level courses may spend an entire term covering a narrower topic in more detail. Some 100-level courses must be completed before you may take upper-level work in that subject. Check your catalog and ask your advisor for help.

- **Credit Hour** *See* Quarter hour.

- **Curriculum** All courses required for your degree. Some colleges refer to all courses in the catalog as the curriculum, and many schools provide students with curriculum outlines or curriculum sheets in addition to the catalog. These sheets show what courses you must take and may indicate the order in which you must take them. That order is called "course sequencing."

- **Dean** A college administrator who may have been a professor. Some deans are academic deans, which means they head colleges. Some colleges and universities have a dean of student affairs, a dean of business affairs, and deans of men and of women. The academic dean is a person who oversees your degree program. He or she can grant exceptions to academic policy. The other types of deans are executives who may or may not work directly with students, although most work in student services. Some deans may have associate or assistant deans to help them.

- **Dean's List** If you make high grades, you'll make the Dean's List at the end of the term. This is an academic honor and looks good on your résumé and on applications for graduate study. See what your school requires for you to make the list, and make it as many times as you can.

- **Deficiency** This word can mean more than one thing. You may be told you have a one-course deficiency that you must make up before graduation or entrance to a particular program. Your grades may be fine, but the deficiency exists as a prerequisite for what you want to do. Deficiency can also mean that your grades are so low that you may not be permitted to return to school.

- **Department** A college is often organized into academic departments. For example, a group of history faculty will develop a curriculum for students studying history. The history department will offer all history courses for every student at the school, including history majors.

- **Dismissal** At most schools, dismissal means the same thing as suspension, and you will be told to leave the school for academic or disciplinary reasons. College catalogs explain the circumstances for dismissal, and you should learn these rules and obey them. Dismissal or suspension usually is noted on your official record or transcript, and the requirements to reenter college will vary. *See also* Leave of absence and Probation.

- **Dissertation** One of the final requirements for the highest academic degree a student can earn in most fields, the doctorate, or Ph.D. In some fields, the dissertation is book length. The graduate student is expected to break new ground in research and must defend her or his dissertation before a faculty committee. *See also* Graduate student.

- **Doctoral Degree** Requires additional years of study beyond the bachelor's and/or master's degrees, and is awarded upon successful completion of course work, the dissertation, and orals. Most of your professors probably have a Ph.D. (doctor of philosophy); other types, including the M.D. (medical doctor) and J.D. (doctor of jurisprudence) also require extensive study.

- **Dormitory** *See* Residence hall.

- **Drop** Most colleges allow students to drop courses without penalty during specified periods of time. Dropping a course can be dangerous if you don't know the proper procedures, since you'll need to complete certain forms and obtain official signatures. If you're receiving financial aid, your status may change if you drop a course. Finally, dropping courses certainly will affect your graduation date.

- **Electives** Students who say, "I think I'll take an elective course," may think that electives differ from other course requirements. This is only partially true, for electives are required for graduation for most college degrees. An elective is a course you may select from an academic area of interest to you. The course will not count in your core, major, or minor/cognate. Each college decides the number of electives you may take, and you may take them at any time. Ask your advisor if he or she recommends that you complete core courses before choosing electives.

- **Evaluation of Courses** *See* Validation of credits.

- **Extracurricular (Cocurricular)** A word describing activities, clubs, or organizations you may join and participate in, above and beyond your academic courses. Such activities provide fun and friends and also look good on your résumé, but keep in mind that some are more valuable than others. Ask a counselor for advice, since certain activities may lead you into career choices. Activities include student government, student media, clubs, volunteer work, and faculty/student committees.

- **Faculty** All the teachers at your college. The names of faculty positions and the ranks held by individuals will vary. *See also* Professor.

- **Fees** At most colleges, fees are costs that are required in addition to tuition. Fees may be charged for housing, health, labs, parking, and many other things. Most college catalogs give a good idea of what fees you'll have to pay and when you must pay them. *See also* Tuition.

- **Final Exams** Some schools call them comprehensive exams and hold them during an examination week, a period when your instructors may find out how much you've learned from them. Most finals are written rather than oral. Professors usually tell students about finals near the beginning of the term, and not all professors require them. A final may count as much as one-half of your grade, or it could count much less. Some schools may also schedule midterm exams.

- **Financial Aid** A complicated subject in recent years. Most colleges have a financial aid office to provide information to students on scholarships, grants, and loans. Some forms of financial aid are gifts, but others are loans that must be repaid with interest. Some aid is offered only to new freshmen, and you must apply before college begins to be eligible. Many grants and loans are provided through federal government assistance, and government regulations control this money. To determine your eligibility for any aid, see your financial aid counselor as early as you can.

- **Fraternity** *See* Greeks.

- **Full-Time Student** Students enrolled for a specified number of hours, such as twelve semester hours or more. At most schools, part-time students receive the same benefits as full-time students. At others, part-time students may receive limited health care and no athletic tickets. Ask your advisor about the advantages of going full time, but remember, if you must work, raise a family, or handle other obligations, a part-time program may be the more sensible one to pursue.

- **Grade-Point Average (GPA)** Sometimes called the cumulative average or grade-point ratio (GPR). Most colleges base grades on a four-point scale, with points assigned to each grade (A = 4, B = 3, C = 2, D = 1, F = 0). To compute your GPA for one term, you need only complete three simple mathematical steps: multiply, add, divide. *Multiply* the number of points representing the grade you receive for each course times the number of credit hours for the course. *Add* the points for all courses to determine the total number of points you've earned for the term. *Divide* the total points by the number of credit hours you attempted that term. The result will be your GPA. Some colleges complicate this with a three-point system or by using grades in addition to A through F. College catalogs explain the system at individual schools.

- **Grades or Grading System** Most schools use the A through F system. A is the highest grade and F means failure. A through D are passing grades for which you will earn points and credits. If you ever transfer colleges, however, the D grades may not transfer. D's and F's are bad because most colleges require a minimum 2.0 GPA, or C average, for graduation, and you might lose financial aid, housing, and other benefits when your GPA falls below a certain level. Bad grades and low GPAs also lead to dismissal or suspension. Some schools have a pass/fail grade (P/F or S/U) and an incomplete grade (I), the latter representing work not completed during the term it was taken. Learning the grading system of your college is one of your first assignments.

- **Graduate Student** A person who has earned at least a bachelor's degree (B.A. or B.S.) and is presently enrolled in a program granting a master's degree (M.A. or M.S.) and/or a doctorate (Ph.D.). Students in law school, medical school, and other specialized programs beyond the bachelor's level are also classified as graduate students.

- **Greeks** Used to describe students who join fraternities or sororities. Discuss the possibility of becoming a Greek with someone whose opinions you value.

- **Higher Education** Any college courses you take or any degree you earn after completing high school (secondary education). Also called postsecondary education.

- **Honors** Most colleges recognize good grades in the form of academic honors. Dean's List is the most common award. Honors are also awarded at graduation to superior students, and the following Latin words are used: *cum laude* (with praise), *magna cum laude* (with great praise), *summa cum laude* (with highest praise).

- **Hours** Another word for credits. If you enroll for fifteen hours this term and pass all five of your three-hour courses, you'll earn fifteen credits. There is often a relationship between the number of hours you spend in the classroom each week and the number of credits you can earn from the course. After you accumulate the proper number of credits/hours, you will graduate with an associate or bachelor's degree.

- **Incomplete** *See* Grades or grading system.

- **Independent Study** Can mean at least two things. An independent study course is one in which you complete course requirements on your own time, under the direction of a professor, and outside a classroom setting. This term may also describe some work you've done, either by yourself or with others, that is creative and that shows your ability to work with minimal direction.

- **Instructor** *See* Professor.

- **Internship** An arrangement that permits students to work and receive college credit in their major. Internships are required for graduation in some fields, such as psychology, nursing, and medicine. Prerequisites must be completed before you may take an internship, and you must complete an application and obtain the proper signatures before you will be allowed to intern.

- **Junior** *See* Class standing.

- **Junior College** *See* Community college.

- **Laboratories** Science courses often come with laboratories. Many large universities call other learning experiences "laboratories." For example, courses in foreign language, computer science, education, psychology, and journalism may have labs. Many courses require labs whether you want to take the lab or not, but in other cases labs may be optional. Check your catalog to see what labs are in store for you.

- **Leave of Absence** Another way to say you've withdrawn completely from college. Most students take a leave of absence while still in good academic standing, with the intention of seeking readmittance at a later date. Remember to read the rules and regulations in your catalog because colleges have different ideas about the meaning of a leave of absence.

- **Lecturer** *See* Professor.

- **Lower Division** Many colleges and universities have divided their academic programs into lower and upper divisions (also called pre-professional and professional). Your standing depends on the number of hours you've accumulated, prerequisites completed, forms completed and signed, and grade-point average. Students in the upper division usually enjoy greater privileges and certainly are closer to graduation.

- **Major** Your field of specialization in college. As much as 30 percent of the courses you need for graduation may fall into this category. Major courses usually carry higher course numbers. Your advisor will explain the requirements of your major to you.

- **Master Schedule** *See* Schedule of classes.

- **Master's Degree Students** Students who have chosen to continue their education in either a Master of Arts (M.A.) or Master of Science (M.S.) program. Master's students may have entered a different program from the one in which they earned their bachelor's degree. Comprehensive exams, a thesis, and/or practicums and internships may be required. *See also* Thesis.

- **Matriculate** An uncommon term, used by the admissions office. It means you've applied for a degree program, have been accepted in that program, and have enrolled for classes. At that point, you're considered matriculated.

- **Minor** A group of courses that may or may not be required for your degree. Not all colleges require a minor. Your advisor may tell you that your minor must be "academically related" to your major, as government is to history. Minors may also consist of courses taken in a professional school, such as business administration.

- **Oral** An examination during which your professor will ask you questions about your class and you will answer aloud. Undergraduate students usually don't have to undergo orals.

- **Orientation** Most colleges now set aside a single day, several days, or even longer for orientation. During this period, new students and their parents are introduced to academic programs, facilities, and services provided by the college. Orientation may also include academic advisement and preregistration for classes.

- **Part-Time Student** *See* Full-time student.

- **Pass/Fail or Pass/No Pass or Satisfactory/Unsatisfactory** Many colleges allow you to take certain courses on a pass/fail system. By passing the course, you will earn credits toward graduation, but the grade will not count in your GPA. Pass/fail grades do not have grade points assigned to them. Most schools will not allow you to take core courses, major courses, or minor/cognate courses on this system, but may allow free electives as pass/fail options. To take courses pass/fail, you must fill out the proper forms before the established deadline in the term.

- **Placement** Several definitions are appropriate here. Placement tests tell academic departments what level of knowledge you've achieved in their subject. A college placement office can help you in résumé writing and interviewing. This office may, with your permission, keep a job file on you and release information to prospective employers upon request. Recruiters from business and industry often recruit graduating seniors through college placement offices.

- **Practicum** Generally, a practicum experience covers a limited amount of material in depth, rather than trying, as an internship does, to provide an overview of an area. The terms may be used interchangeably, however, and refer to practical types of learning experiences, usually for college credit.

- **Preregistration** Many colleges employ preregistration systems (often computer-assisted) to simplify the process of signing up for the courses. Preregistration usually occurs in the middle of the term prior to the one you're registering for. This early registration also tells colleges what courses students want, when they'll want them, and what professors they request. Preregistration gives students a greater chance of receiving the courses and sections asked for.

- **Prerequisite** A prerequisite is a course or courses that must be completed as a condition for taking another course. Catalogs state prerequisites. Often a GPA or class standing may constitute a prerequisite for certain classes.

- **President** The chief executive officer of the university or college. Presidents report directly to governing boards (trustees). Unless you attend a small school, you won't see this person often, except at official functions such as commencement.

- **Probation** A warning that you are not making satisfactory academic progress toward your degree. Probation is followed by suspension/ dismissal unless the situation is corrected. Probation may also exist for disciplinary reasons.

- **Professor** College teachers are ranked as teaching assistant, instructor, lecturer, or professor. Professor is the highest rank and includes three levels: assistant professor, associate professor, and (full) professor. To avoid confusion, note how your teacher introduces himself or herself the first day of class. When in doubt, use "professor." While most professors have earned a doctoral degree, this is not a rigid rule for holding professorial rank.

□ **Proficiency Exam** A test used to measure whether or not you've reached a certain level of knowledge. Such exams may allow you to exempt, with or without credit, certain lower level courses. Math and foreign language departments make use of proficiency exams.

□ **Quarter Hour** A unit of credit given at colleges whose terms are called quarters, which last approximately ten weeks. *See also* Semester hour.

□ **Quarter System** Colleges operating on this system have four terms, or quarters: fall, winter, spring, and summer. If you attend full time and plan to finish in four years without attending summer school, you'll take courses for twelve quarters. *See also* Semester system.

□ **Registrar** The college administrator who maintains your transcript, directs the registration process, and performs other academic duties as assigned by the faculty. When faculty submit final grades, the registrar posts them to your transcript, and mails you a copy.

□ **Registration** The act of scheduling your classes for each term. Whether you preregister or sign up just prior to the term, you should seek academic advisement first to be certain you're taking the proper courses. When in doubt, ask your advisor first! *See also* Preregistration.

□ **Reinstatement or Readmission** A return to college following suspension or a leave of absence; you must apply for reinstatement or readmission. In some cases you'll be readmitted with no restrictions. If your GPA is low, you may be readmitted on probation. Check the academic regulations at your school.

□ **Residence Hall** A fancy term for dormitory, a residence hall is operated by the college as student housing. Ask your residence hall or dorm counselor to explain the rules that apply to your place of residence on campus.

□ **Residency** State-supported colleges and universities charge a higher tuition to students who do not reside (maintain residency) the year around in the same state and who are not considered legal residents of that state. If you live in the same state in which you attend college, you have residency in that state and are eligible for in-state tuition, provided you meet other specific requirements of your school.

□ **Sabbatical** A period of paid or semi-paid release time awarded every six or seven years to professors, who are expected, during this period, to conduct academic research or writing that makes a contribution to their academic discipline.

□ **Schedule of Classes** Also called a master schedule, this is a listing of all classes that will be offered during the coming term, including days and times of class meetings, name of instructor, building and room, and other registration information.

- **Scholarship** A financial award made for academic achievement. Many scholarships are reserved for new freshmen and may be renewed annually, provided grades are satisfactory. The money is applied to tuition.

- **Section** The different classes offered for a single subject. For example, a large college might offer fifty different sections of freshman English. Depending on the section you register for, you may have a different teacher, different textbook, and different meeting time than your friends who are taking different sections of the same course.

- **Semester Hour** The unit of credit you earn for course work that takes a semester to complete. Many college courses carry three credits, or semester hours.

- **Semester System** As opposed to the quarter system, a semester system consists of a fall semester, a spring semester, and summer school. A full-time student can complete a bachelor's degree in eight semesters without attending summer school.

- **Seminar** A class containing fewer students than a lecture class, in which the teacher leads discussions and all students participate. The majority of classes in graduate school are operated this way, although you'll find seminars in undergraduate programs as well.

- **Senior** *See* Class standing.

- **Sophomore** *See* Class standing.

- **Sorority** *See* Greeks.

- **Special Student** In most colleges, this is a student who has not matriculated (has not been accepted into a degree program). A special student may have one degree, but may wish to continue his or her education by selecting courses without regard to a degree program. Military personnel are often admitted as special students. Special students may be exempted from certain prerequisites, but they can't receive financial aid or free athletic tickets.

- **Student Teaching** An internship that all education majors must complete before graduation.

- **Student Union** A building, also called the student center, where you can eat, see a movie, meet friends, and take part in extracurricular activities.

- **Summer Session (Summer School)** For students who wish to make up deficiencies, get ahead, or just can't seem to get enough of school.

Classes meet every day for longer periods than during the regular sessions. Since things move quickly, good academic advisement is essential before you consider summer school. You may also take summer courses as a transient student at another school, provided your advisor has given you prior approval. Since many schools will not let you take courses you failed at another school, be careful.

- **Suspension** *See* Dismissal.

- **Syllabus** One or more pages of class requirements a professor will give you on the first day. The syllabus acts as a course outline, telling when you must complete assignments, readings, and so on. A professor may also include on the syllabus her or his grading system, attendance policy, and a brief description of the course. Be sure you get one and use it.

- **Technical (Tech) Schools** Technical education systems established by many states offer specialized two-year degrees and certificates. While these schools may be accredited, course work may be so technically oriented that it won't transfer to a bachelor's degree program. If you plan to attend a tech school, be certain to ask about the "college parallel curriculum." *See also* Associate degree.

- **Term Paper** Not all college courses require one, but when you're assigned a term paper, you should treat it as a very important portion of the course. The instructor may give you the entire term to research and write a term paper—hence, its name. Be certain to know which style manual your teacher prefers, and follow it.

- **Thesis** A longer research paper, usually written as partial fulfillment of the requirements for a master's degree. Some schools still require a senior thesis of graduating students.

- **Transcript** The official record of your college work, which is maintained and updated each term by the registrar. Your courses, grades, GPA, and graduation information will be included in your transcript.

- **Transfer Credit** If you should transfer from one college or university to another, the number of courses the new college accepts and counts toward your degree are your transfer credits.

- **Transient Student** A student who receives permission from his or her regular college to take courses (usually in the summer) from another college.

- **Tuition** The money you pay for your college courses. *See also* Fees.

- **Upper Division** The opposite of lower division and much closer to graduation. *See also* Lower division.

- **Validation of Credits** Procedure in which a school determines which credits from another school may be transferred. Despite good grades, not all of your courses may be accepted. A grade of D normally will not transfer. If you ever consider transferring from one college to another, it's your responsibility to learn which courses and grades will transfer.

- **Withdraw** Although you may withdraw from one course, this term usually denotes the dropping of all courses for one term and leaving school for whatever reasons you may have. Withdrawal requires a form and signatures, and if you don't follow the prescribed procedure, you may receive failing grades on all courses, which could place you on academic suspension. Withdrawal in good academic standing, following established procedures, will allow you to request readmission later. *See also* Reinstatement or readmission and Leave of absence.

Index

Costs of college education, 279–80
Critical thinking, 109–20. *See also*
    Rational thinking
    analysis and, 115–16
    beyond college, 116–18
    in college, 112–14, 169
    deductive and inductive reasoning,
        114–15
    liberal arts and, 110–12
    self-definition and, 119–20
    self-discovery and, 118–19
Curriculum, 30–34
    Brooke Shields's, 30–31
    choice of courses, 31
    core, 36–37
    elective, 38
    faculty and modern, 32–34
    liberal arts, 110–12
    liberal arts vs. career-oriented,
        36–38

Deductive reasoning, 114–15
Dialectical process, 113
Diaphragm, 235
Dictionary of Occupational Titles, 144
Diet. *See* Nutrition
Douching, 235
Drafts, written, 103, 105–6
Drug(s), 248–51
    controlling illegal, 249–50
    trends in the use of, 248–49
Dwyer, John, gift from academe to,
    27

Eating better. *See* Nutrition
Eating disorders, 229–30
Educational attainment, relationship
    to career opportunities and in-
    come, 19
Einstein, Albert, gift from academe
    to, 32
Encyclopedias, information retrieval
    from, 82–84
Essay exams
    focusing on structure in, 104–5
    studying for, 51–52
Essayist attitude, 100
Ethical behavior, effect of higher edu-
    cation on, 20

Ethical communication, 195–99
Exams. *See* Tests
Exercise, 223–34, 230–32
Explanation and argumentation, in
    reading and writing, 98

Faculty. *See also* Professors
    early, vs. modern curriculum,
        32–34
Fallacies in thinking, 126–31
False cause, 130
Family life, effect of higher education
    on, 20
Finances, 16, 277–93
    application for financial aid,
        282–83
    budgeting when living with
        friends, 219
    managing personal funds, 283–89
    paying for college education,
        279–82
    student loans, 289–92
Financial aid programs, 278, 280,
    281–82
    for adult students, 302–3
    application process, 282–83
Freshmen, factors affecting the suc-
    cess of, 6–7
Fromm, Erich, 189

Genital herpes, 238
Genital warts, 238
Gifts of Academe
    Barth, John, 36
    Dwyer, John, 27
    Einstein, Albert, 32
    King, Martin Luther, Jr., 34
    McCarthy, Mary, 33
    Martin Luther, 29
    Mehta, Ved, 37
    Newton, Isaac, 30
Goals
    establishing measurable, 167–68
    life, and career planning, 141,
        142(fig.), 149(fig.)
Gonorrhea, 238
Grade(s), improving through writing,
    93–96
Grade point average (GPA), 9, 94

Luther, Martin, gift from academe to, 29

McCarthy, Mary, gift from academe to, 33
Major. *See* Academic major
Marijuana, 249
Mehta, Ved, gift from academe to, 37
Memory, improving, 47–49
Mill, John Stuart, 27–28
Minority students, 155–74
   admission to college and academic success, 165
   challenge of higher education for, 157–58
   experiences of, on white campuses, 161–65
   historical considerations of education for, 158–61
   learning to thrive at white colleges, 166–71
Money management, 278, 283–89. *See also* Finances
   three-step budgeting, 284–89
Morning-after pill, 235
Morrill Act of 1862, 14, 29
Multiple-choice exams, studying for, 53

Narration, in reading and writing, 97
Networking with friends and colleagues, 198–99
New students, 15
Newton, Isaac, gift from academe to, 30
Nontraditional students, 15. *See also* Returning students
Notetaking, 47–49
   writing and, 99–100
Nutrition, 222–23
   eating better, 227–29
   self-assessment, 224–26
   whole vs. processed foods, 227

Open admissions policy, 3, 4, 14
Oral contraceptives, 234

Patterson, Charlotte, 10–11

Peer pressure, 215, 233
Periodicals, information retrieval from, 85–87
Personality characteristics, and career planning, 140–41, 144–50
Pill, contraceptive, 234
Premises, logical, 115, 124, 126
Presentations, giving classroom, 89–90
Princeton University, 28, 30–31
Private writing, 93, 102–3
Professors, 57–67. *See also* Faculty
   academic freedom and, 63
   academic standards and, 65–66
   expectations of, toward students, 66–67, 163–64
   as former students, 58–59
   vs. high school teachers, 59–60
   interest in students, 60
   reasons for choosing teaching, 60–61
   student relationships with, 62–63
   tasks of, 61–62
   tenure and rank, 64–65
Program management, 206–7
Public writing, 93, 102–3
   planning for, 103–5

Racism on college campuses, 164–65
Rank, academic, 64–65
Rational thinking, 121–32
   correct and incorrect reasoning, 122–23
   fallacies in thinking, 126–31
   learning through arguments, 124–26
   logic of correct writing, 123–24
   logic of learning, 124
   need for correct reasoning, 122
Reading
   relationship to writing, 95, 96–99
   of textbooks, 49–51
Rejection, fear of, 195–97
Relationships, 186–200
   with academic advisor, 71–73
   ethical communication, 195–99
   interpersonal communication, 189–95